# *ACCESSing School*

## Teaching Struggling Readers to Achieve Academic and Personal Success

Jim Burke

HEINEMANN
Portsmouth, NH

**Heinemann**

A division of Reed Elsevier Inc.
361 Hanover Street
Portsmouth, NH 03801–3912
www.heinemann.com

*Offices and agents throughout the world*

The author and publisher wish to thank those who have generously given permission to reprint borrowed material:

"College Dream" by Dwana Bain copyright © 2004 by *The Independent,* April 10, 2004. Reprinted by permission.
"Empowering Speech" by Lanelle Duran copyright © 2004 by *The Independent,* May 4, 2004. Reprinted by permission.
"Messages from the Heart" by Dwana Bain copyright © 2002 by *The Independent,* December 21, 2002. Reprinted by permission.
"Reading Is Right on Track" by Sabrina Crawford copyright © 2004 by *The Independent,* October 12, 2004. Reprinted by permission.
Excerpt from *Reader's Handbook: A Student Guide for Reading and Learning (9–12)* by Jim Burke, Ron Klemp, and Wendell Schwartz. Text copyright © 2002 by Great Source Education Group, a division of Houghton Mifflin Company. Reprinted by permission. All rights reserved.
Excerpt from *Realizing the College Dream* by the ECMC Foundation and the Center for Educational Outreach at the University of California, Berkeley. Copyright © 2003 by the Educational Credit Management Corporation. Reprinted by permission.
"Students Learn Lessons on Esteemable Acts" by Dwana Bain copyright © 2003 by *The Independent,* November 1, 2003. Reprinted by permission.
"Teaming Up for Success" by Sabrina Crawford copyright © 2003 by *The Independent,* June 3, 2003.

**Library of Congress Cataloging-in-Publication Data**
Burke, Jim.
    ACCESSing school : teaching struggling readers to achieve academic and personal success / Jim Burke.
      p. cm.
    Includes bibliographical references and index.
    ISBN 0-325-00737-3
    1. School improvement programs.   2. Academic achievement.   3. Reading (Secondary).   I. Title.
  LB2822.8.B87 2005
  428.4'071'2—dc22                                     2005007556

*Editor:* Lois Bridges
*Production:* Abigail M. Heim
*Typesetter:* Kim Arney Mulcahy
*Cover design:* Judy Arisman, Arisman Design Studio
*Manufacturing:* Louise Richardson

*About the Cover:* Tony Arteaga (*left*) and Nelson Tejada pose minutes after graduating from Burlingame High School. Tony entered high school and was placed in ACCESS; when he graduated four years later, he was president of the Cultura Latino club and received several scholarships. He enrolled three months later in the local community college. Entering as a freshman, Nelson was placed in Burke's honors English class based on his prior teacher's recommendation. Though he clearly had potential, he needed to develop the academic literacies to succeed. After nearly failing the class first semester, he learned the skills he needed to graduate four years later and be accepted into the California State University system.

Printed in the United States of America on acid-free paper

09  08  07  06  05   RRD   1  2  3  4  5

**To** the faculty, staff, and administration at Burlingame High School, and to all the ACCESS students:

You are my most important teachers.

*P*erhaps more significant than what [our teachers] taught is what they believed. . . . They held visions of us that we could imagine for ourselves. . . . They were determined, despite all odds, that we would achieve.

—Lisa Delpit, *City Kids, City Teachers*

*D*iving In: [The teacher] who has come this far must now make a decision that demands professional courage—the decision to remediate himself, to become a student of new disciplines and of his students themselves in order to perceive both their difficulties and their incipient excellence. . . . Diving in is simply deciding that teaching them to write well is not only suitable but challenging work for those who would be teachers and scholars in a democracy.

—Mina Shaughnessy

# Contents

# *Foreword*

Each day there are more than three thousand excellent reasons to read this book you now hold in your hands. More than three thousand reasons daily. What are those reasons? They are the three thousand plus students who drop out of high school every day.[1]

You've probably known or taught some of those students—maybe more than you'd care to admit. They are more often Latino and African American students than White and Asian students. They are more often boys than girls and more often from homes that struggle financially than those that do not. They are likely to be part of the eight million struggling readers found in grades 4–12 across this country.[2] They come to school reluctantly, angrily, timidly, and sometimes only occasionally. They require differentiated instruction and easier reading materials, yet they face the same high-stakes tests as their higher-achieving cohorts. Some may arrive hungry and tired. Some speak Spanish or Vietnamese or Chinese or Hmong fluently but stumble through the easiest English phrases. They are students just like Ben.

Ben is one of the many adolescents who does not see high school as a doorway to a successful future but instead sees it as a place of humiliation where daily work spotlights inadequacies and high-stakes tests confirm failure. He is part of the nearly 70 percent of all ninth graders who enter that transition grade reading below grade level.[3] He's one of those kids you've seen far too often—some days

---

1. Alliance for Excellent Education. *Left Out and Left Behind: NCLB and the American High School.* (Washington, DC, 2003), p. 3. Accessed online at http://www.all4ed.org/publications /NCLB/NCLB.pdf

2. National Center for Education Statistics (NCES). *Nation's Report Card: Reading 2002.* (Washington, DC: US Government Printing Office, 2003.) Accessed online at http://nces.ed.gov /pubsearch/pubsinfo.asp?pubid=2003521

3. This number is based on the National Assessment of Education Progress scores in reading for grade 8 in 2003. 26 percent of eighth graders scored below the basic level and 42 percent scored only at the basic level. Consequently, 68 percent of entering ninth graders entered below the proficient level, only 29 percent scored at the proficient level, and 3 percent scored above the proficient level. You can view the entire report online at http://nces.ed.gov/nationsreportcard/reading/results2003/.

apathetic, other days angry, occasionally honest with his fears, more frequently defiant about his situation. In addition to reading below grade level, he struggles to write essays, finds algebra confusing, and declares his history textbook overwhelming. He has little encouragement for day to day success from his parents and no expectations from himself that he'll do anything after high school beyond "hang out, maybe get a job." While statistically Ben is not yet a school dropout, emotionally, socially, and academically he is.

As a teacher, a researcher, and the Chair of the National Adolescent Literacy Coalition, I know far too well the costs of failing Ben and students like him. I don't use the word "failing" as a synonym for retaining. I mean failing in the truest sense of the word—failing to teach Ben the skills he needs to be successful as a student in school, as an adult in his community, as a contributor in the workforce, and perhaps as a parent someday (if not already). Today's academic failure of these adolescents becomes tomorrow's economic and social problems for this country. This national crisis of our students' academic needs is far too serious, far too insidious, and has far too many consequences for us to ignore. Yes, there are three thousand plus excellent reasons for you to read this book and their names are Ben, Maria, LaTonya, Derek, Juan, Choi, Rafael, Victor, Sok, Mike, Luis, Mei, Isabella, Amanda, George, and. . . .

But why read *this* book? What sets this book apart from the many others you can find on motivating adolescents, on restructuring high schools, on providing programs that promise success? The answer is simple. *This* author takes us deep inside his ACCESS class, a class designed solely to help high school students like Ben gain the academic competencies needed to be successful in school. He shows us how to help students with reading, writing, studying, note taking, goal setting, and motivation. He shows us how to help those students in the bottom quartile find success not only in their language arts class but in all their content classes. There's no standing at the doorway peering in with this book, no wondering just how this or that was accomplished. From the first page you are thrust into the heart of the classroom, and there you discover that heart is at its center. You read *this* book because it is by Jim Burke, a master teacher who now shows us step-by-step what he does to help his students who teeter on the precipice of failure to regain their balance and head toward academic success. You read *this* book because it will change how you help students who need help the most.

When looking at the components of a program designed to encourage academic success for those most likely to fail, there's little argument about the essential elements. Of the many components, successful programs do the following:

1. Set high expectations and offer a rigorous curriculum for all students, even those who struggle with basic academic skills
2. Offer instruction that is direct and explicit, guided by research, and fosters active participation by the family and community
3. Focus special attention on the transition years (sixth and ninth grades)
4. Extend or provide additional time for literacy development
5. Provide appropriate grade-level materials
6. Integrate reading with writing
7. Encourage students to participate in cross-age tutoring programs
8. Require that students participate in daily sustained silent reading
9. Provide instruction for how to read and write both narrative, literary texts and expository, informative texts

Those requirements are never far from my mind as I evaluate programs, visit classrooms, talk with superintendents and principals, and watch teachers in action. They won't be far from your mind as you read about Jim's ACCESS classes, in which he attends to each of these necessities. With specific information ("Here are the emails I sent to the principal") and broad underlying beliefs (from philosophy toward teaching and learning to thoughts about the power of a single, individual teacher), ACCESS gives you access to a master teacher at work. This book, though focused on one teacher in one school with one group of students, shows all teachers what can be accomplished. I believe such individual stories are necessary because, while the collective voice gives us community, it is the individual voice that gives us strength. Jim's voice gives us much strength, much strength indeed.

Kylene Beers
Senior Reading Researcher, School Development Program, Yale University
Chair, National Adolescent Literacy Coalition
Author, *When Kids Can't Read: What Teachers Can Do*

# *Acknowledgments*

I have been blessed with mentors and allies since I entered teaching, and the work described in this book stems from the influence of those people. While this book examines the workings of a program I have created over the last few years, the principles of this course are derived from lessons I learned years ago. I began my teaching career at a private school for kids with developmental disabilities, where great teachers taught me to believe in the possibilities within each student. Years later, when I received my first job teaching English at Castro Valley High School, I was assigned, as new teachers so often are, to teach remedial English to a group of kids no one else seemed to want to teach. A few were special education kids; a couple were ESL students; a few were disaffected; and others had problems unknown even to themselves. It was those students, in that class, that taught me that kids—*all* kids—could do great things. I owe those students a huge debt of gratitude.

At Burlingame High School, and in my district, I must thank those who have taught me what is possible and have helped me make it so through their support and guidance. The teachers at my school are a dedicated group of professionals who have helped me shape the ACCESS program, often in invisible, informal ways while chatting around the photocopy machine early in the morning. A few—Diane McClain, Steve Mills, Michelle Riley, Rebecca Shirley, and Elaine Caret—have made substantial contributions to my own thinking, again through occasional conversations or their own efforts on behalf of the kids in my ACCESS program. The administrators, particularly my principal, Matt Biggar, and the assistant principal, Jackie Estes, have been exemplary from the beginning, not only helping me improve the program but also understanding what I was trying to accomplish through it. The counselors—Jean Marie Buckley, Karen Latham, and Bill Smith—have been great advocates for the program and my students all along; without their guidance and commitment, the program would not succeed. Mario Mora, the Latino outreach coordinator, has become an important influence and companion; I am grateful to him for helping me better understand the culture and needs of Latino students and their families through our collaborations and conversations in the last two years. I must single out three people for their contributions to the program: Lori Friel, Sue Glick, and Beth Pascal. These three women, as the book will repeatedly demonstrate, have helped to define the program and my role in it. They do this by constantly showing me what is possible, especially when I have initial doubts. This program is not my program; nor are its guiding principles mine; rather, the program is something we have created together through five years of collaboration, discussion, and friendship.

At the district level, I must thank the following people for their investment of time and faith in my work with the ACCESS program. Superintendent Sam Johnson and his predecessor, Tom Mohr, have never wavered in their commitment to the program. Assistant Superintendent Mark Avelar has also repeatedly demonstrated his investment in the program and the kids in it. Joan Rossi, the district's reading specialist, has been a great resource and advocate for not only my program but those at the other schools. I also wish to thank the reading teachers at the other schools, especially Patty Reik, for all I have learned through their example and our discussions these last five years. They are a remarkable group of dedicated teachers. Finally, I wish to thank Jeannie Kwong for all she does to ensure that the right kids find their way to my program; for months she is out in the field assessing kids at other schools to find those who need what my program has to offer.

Lois Bridges, my editor of many years, guided me through the writing of this book. No writer ever had a better editor, advocate, or friend. In addition to Lois, I wish to thank those at Heinemann who made this book possible: Abby Heim, Maura Sullivan, Amy Rowe, Brita Mess, Pat Carls, Eric Chalek, and Louise Richardson.

During the year I wrote this book, my family gave me the time and peace needed to work. My wife, Susan, is invaluable during the writing of any book, for she listens, questions, and always supports, helping me understand what I am trying to say while supporting my efforts to say it.

# Prologue: ACCESSing School

It's best to begin with the end toward which it all moves: graduation. It is a warm evening in early June; families mingle outside the auditorium where they have come to celebrate young adults' transition from adolescence and high school to . . . college? Work? Military? Confusion? For now, however, it is a moment to relish, one parents and friends, relatives and teachers have come to witness, a moment that was inevitable for most but not for all. While I come to celebrate all the students I have taught, one group tonight means more to me than any before: the students who four years ago entered Burlingame High School and were placed into my ACCESS (Academic Success) program because they lacked the skills and knowledge necessary to succeed in high school.

Just before my colleagues and I permit the eager families to enter, I run in and claim a seat in the front row, pausing to chat with different students from the band, all of whom were in my honors English class and all of whom I enjoy and respect. They are passing around the bottles of bubbles that the band members blow from the orchestra pit when the names of graduating band members are called out, a tradition that has existed since long before I arrived at the school thirteen years ago. Having secured my seat—a serious breach of teacher decorum, for such seats should go to students' families—I resume my station at the front doors just as the principal tells us to let people in.

My colleague Diane McClain and I collect tickets from the parade of family members streaming through the glass doors. We each pause at different moments to marvel at former students who have come to celebrate a sibling's graduation, or to exchange a few brief enthusiasms with different parents. Soon enough everyone is inside and the band begins to perform its prelude to the ceremony. Outside, unobserved by parents, the 319 graduating seniors assemble, their robes fluttering in the breeze like flags of the countries each student represents tonight. Looking at them, I think of the unwritten story of the years ahead—years of life and love, challenges and choices, promises and problems—which we have prepared them for in the four years they spent at Burlingame High. I leave my post to claim my seat so I don't miss a moment—or a shot, for I have brought my camera tonight, something I've never done before.

As the preliminary events—songs and speeches—take place, I review pictures on my digital camera from Senior Awards Night, which took place earlier that week. Images of Brian and Jessica standing proud with the other sixty-five recipients of the President's Academic Excellence Award. A photograph of Jorge accepting his soccer scholarship to a state college. Several pictures of Tony Arteaga going up to receive La Cultura Latina Scholarship and the College of San Mateo scholarship for a promising Latino student. Among the other photographs I look at are several of Maricela Vega and me as I present to her the first ACCESS College Scholarship, money she has already used to complete her application process for the University of California, which subsequently accepted her for the fall, making her the first member of her family to attend college.

As the principal begins calling off names of the different graduates, I sit up and listen for certain names, smiling and applauding when familiar kids step out under the lights and present themselves before the audience. Eventually the principal announces the first of my ACCESS students to graduate: Paulina Gavilanez, whose family came to the United States from Central America years ago. Everyone else sees a beautiful young Latina beaming with pride as she steps forward to receive her diploma, but I see something different, something more. I see the young woman who worked hard to learn how to "do school"; who stepped up when I asked for volunteers to work with developmentally disabled kindergartners (see Figure 1); whom I took to the local community college for a Latina Literature day and who said, upon getting out of my van and seeing the throng of college students, "Oh my God, they look just like me." And so they do, for she will be one of them in the fall. (See Figure 2.)

Other students come up—Emily, Daniel, Dominic, Zack, Danielle—and I marvel at all they have done to reach not just this moment but all those that will follow: nearly all of them are entering into some form of postsecondary education. When Tony Arteaga steps up, his eyes glisten with emotion and pride; behind me I hear his family yell his name, and everyone claps. He entered school reading at the sixth grade level and leaves it having resurrected La Cultura Latina Club. As the club's president, he accomplished many important goals while also serving as a member of the yearbook staff and working at his father's garage after school.

Still other ACCESS students—Meagan, Jessica, Tommy, Dana, Maricela—step out to get the praise (and diplomas!) they have earned. As we near the end of the ceremony, the last row inches forward. In the midst of the throng stands a young man with wiry hair and a pained but proud smile: Jorge Rodriguez. Everyone around me sees a happy boy about to receive his diploma, but I see a

FIGURE 1. Paulina, when she was a freshman, working with kindergartners at Washington Elementary School.

young man who worked with Down's syndrome children as a freshman; who stood before the faculty one morning as a freshman and spoke movingly about the importance of such work; who entered high school reading at the sixth-grade level but overcame those challenges to excel and win a soccer scholarship at California State University at Sonoma. I see a young man whose eyes shine with tears he won't let fall, who steps out before the audience and looks toward a sky he cannot see and holds up his hands in prayer and gratitude for the mother who died two nights before her first son graduated from high school and became the first one in his family to attend college.

As the ceremony moves toward its conclusion, I cannot help but think of those ACCESS students who are not present and wonder where they are and what will happen to them. Some have kept in touch: Allison Molina and Angie Velez moved away but maintained their focus, navigated the initial obstacles, and moved toward college. Others, like Mike and Steve, ended up at the continuation school because they fell so far behind that they could not graduate

FIGURE 2.    Paulina and me at graduation.

otherwise. But they did work—and graduate. Still others never returned, just disappeared: Chantierra, Shane, Kevin, a few others.

After circulating among the graduates to shake their hands and tell them one last time how proud I am of them, how grateful I am for all they taught me over the last four years, and after giving Jorge a big hug and telling his father how sorry I am for his loss, I walk down the street to my dirty truck and begin the drive home. The school year is done: my grades are in, my room is cleared out, my keys returned. Driving home, I think not of the summer months to come, but the year ahead, wondering what I can learn from those who just graduated that can help those who will arrive in only a couple of months on the shores of this country called Academia, where the customs are so foreign, the language so unfamiliar, the conventions so invisible—a place where, despite these challenges, they must learn to live so that they might not just survive but thrive, as the kids who graduated tonight did and will no doubt go on to do. (See Figure 3.)

As I near my home in San Francisco, I see the elegant Golden Gate Bridge, its lights describing its beauty against the darkness. My ACCESS students crossed from one place to another, but I am not the author of their success. Indeed, I am like one of the pillars of that bridge they crossed to get to this moment, a bridge made strong by the contributions of other teachers, family, coaches, clergy, and friends. I do believe, however, that the ACCESS program offers useful insights into academic success and helped these graduates learn not just how to cross bridges but to build their own. As Magdelene Lampert wrote of academic success:

> Although some students show up at school as "intentional learners" —people who are already interested in doing whatever they need to do to learn academic subjects—they are the exception rather than the rule. Even if they are disposed to study, they probably need to learn how. But more fundamental than knowing how is developing a sense of oneself as a learner that makes it

FIGURE 3.  Jorge Rodriguez right after graduation from high school.

socially acceptable to engage in academic work. The goal of school teaching is not to turn all students into people who see themselves as professional academics, but to enable all of them to include a disposition toward productive study of academic subjects among the personality traits they exhibit while they are in the classroom. If the young people who come to school do not see themselves as learners, they are not going to act like learners even if that would help them to be successful in school. It is the teacher's job to help them change their sense of themselves so that studying is not a self-contradictory activity. One's sense of oneself as a learner is not a wholly private construction. Academic identity is formed from an amalgamation of how we see ourselves and how others see us, and those perceptions are formed and expressed in social interaction. How I act in front of others expresses my sense of who I am. How others then react to me influences the development of my identity. (2001, 265)

The principles outlined in this book, as well as the story of ACCESS, offer teachers insights into a process and a program designed to help students very much like the kid I once was. It is a program that provides possibilities, one that teaches them what they can expect from themselves if they can take those risks that Jorge, Maricela, Tony, Megan, Brian, and many others did so that they might gain access not only to school but to a better life. Thus the work I describe in this book is, of course, professional, but it is also very personal, for each day the teacher I am has the chance to help kids like the student I was build the bridge that leads to the person they want to become.

# ONE
## *Introduction*
### The Traits of Effective Academic Success Programs

Robert Moses, founder of the Algebra Project, huddles around a pizza and talks with two high school students about how a graphic calculator and their expertise with it can change their lives.

Kurt Wootton, creator of the ArtsLit program at Hope High, directs a group of students in a performance of Shakespeare's *Othello* at Brown University. While most of their friends are working summer jobs or looking for trouble, these 160 kids are spending four hours every day memorizing lines, keeping journals, and engaging in thoughtful discussions with each other and the professional actors and directors who serve as mentors to the program.

Four seniors gather around a table after school at the ReSOARce Center, talking about their trip the previous day to Santa Rosa Junior College, where they spoke with college students and faculty about the demands—and advantages—of attending college. But these students need no convincing: today they are meeting with the SOAR (Successful Options for Academic Readiness) tutor whose specialty is the SAT for a last-minute prep session before they break off to join the specific academic tutoring sessions that meet every day after school.

Fausto and Darnell leave the elevator and look for the hundredth time at the wall of college acceptance letters as they move toward the classrooms at the HEAF (Harlem Educational Activities Fund) headquarters to get individual help on their academic classes. Passing the Oasis Room, they see kids reading, playing chess, writing. Fausto stops by the Onward! Office while Darnell checks in with the College Quest advisors regarding the upcoming admissions process. Entering the classroom area, they tell the SAT prep tutor they need to get some quick help on some economics homework, and then they'll catch up. The teacher smiles and says it's good to see them working so hard.

And in room 82, my classroom, a freshman girl named Simone, who rarely spoke the whole first semester, approaches the podium to speak. It is June, everyone's last day in the ACCESS (Academic Success) program, and she, along with the others, has come to share what she has learned over the last year:

> Throughout this freshman year I have learned a lot from this ACCESS class. I learned how to read better and I even brought up my reading ability by three grade levels in one year. I went from not wanting to read a book to reading three books in one semester.
>
> Learning how to read better was not the only thing I learned. I also learned strategies on studying for a test. Like in History we had a map test and so I took a blank map, filled in everything I knew and then after I would get the list of things I needed to know and find out which ones I had missed and study the things I did not know. Just like we did in ACCESS earlier that day. Another time me and a couple of kids in our class played Jeopardy, just like we did in our history class that morning, to help us study for a test the next day. After using those studying strategies both of those test scores were my highest.
>
> Later in the year we started the program Toastmasters. That is when I learned to speak in front of a group of people and feel comfortable while speaking. But it's not just speaking that's important. You also have to listen to what someone else is saying while they are giving a speech so you know what the person is talking about. But while you are speaking you have to speak loud enough, and clearly, so everyone can hear you and understand what you are saying. It's also to teach you not to fidget with anything or move around a lot. You also have to have eye contact with your audience. Before doing all this you have to write an organized speech so it is easy for you to read it and to give a good speech.
>
> I was also taught not to give up because if you give up you will never succeed. So I do everything the best I can and if I do bad, I know I have done something wrong, so I go back and figure out what that thing was and fix it. So then next time I won't make the same mistake and succeed. Like when I competed in a gymnastics meet and I fell off the beam while doing a cartwheel. After I figured out that my hips weren't squared, I fixed that next time and didn't fall off. It's like Mr. Burke says, "Success is not an accident."

What do all of these programs have in common? Let's examine first what they do *not* have in common. Some of the programs are classes, but usually not in the traditional configuration: some are semester- and yearlong courses taught by certificated teachers; a few are after-school programs run by teachers and adult mentors who establish a sanctuary in classrooms, libraries, community centers, or donated corporate offices. Certain programs focus overtly on academic essentials—note taking, reading, study skills—while others concentrate on everything from humanities and debate to business and chess, embedding the previously mentioned academic essentials into these more authentic contexts. One program serves Latino students in general, another Latina girls in particular. A program in California accepts children whose parents have not attended college; a course in St. Louis includes all incoming freshmen and, for the next nine months, teaches them everything they need to know about the academic world. Finally, some kids in such programs are unmotivated, but not all; others have special needs, but are not special education students or English language learners.

All of these programs, however, work with kids who struggle, whose success in middle and high school is not guaranteed, especially if they receive no support. All students in these programs need help with various academic essentials such as organizing, studying, testing; most tend to need intensive guidance in the areas of reading, writing, and mathematical reasoning. Such programs also typically have teachers who believe in these kids and the ability of that program to help these students. Teachers of such programs might just as easily be called mentors, coaches, guides, counselors, or masters; the students themselves are more like apprentices learning the craft of "doing school." Though there are certainly exceptions, the kids in these programs are not wealthy and often come from families that do not expect or support academic success. In the end, what these programs have in common is that they have *worked*, getting kids into Harvard and Spellman, but also helping them enter community colleges and graduate from high school, achievements many people thought were impossible when those students first entered high school.

These programs and their students share certain narrative elements. In *Conversational Borderlands: Language and Identity in an Alternative Urban High School* (2001), Betsy Rymes examines both dropouts and "drop ins" (students who return to school committed to achieving academic success) as well as one school's program, focusing on the role that narrative plays in both the individual's and the institution's success. Listening to "dropping in" stories of academic success from kids who were "exclusively low-income, ethnic minorities, many of whom had spent time in jail or juvenile hall, had babies, or were gang members," Rymes identified five common elements to their success narratives:

1. Abstract (not always present) [akin to exposition in a story]
2. Central Problematic Experience [akin to conflict in a story]

3. Response (usually psychological) and Turning Point [akin to climax]
4. Consequence (usually a return to school, a new role as advice-giver) [falling action and resolution]
5. Coda (not always present) [akin to an epilogue] (78)

In short, Rymes found that successful students had a "problematic experience" with their former self, which forced a realization that this was not who they really were or wanted to be; they were "on the wrong path," as one boy said. Successful students within such programs tend to distance themselves from that former self (i.e., have a "psychological response") and create some new self (the "turning point") that offers more hope, a result more consistent with the person they want to become or the role (within their family or the community) they want to play. The consequence of this turning point is that they create a role and then seek a program or person who can help them make this new story about themselves come true. Some programs attempt to *cause* that problematic experience by creating an awareness of where the students' choices will get them; other programs serve those students who have come to such realizations on their own. All of the students, however, need the support, guidance, and resources such academic success programs provide.

Rymes reinforces the role of narrative by referring to the high school students in her study as "authors," thereby implying that the students must accept responsibility for creating a new story of who they are or will become. Yet these authors still need editors—that is, mentors and guides—to help them shape their story as they work through the multiple drafts of self to, as one boy said, "get [himself] straight." Like any author or athlete determined to succeed, they must give the program and their teacher permission to push, challenge, and ultimately shape them, to develop in them the "Four Cs of Academic Success": commitment, content, competencies, and capacity (Burke 2004). One additional aspect of these programs merits mention: The successful students, because they give these programs permission to help them succeed, feel a strong sense of identification with and devotion to the programs; the students want to help the program's proposed story of success come true as well, so they tend to commit time and energy to not only their own success but also the program's. It is the one way they can show their gratitude for what the program has given them.

The kids in these programs, as well as the programs themselves, are what Sternin calls "positive deviants" (Sparks 2004, 49). These programs succeed where others have not, with kids whom others have not been able to help, under conditions that have constrained and ultimately defeated others. This concept of the positive deviant (PD) comes not from education but from, of all places, the organization Save the Children and its work on starvation in Vietnam. Jerry Sternin, who works for Save the Children and developed the model, describes PDs this way: "Positive deviants are people [or programs] whose behavior and practices produce solutions to problems that others in the group who have access to exactly the same resources have not been able to solve" (Sparks 2004, 49). Sternin outlines "the 6 Ds of the Positive Deviance Approach":

1. Define
   - What is the problem and what are the perceived causes and related community behavioral norms?
   - What would a successful solution/outcome look like (described as a behavioral or status outcome)?
2. Determine
   - Are there any individuals or entities in the community who already exhibit [the] desired behavior or status (identification of positive deviants)?
3. Discover
   - What are the unique practices or behaviors that enable positive deviants to outperform or find better solutions to problems than others in their community?
4. Design
   - Design and implement an intervention that enables others in the community to experience and practice new behaviors (focus on doing rather than transfer of knowledge).
5. Discern
   - What is the effectiveness of the intervention (determined by ongoing monitoring and evaluation)?
6. Disseminate
   - Make the intervention accessible to a wider constituency (replication/ scaling up). (Sparks 2004, 49)

How do we then define the problem of academic success? What *is* the problem for which these different academic success programs are the solution? Some identify skills as the urgent need; still others emphasize motivation. In truth, it is inevitably both, though some programs are for more motivated kids whose skills need to improve if they are to achieve the success they desire (e.g., in advanced courses). The authors of *Reading for Understanding: A Guide to Improving Reading in Middle and High School Classrooms* (Schoenbach et al. 1999) write about what they call "the quiet crisis":

> Meeting the challenge of higher academic standards is difficult in all the academic domains. In reading, national tests reveal that although the majority of U.S. students can read at a "basic" level, they cannot read and comprehend the types of higher-level texts essential to an individual's success in an information-based economy. Such tests tell us what most secondary teachers already know: students' limited reading proficiency keeps them from accomplishing the challenging work necessary to meet high academic standards.
>
> Teachers who work with low-achieving students often feel particularly frustrated by poor reading. They may feel especially overwhelmed when contemplating the distance between the expectations set out in reform documents about what students should know and be able to do in each subject area.
>
> But low academic literacy is by no means an issue only for poorly performing students. Even among those who do relatively well in class and score reasonably well on standardized tests, teachers can point to students who have difficulty comprehending and interpreting class texts, who fail to complete reading assignments, and who seem unlikely to become independent, lifelong readers. (4)

While this passage focuses on reading, it's important to note the program's more global emphasis on *academic* literacy and the need to teach students to think and work like apprentices so they can achieve academic success. *Realizing the College Dream*, a program started in Oakland, California, in collaboration with the University of California, offers a different perspective on the problems that many students must overcome if they are to succeed in school and outlines the three principles that guide the organization's efforts to help students obtain that success, as shown in Figure 1.1.

Such programs are all the more important in light of increased expectations by both the government and universities. Consider the initiative from the California Department of Education, beginning on page 9.

## Preface

**Realizing the College Dream** is a curriculum guide that supports teachers, counselors and community-based organizations in their work to increase the expectations of attending college by low-income and first-generation college students and their families. The lessons and workshops provide students with an opportunity to think of themselves as future college students and to debunk the myth that they can't afford college.

The guide is geared for middle school and community college students and adult learners, as well as parents and family members. It can be used in a variety of settings including classrooms, after-school programs, Saturday programs, and community and faith-based programs.

Sections A and B focus on students. The lessons can be used in their entirety, in the order presented, or adapted to fit your students' specific needs. In addition to covering material dealing with attaining higher education, each lesson is aligned with the national high school curriculum and skill standards in English/language arts, mathematics, social studies, and/or technology.

Section C is geared for families of college-bound youth and focuses on helping families of low-income and first-generation college students, most of whom have not experienced higher education themselves, understand the importance of attaining higher education. It goes on to outline practical step-by-step information on the process of how families can help their children realize the college dream.

When it comes to believing that students can access college, real and perceived barriers not only confront many first-generation students and their families, but also seem insurmountable.

## Here are the Facts

1. Low-income and first-generation students often live in communities where young people take jobs immediately after high school and do not see the value of going on to college if they are "making money now." Students benefit from identifying immediate and long-term educational and social goals through activities that illuminate future possibilities, such as researching careers that have increased earning potential.

2. The average parent or student believes college costs twice what it actually does, according to research. Also, many students and families do not understand financial aid, including eligibility and the kind of aid available. Misconceptions about public institution college costs are particularly acute, and recent media attention on rising college costs unnecessarily discourages students and their families.

3. Only 19 percent of low-income eighth graders will go on to complete an associate's degree or above, compared with 76 percent of high-income students. Now more than ever, employers are demanding an educated and skilled workforce. Opting out of postsecondary education significantly reduces a student's opportunities and results in diminished economic standing, which ultimately reinforces cycles of underemployment.

FIGURE 1.1. Preface for *Realizing the College Dream*. Reprinted with permission of the ECMC Foundation. (continues on next page)

**Realizing the College Dream** is guided by three principles:

1. Educate students and their families about the social and financial benefits of a college education, and provide information about financial aid to students and their families;
2. Expose middle school and high school students to college students, faculty, and campus life; and
3. Create instructional strategies that are hands-on and interactive, with the content and skills aligned with the national high school curriculum and skill standards.

**Realizing the College Dream** is divided into four sections.

The first three sections introduce a set of lessons and workshops that contain the following elements: introduction, learning goals, target audience, timing, materials needed, activities, supplemental materials, references, bibliography and websites (as appropriate). In addition, the lessons include the national high school curriculum and skill standards addressed in each lesson/workshop, and lesson-specific handouts for duplication or overheads. The fourth section, the Appendices, contains a handout for use throughout the curriculum. **The More You Learn, The More You Earn,** a template for an individual academic action plan, and sample program evaluation tools.

### Section A. Thinking of Yourself as a College-Bound Student
Lessons and Workshops for Students

This section asks students to dream about the future. First, they are asked to determine how much money they will need to develop the life-style they see for themselves, and then to explore jobs and career options. Both lessons point to the need for a college education to achieve their goals. Three experiences then take students into the world of higher education, by first researching all available options, then "experiencing" college through the eyes of students like themselves, and finally through role-playing as admissions directors so that they will understand more deeply the criteria and college-entrance requirements.

### Section B. Debunking the Myth that "You Can't Afford College"
Lessons and Workshops for Students

This section guides students through the process of learning about financial aid and why investing in college is a value-added expense. Activities give students an experience in understanding how their values about spending money can affect the future, and how to compare the financial aid packages offered by different colleges.

### Section C. Getting Involved and Staying Involved
Workshops and Presentations for Families of College-Bound Youth

This section gives families the information they need to help their students prepare for college as well as what can be expected when they attend college. It also provides a step-by-step guide on how to develop a financial aid workshop to be used by teachers, counselors, and community or faith-based workers for students and families.

### Section D. Appendices
This section contains statistics on earnings grouped by educational level to show the positive economic impact of education, a sample individual action plan for high school students, and questionnaires to assess the **Realizing The College Dream** curriculum.

ECMC Foundation sincerely hopes that students and families benefit from the lessons and workshops offered in this guide and that the lessons learned will be used to realize the dream of a college education.

FIGURE 1.1. *Continued.*

## High Performance High School Initiative: Improving High Schools from the Inside Out

*We can no longer limit the adult opportunities of our students because of our failure to provide them both challenges and support in high school . . . It's time to change high schools from the inside out.*

—State Superintendent Jack O'Connell

### The Problem

Over the past five years, California's public high school enrollment has increased by 14 percent and is projected to increase by a like amount over the next five years. Yet less than 10 percent of high schools have reached the optimal level of 800 on the Academic Performance Index (API), and on average, high schools have met their annual API growth targets only about 40 percent of the time. The majority of California's high school students are not reaching the academic levels needed to succeed in the workplace, in college, or as effective citizens. Nearly two-thirds of high school students are not adequately prepared to enter college or transition to a career. There remains a huge mismatch between the highly skilled technical jobs available throughout the economy and the lack of individuals emerging from the education system with necessary academic and technical skills.

### Solutions

State Superintendent Jack O'Connell is proposing a new High Performance High School Initiative aimed at focusing high schools toward the primary role of preparing students for admission to college or transition to a career. O'Connell's High Performance High School Initiative will confront the challenge of improving high school performance and begin a process of fundamental change by:

IMPLEMENTING HIGH EXPECTATIONS FOR ALL STUDENTS
- Require all students to take courses required for college entrance, known as "A–G" requirements.
- Increase the number of students enrolled in academically rigorous courses such as Advanced Placement and International Baccalaureate programs.
- Encourage and assist high schools to expand successful college prep programs, such as AVID, Puente, and career paths and academies.
- Provide early intervention so that struggling students can be prepared for postsecondary endeavors.

## DEVELOPING WORLD CLASS TEACHERS AND SITE ADMINISTRATORS

- Give incentives to high schools to provide sustained, standards-based professional development.
- Mentor and support all beginning teachers and principals.
- Encourage school districts and universities to create leadership development programs to meet the need for qualified new principals.
- Make it easier to recruit qualified new principals from the business community.

## DEVELOPING WORLD CLASS INSTRUCTIONAL MATERIALS

- Guide high schools toward standards-aligned instructional materials by a state "seal of approval."

## SUPPORTING SUCCESSFUL TRANSITIONS TO POSTSECONDARY EDUCATION

- Plan in middle school to assess and identify students needing targeted intervention and those who are ready to accelerate into the high school curriculum.
- Expand career academies such as health, fire science, government, and manufacturing that allow students to explore careers, work as interns, and prepare to continue their education in college or transition to employment.
- Implement CSU Early Assessment programs, Early College High Schools, written agreements, or compacts to increase student access to postsecondary-level options.

## NURTURING AND DEVELOPING A COMMUNITY OF SUPPORT TO FOSTER HIGH STUDENT ACHIEVEMENT

- Promote community support to implement innovative programs and approaches.
- Include parents, businesses, higher education institutions, community-based organizations, and public agencies.
- Convene a summit to focus on launching and implementing the high school initiative. (O'Connell 2004)

More and more, initiatives like this drive decisions in my own district as well as those of colleagues of mine. I know one teacher who works at a very troubled high school in Los Angeles where the principal has made the University of California admission requirements the graduation requirements at his school of nearly three thousand students. It is a noble goal and certainly embodies high expectations, but one must also put in place the resources and programs, such as those I discuss in this book, to help students achieve those goals.

Before outlining the common traits of effective academic success programs, I want to discuss the Four Cs of Academic Success (Burke 2004). The Four Cs place the previous comments about reading and school success in the larger context of competencies (i.e., skills) that students must have to succeed in school, and they emphasize that reading, for example, is only one piece of the academic puzzle. Figure 1.2 provides a summary of the Four Cs.

It is within this framework of the Four Cs that I offer the following analysis of academic literacy programs. My hope is that the analysis will provide a road map for those creating or adapting such programs in their own schools. I will use this framework to examine my own program and its effectiveness for incoming high school students reading seriously below grade level.

Effective academic success programs:

## 1. DEVELOP STUDENTS' AND OTHERS' *COMMITMENT* TO ACADEMIC SUCCESS.

The teacher:

- Begins where students are and provides instruction and experiences that will reliably get them where they need to be.
- Establishes and maintains high expectations.
- Develops a student's identity as someone who can and does succeed at academic work.
- Maintains faith in *all* students' ability to succeed as well as in the methods and materials used to achieve such success.
- Fosters a sense of community within the classroom and a feeling of pride that students are a member of that community. (Through this process, a new, viable identity emerges, which the program supports.)
- Enlists various mentors, masters, and advocates who contribute their gifts and support the students' immediate academic and long-term personal success.
- Reaches out to key constituents—teachers, administrators, counselors, mentors, parents, and students themselves (9–12)—to ensure present and future success outside the program and to serve as advocates and guides through such processes as the college application process.
- Constantly creates and reiterates the context for why academic success matters, what it leads to, and why students need to possess certain knowledge or skills.

# THE FOUR Cs OF ACADEMIC SUCCESS

## Commitment

*Commitment* describes the extent to which students care about the work and maintain consistency in their attempt to succeed.

Key aspects of **commitment** are:

- *Consistency:* Everyone can be great or make heroic efforts for a day or even a week; real, sustainable success in a class or on large assignments requires consistent hard work and quality conscience.

- *Effort:* Some students resist making a serious effort when they do not believe they can succeed. Without such effort, neither success nor improvement is possible.

- *Emotional investment:* Refers to how much students care about their success and the quality of their work on this assignment or performance. Directly related to perceived relevance and importance. This is what Jaime Escalante calls *ganas*, which means "the urge to succeed, to achieve, to grow."

- *Faith:* Students must believe that the effort they make will eventually lead to the result or success they seek. Faith applies to a method or means by which they hope to achieve success.

- *Permission:* Students must give themselves permission to learn and work hard and others permission to teach and support them if they are to improve and succeed.

## Content

*Content* refers to information or processes students must know to complete a task or succeed on an assignment in class. Domains include academic, social, procedural, cultural, vocational, ethical, and cognitive.

**Content** knowledge includes:

- *Conventions* related to documents, procedures, genres, or experiences.

- *Cultural reference points* not specifically related to the subject but necessary to understand the material, such as:
  - People
  - Events
  - Trends
  - Ideas
  - Dates

- *Discipline- or subject-specific matter* such as names, concepts, and terms.

- *Features, cues, or other signals* that convey meaning during a process or within a text.

- *Language* needed to complete or understand the task.

- *Procedures* used during the course of the task or assignment.

FIGURE 1.2.   The Four Cs of Academic Success from *School Smarts: The Four Cs of Academic Success* by Jim Burke, © 2004 (Heinemann: Portsmouth, NH).

A full-size, downloadable version of this form is available on the *ACCESSing School* page of the Heinemann website, at www.heinemann.com.

*May be copied for classroom use. ACCESSing School by Jim Burke (Heinemann, Portsmouth, NH), © 2005.*

## THE FOUR Cs OF ACADEMIC SUCCESS

### Competencies

*Competencies* are those skills students need to be able to complete the assignment or succeed at some task.

### Capacity

*Capacities* account for the quantifiable aspects of performance; students can have great skills but lack the capacity to fully employ those skills.

Representative, general **competencies** include the ability to:

- *Communicate* ideas and information to complete and convey results of the work.

- *Evaluate* and *make decisions* based on information needed to complete the assignment or succeed at the task.

- *Generate* ideas, solutions, and interpretations that will lead to the successful completion of the task.

- *Learn* while completing the assignment so students can improve their performance on similar assignments in the future.

- *Manage* resources (time, people, and materials) needed to complete the task; refers also to the ability to govern oneself.

- *Teach* others how to complete certain tasks and understand key concepts.

- *Use* a range of tools and strategies to solve the problems they encounter.

Primary **capacities** related to academic performance include:

- *Confidence* in their ideas, methods, skills, and overall abilities related to this task.

- *Dexterity,* which allows students, when needed, to do more than one task at the same time (aka multitasking).

- *Fluency* needed to handle problems or interpret ideas that vary from students' past experience or learning.

- *Joy* one finds in doing the work well and in a way that satisfies that individual's needs.

- *Memory,* so students can draw on useful background information or store information needed for subsequent tasks included in the assignment.

- *Resiliency* needed to persevere despite initial or periodic obstacles to success on the assignment or performance.

- *Speed* with which students can perform one or more tasks needed to complete the assignment or performance.

- *Stamina* required to maintain the requisite level of performance; includes physical and mental stamina.

FIGURE 1.2. *Continued.*

## 2. DEVELOP STUDENTS' *CONTENT* KNOWLEDGE SO THEY CAN COMPLETE ASSIGNMENTS AND PARTICIPATE IN ACADEMIC ACTIVITIES.

The teacher:
- Develops students' general academic and subject-specific language so they can understand and complete assignments.
- Teaches students the rules—spoken and unspoken—that govern school (i.e., facilitates the students' enculturation).
- Expands students' knowledge of the world through exploration, investigation, and conversation about ideas, events, people, and places.
- Respects and makes use of students' knowledge and experience outside the classroom in order to help them feel more comfortable and successful inside the classroom.
- Recognizes that content is both structured and opportunistic, responsive to emerging situations to help students succeed *now*—and in the long run.
- Develops, through reflection, knowledge (regarding instructional and programmatic practices) about what works and why to create an ongoing cycle of continuous improvement.
- Teaches social customs and conventions students will need to succeed in the world they are preparing to enter.

## 3. DEVELOP STUDENTS' *COMPETENCIES* IN THOSE AREAS ESSENTIAL TO ACADEMIC SUCCESS IN GENERAL AND THAT TEACHER'S CLASS IN PARTICULAR.

The teacher:
- Teaches students strategies they can use to do their work successfully.
- Accelerates instruction while making sure that everyone, especially those who need additional support, understands and learns the lessons.
- Transcends specific subject context to help students see and learn how to use these skills in a broad range of academic, vocational, and personal circumstances.
- Demystifies successful performances, processes, and products by having students analyze how certain results were achieved (i.e., what they did, how they did it, and why it worked).
- Employs or draws on a range of methods—sometimes idiosyncratic or nontraditional—to help students understand, apply, and remember important ideas and procedures.

- Trains students to use certain organizational techniques to better manage their time, demands, and resources so they can focus on learning the academic content of a course.
- Requires and teaches students to communicate what they learn and how they solve problems using a variety of written, spoken, and graphic techniques.
- Provides access to and instruction in the use of advanced learning tools such as computers and graphic calculators and research facilities such as libraries and laboratories.

## 4. DEVELOP STUDENTS' *CAPACITY* TO MEET THE DEMANDS OF VARIOUS ACADEMIC TASKS.

The teacher:
- Emphasizes fluency and dexterity, developing through many different ways the ability to see and understand problems from multiple perspectives and solve them using a range of strategies and techniques.
- Develops students' ability to generate explanations, hypotheses, ideas, questions, and solutions.
- Addresses the need not only to learn to do certain tasks but to do them quickly and for long periods of time so that the student may, for example, succeed on lengthy state tests.
- Builds up students' confidence in their ability to do what teachers ask and assign.

While the Four Cs offer a useful framework for analyzing academic success programs, it's not complete, for there are a few stray factors that don't fit neatly into the box. Successful programs honor and adapt themselves to the local culture of the school and its community. Thus they inevitably have clearly articulated principles that shape the curriculum and teaching practices, but they are not "canned." They are often the result of charismatic teachers (one thinks of Jaime Escalante), but if they are to evolve into successful programs that can sustain themselves, they must develop techniques others can learn and apply to achieve consistent and significant results. Effective programs tend, as Sternin pointed out earlier, to work with what they have instead of relying on outside assistance that can dry up and render the program unable to continue (e.g., if grant funding runs out and the district is not willing to pick up the cost of continuing the program). Thus effective programs typically draw on their own local intellectual resources, which makes for more frequent and effective collaboration; moreover, such ongoing discussions result in a more coherent, cohesive framework by generating a set of common terms, practices, and values. Finally, effective programs use performance data from different sources but for similar ends: to refine the program's structure and improve instruction in order to achieve both short- and long-term results. In short, they use the data to ensure that what they do makes a difference, or as Mike Schmoker (1999) writes, "they are concerned with processes only insofar as *these processes affect results*" (5).

# TWO
# *ACCESS*
## A Program Overview

It's the seventh week of the second semester and I'm sitting with the Michael, the biggest kid in my class, who is trying not to let everyone see that he is crying. He has worked very hard this semester to succeed; he's been proud of his scores; he's taken risks, visited college campuses, and received generous praise from people he has met (e.g., a college president and professors); and he's missed many days of school because his parents took him on vacations or let him stay home when he should have been in school. Still, he is completely surprised by the row of Fs on the progress report I am showing him. I received an early copy of it from the data clerk; tomorrow the real progress report will arrive at his house. Frankly, I am as surprised as he is. I've been monitoring his efforts, showering him with praise for keeping on top of things (especially in Algebra). But slowly we are both learning how school works, realizing for the hundredth time that *everything* matters, that success demands a steady vigilance, often at those moments when you don't have it to offer or when it seems to matter least.

Meanwhile, Patrick and Vito are getting tutored by Andrew, the elite junior I recruited to help kids with their math classes since the semester grades show that many kids in my class are failing or earning a D in Algebra (though *not* in greater numbers than the overall freshman population). I just finished speaking to Patrick about his progress report, which we agreed showed important progress after six weeks of unprecedented hard work: the D+ in Algebra represents a 30 percent increase in his academic performance over the last semester. In another corner of the room, Ryan and Chris search the Internet for images to use in a time line for their Modern World History class. Four kids are gone: They go once a week to tutor kindergartners in Ms. Bogdis' class at the elementary school two blocks away. Two of the kids who go, Aline and Carlos, play an especially important role there when they go: they speak Spanish and can help the kids in her class who speak almost no English.

While I talk with kids at my conference table at the front of the room, Carl slumps at his desk, using the novel he should be reading for English as a pillow to rest his head. I could nudge him—I'm that close to him—but instead I let him be. He's been depressed lately and we've talked about why: family problems. Yet he is doing his work this semester. Perhaps seeing all his buddies drift away one by one over the last six months has made him realize that he has to take advantage of the opportunity that his friends lost when they got expelled, moved away, or were reassigned to special education.

Karina, on the other hand, is absorbed in her history homework, alternating between solo work and a group of classmates she consults when she needs help. After failing her classes the first semester, she transferred into my class and immediately gave herself permission to make changes, changes that have stuck and resulted in dramatic improvement on her progress report: from a .333 GPA first semester to a 2.1 on the first progress report of the second semester. Daniel Finnegan and Sergio Torres made similar turnarounds after the first semester, which is why I encouraged them to go out on the job-shadowing opportunities available today. Daniel is spending the day with the police department, and Sergio went to the automobile manufacturing and design plant to further investigate his passion for cars for the day. Next week we're all going on a trip to the local community college so the kids can see what a college campus looks like and, moreover, see that the people who go to such colleges look just like they do.

To an outsider, what is going on might seem anything but remarkable and certainly not exemplary. Movies have taught us to expect dramatic moments, the kind underscored by emotion-arousing music, that signal complete transformation and send us out of the theater sighing, inspired by how those kids' lives were changed by that incredible person, the teacher, who came into their lives. But this isn't the story I have to tell. Instead, mine is a collection of small moments, yet moments no less of wonder—the girl who raises her hand (twice!) to contribute to a class discussion after six months of silence; the boy who begins to do the most obvious thing imaginable: turn in his work; the kids who earn the highest grade they have ever received on their history exam: a C−, which we celebrate before working even harder to do better, for we are in this together.

Meanwhile in the back of the room, two boys are passionately engaged in a game of chess, as they are whenever they get the chance, their thoughtful faces slung in their hands, eyes reading the opposition, minds churning, thinking, plotting. And Amanda, in the closing minutes of class (during which she once again did no work) has taken up my markers and written, "Amanda is hot and sexy," on the board, which she then erases, only to replace it with "Amanda is cool!" which she also erases before leaving at the bell with only "Amanda" on the board and a sad, lost look in her eyes.

At the bell, some stay to work, talk, hang out; others shuffle out, saying, "See you tomorrow, Mr. Burke!" or asking if they have to give their speech for Toastmasters on Friday. While the next period of ACCESS doesn't start for twenty minutes, many of the kids spend the recess period in the class where they have come to feel at home and have learned how to do school. I pull out an apple and sit at my conference table, looking at the roster, noting the names of those who are not here any longer. Juan, Pedro, Jenny, Gianna, Janae. Each gone for a different reason: Juan to his mother's in Sacramento, Pedro to a new school after his parents bought a new house outside the district, Janae out of the ACCESS program because she excelled so much after one semester, and Gianna because she couldn't handle the stigma of being in a class that marked her as different in any way.

Finally, I reach for the paper from Fanny, a girl new to the school, whose silence and sudden arrival in the middle of the year suggest a story. I asked her to tell me what I should know to allow me to help her settle into the school and teach her well. She wrote:

> Now, I still can't forgive myself for what I did. I made my mom sick, she had heart surgery two weeks ago, because I had too many trouble; I made her so mad, sad, and unhappy. However she still cares about me a lot, still trying to make me good, and still loves me a lot. To me, she's the best mother in the world, and will always be.
>
> I'm from the city [San Francisco], and the reason why I moved here is because I was bad, and all my friends are bad. I was in a gang, we do all the bad stuff as you can think, or maybe I should say we never do good stuff. Last time we went to a gang fight, I don't know why the police came, and almost all of us got pulled over. My mom was so tripping about it, and she was so sad, she told me to quit the gang, and be good. But I didn't want to, because it's easy to get in the gang, and hard to get out, they got so many people. And I thought it was so cool, so I didn't quit.
>
> My mom got mad, she quit her job to make sure that I go home on time, and not going out to chill with my friends. She took my money away, and my cell phone, too, she didn't let me go online, and talk on the phone. I don't like that, so I got so pissed. I told my friends about it, they said I shouldn't always follow what my mom said, and don't be a mammy's girl, I thought they were right. They told me to run away, mom was so worry about me, she didn't sleep well, and eat well. She was looking for me the whole time, but she couldn't

find me, and she got sick, so she called the police. And they found me in five days. I got trouble for that. So we moved here as soon as possible.

   If I got a chance, I would never join the gang, and be bad, but now it's already too late. Now, I just hope my mom can get well, and I'll try my best to be a good student.

Fanny entered our school and the ACCESS program reading at the sixth grade (with only four months of school left) and with a cumulative GPA of roughly 0.0; when the last bell rang four months later, she was reading at the eighth grade and her GPA was 2.75, but what mattered most was the smile that began to appear on her face as she realized it was not "too late" and that her "best" was paying off, that her story was not finished, that it could, in fact, be revised, improved upon—as could she.

   But I don't know how it will turn out when I first read Fanny's story. After I finish reading her story, I get up, grab the set of progress reports for *all* students who are or have been in ACCESS in the past three years, and walk toward the office to see if I have any mail. I stop along to way to check in with former ACCESS students, celebrating with them their success or expressing concern and giving encouragement if they are getting into hot water ("Tanisha! How are you? What's going on with your math class? You got a B in math last year!"), reminding them that it's not too late, and that I am, even though they no longer have a class with me, available, or as they would say, "there for them."

   In my box I find a completed survey I recently gave to all the ACCESS students who are seniors, for they are the first group of ACCESS kids to graduate. Question 5 on the survey asked kids to identify a person, class, or experience that made the biggest difference for the student in the last four years. Dominic Mitchell, a shy, awkward, friendly boy wrote:

> I think that the ACCESS class helped me grow my academic ability to do bet-
> ter in school. Mr. Burke really influenced me to keep my grades up and to
> look into college to start my career. We really need to strengthen the ACCESS
> program so that more people become involved in the class and hopefully look
> into their careers and make the right choices. I think that all the guest speakers
> we had helped me in a way to find what the outside world is all about and how
> to manage your way to success. Another person that helped me change my
> ways around school was a really good friend of mine named Jessica who is cur-
> rently a junior at Burlingame [and a former ACCESS student; see article in
> Figure 2.1, page 28, in which she is featured]. She really helped me along the
> way to do better in school and to succeed. She is the kind of person who was
> always there for me and would always help me on my homework whenever I
> needed help. So these two people changed who I am today at Burlingame.

I want to be able to tell you that I have cracked the DNA of academic success and can ensure that your own program will produce kids like Dominic and Jessica, but I can't do that. I do not have a solution to offer you; instead, I have my story and the stories of my students. All solutions must be local, for while kids are kids, each school and community represents its own unique challenges. Thus I offer the following story of my program, along with our methods and materials, in the spirit of George Bernard Shaw's assertion that any writer who writes honestly about his own town writes about all towns, and any writer who writes the truth about one person tells the story of all people.

## *What* Is *ACCESS?*

The name of the program itself marks the beginning of the story, for it was the very notion of labeling that got me thinking. You will not find *ACCESS* or *Academic Success* on my students' transcripts or in our course catalog, nor will you find either of them on the district's list of approved courses. What you'll find instead is a course called Developmental Reading. *Developmental Reading* is not a name that gets the kids running down the hall to get to class, nor is it one they speak out loud to their friends when they break and say they "gotta get going to class." It reeks of remediation, signals trouble, and generally causes in kids a sense of embarrassment, even shame that marks a private defeat. So the first year I taught the course, I called it Reading Workshop. Ooh—big change.

I doubt, in retrospect, that any kids said, "Hey, gotta go, man, don't want to be late to the reading workshop!" In that class, we read, and read some more, and the kids improved, but their grades did not. We did SSR (sustained silent reading) and read aloud; we did book talks and response logs. They became readers, but only a few, by some good fortune I cannot identify, became *students*. Their reading scores rose steadily all year and, when I retested them in June, were mostly at grade level. Their GPAs were, however, terrible; nothing seemed to transfer. I concluded that while reading was essential to their success, it was not the only source of trouble nor was it the only skill they needed to develop. I concluded that they lacked academic confidence. So during that summer, I developed a more comprehensive program for incoming freshmen, one that would give them access to not only the texts they read but the lectures they heard, the films they watched, the classes they took, and the life they sought. The more I thought about it, the more I realized these kids often did not know what school—or reading for that matter—was *for*, what purpose it served. Thus one day I came up with ACCESS: Academic Confidence Creates

Equality and Success for All Students. I went to bed feeling like I had created something important. When I woke up and told my wife, she asked what ACCESS stood for, and I got confused and forgot the last half. Soon after, I realized that ACCESS equaled ACademic SucCESS, and so the acronym and the concept stayed but the meaning changed. Ultimately, this process of self-definition proved to be important, providing an opportunity to reflect on the guiding principles and long-term goals, not unlike Stephen Covey's "personal mission statement." (Covey 1990)

Many programs out there have created brand names for their ideas. AVID, Puente, KIPP, Accelerated Schools, and others have established distinct names for their programs, building these successful programs on strong foundations made of specific techniques all teachers and students must follow if they are to become part of the franchise, the network. When I began planning this book, I intended to offer ACCESS as a similar solution, a name with specific principles and practices, but then I realized how much began with creating a name for our program, how much ownership that gave me, how much I talked about it to the kids as an example of taking responsibility, not letting the district decide who or what we were about (so long as I still delivered improved reading scores!). So I begin by urging you to think about your own school, your own community, your own students and finding a name that honors something specific to that community or culture. *Puente*, for example, means "bridge" in Spanish, which captures what that program tries to build for the Latino students enrolled in it. Just as I offer you here the story of my solutions, you must create a program that tells the story your community, school, and students' needs, and give it a title (i.e., a name) that has meaning to those *inside* the program as well as those outside who might want to come into the program. Kids will not, to return to an earlier theme, say they "gotta get to Developmental Reading," but they will say out loud, "I gotta go to ACCESS," which sounds somehow different to us both, more hopeful, more ambitious, more interesting.

Jonathan Freedman (2000) describes the process whereby the AVID program arrived at its name:

> Mary Catherine [Swanson, the founder of AVID] would fill those seats with her own students, exposing them to college campuses and cultural experiences that would ordinarily fall far outside of their scope of experience.
> This innovative new program needed a name. Jim [Grove] imagined an average student from a poor, chaotic background, not unlike his own—a bright kid who, despite hurts and insecurities, was avid to learn. Avid comes from *avidus*, meaning "eager for knowledge." Mary Catherine liked the connotations. If AVID was used as an acronym, what might the letters stand for?

Jim rubbed his beard. "*A* could stand for *achievement*," he suggested.

What inner qualities would be required to reach that goal? Students and teachers, Jim and Catherine agreed, would need *individual determination* to overcome obstacles and strive to improve learning. By what path? *Achievement Via Individual Determination.*

"I like the way it flows," Jim said, as the words rolled easily off his tongue.

"Yes, but many programs promise achievement," Mary Catherine warned him, wrinkling her brow. "What we are proposing is to move students forward academically and socially." She closed her eyes and contemplated the ultimate goal that would make this program unique. Suddenly, her eyes flashed open. "*A* is for Advancement!"

"Advancement Via Individual Determination," Mary Catherine enunciated each word distinctly, her voice rising with excitement. "AVID—that's the name!"

Thus, AVID was born. (34)

Flash forward four years to the first day of school. The first class of ACCESS graduates have moved off into their lives (72% of them into college). Twenty-five freshmen shuffle into my classroom, looking around. First, I arrange them by alpha order so I can do my best to know all their names by the next day. Then, I tell them about the name, tell them that we never refer to the class as "Developmental Reading," that this class is about much more than reading. I ask them to get out a sheet of paper and a pencil. Knowing "my people" well enough by this point, I know there will be a couple who have no supplies, kids who think there must be some rule against doing *any* work on the first day of school—or even the first week. On the board, I tape a sheet of binder paper (so they get a clear sense of what I want their work to look like) and draw a T-note format on the page. Atop the left side, I have them write, "ACCESS Is," and on the right side: "ACCESS Is Not." Then I turn out the lights, turn on my laptop and projector, and tell them to use bullets to generate a list of words that define the program. What they see is a five-minute slide show of images from the last four years of the program. I don't say anything. It's just images and music for five minutes. Instead of slamming them with a reading test as they walk in, or passing out a thick course syllabus, or assigning them textbooks, I read with them a story told through images, a story I immediately play again, narrating it out loud the second time through. I stop periodically to remind them to write down what they see, giving them examples of the kind of language they might find helpful to use.

As the slides go by, the pleasant melodies of Philip Glass playing in the background on my laptop, I comment on the images. I introduce students to the stories, the kids, telling them next year *their* pictures will be up there, and I will be telling those kids the story of what we'll do *this* year. Krish Singh, whom I met days before at freshmen orientation day, writes that ACCESS is:

- Helping class
- Working together
- Social
- Learning new things
- Learning how to study
- About how to read better
- Reading a lot
- Speakers
- Field trip to college campus

On the right side, he, like everyone else, writes that it is "not a reading class." After this, I have them write a brief paragraph to summarize what they saw and learned. Krish explains that:

> ACCESS is an important and social way to learn how to be successful, in not just school but in life also. As I watched the slideshow I have seen many people work hard to graduate and to go on in life. I believe that this isn't just a regular reading class. I actually think this is more of a social and learning how to learn kind of class.

Within ten minutes we have worked together to define what the course is and what it has to offer them. My goal that first day is for them to leave wanting to come back, realizing that this class will help them. Still, I need more; I want past students to explain what this class did for them; I also want the kids reading on the first day so that I can establish a culture of high expectations and show them that I will help them meet those expectations. So I pass out a set of letters that the students must read and annotate, choosing "the most important lines" that will help to answer the question, *What is ACCESS and how can it help me?* In this way, I introduce within the first period the following academic essentials: note taking, reading with a purpose, annotating, asking questions, and using techniques like bullets and graphic organizers to help them generate and organize ideas so they will be prepared to write when the time comes. Here are two letters written by kids who did well in my class, but more importantly, continued to do well after they left the ACCESS program. Joanie Naify wrote:

> Dear Incoming Freshman,
>
> Welcome to a great year of new experiences and chances to become who you want to be remembered as. What middle school have you come from? Many

new classmates will be from all middle schools around the area, maybe even some you have never heard of.

I was an incoming freshman from Burlingame Intermediate School and I didn't quite know what to expect as a freshman besides the laughs of other older students such as the seniors, juniors, and sophomores. On the first day of school and throughout the year it wasn't like that at all. Yes, you will be called a freshman, but that's all they will really say. As they say, "Hey it's a freshman," just remember so were they. As I was scared of older classmen, I had been in an art class when I was 1 out of 2 other freshmen. After a few weeks got into the school year, the seniors had talked to me, they were nice and I got to know them. So if you end up in class with older classmen, don't be intimidated. They are all still young just like you.

I learned to be confident. By the end of the year, I learned what it was to be successful and how to achieve it. Setting goals for yourself during your freshman year is a good way to start out a smart year. Even if what is expected of you doesn't get to your head until beginning of second semester, use that knowledge of last semester and end with a great year. Being confident in each and every one of your classes will help you keep up your social life also. Having good friends in your life is also a good start. Pick friends that will be helpful and mindful of the success you want. Your social life shouldn't take over your academic course of the year.

This ACCESS class will help bring up your reading throughout the year. It will help you to understand all types of reading you will encounter here at Burlingame and years to come. This class also gives you the chance to understand life itself. It will help you to know what kind of person you want to become in the near future. Being in this class helped me to become a better person, and to understand all the aspects of life, and how to deal with them. This class has taught me what to do before, during, and after I read. Knowing those simple things it has made me become a better reader. I now understand all the reading I have done, and I plan to keep up this progress.

Well as you have read through this letter, I hope you take either a little or a lot of this in consideration, and if not now I hope one day. I wish I had someone to tell me this when I was a freshman on my first day, but because of this class I have learned it a different way. So as I say good luck, I hope to know you will be able to say, "I can succeed."

Sincerely,
Joanie Naify

And Michael Caroline wrote:

Dear Incoming Freshman:

Welcome to Burlingame High School. BHS is a great school. It is very educating. When I first came to BHS the first day of school I was excited of meeting new people and the different teachers. I was also terrified of the upper classman.

I thought they would punk on me and push me around the lockers, and take my things and throw them to the ground. But I thought wrong. BHS is a very safe and friendly school.

My name is Michael Caroline. BHS has its ups and downs and the good days and the bad days. As each semester went by classes, projects, assignments began to get harder and harder as months pass by. It was really easy for the first few months but as you get into the middle of the year, that's the time all the baby crying should stop. You have to work really hard and do your best in all your classes so teachers and people would like you and respect you. As for myself, I needed a lot of adjusting during my past year as a freshman. I had a lot of struggles, failed my tests, projects weren't that great. But by and by, you start to improve and think more harder, and act more mature. ACCESS is a great class for those who need help in doing your best, and reading, raising your stamina.

High school is a whole different ballpark than in middle school. There are a different set of rules and policies, and much stricter teachers. You don't get babied around in this school. You turn in your work on the exact date it's due, unless it's been extended. As you maybe heard, high school was just fun and games. Well no it isn't. You have to take notes, and work your butt off to pass your classes, or else summer school. Also being ready for finals. Burlingame has fun times. We have football games, basketball games, special events, dramatic plays, and special activities and programs. As you know on Wednesdays all students are to go to school at 9 in the morning instead of 8 because teachers have meeting and etc. So you can enjoy your extra hour sleep, but when you first step in your first class, it's back to work, no more fantasies.

I have learned a lot this year. I learned to study even longer and not just fool around and skim through reviews, to do my best on quizzes and tests even though I don't really know the answer, and to just be yourself for people to like you. I learned all this by my mistakes. Without mistakes you can't fix your problems, and as each month passes by you improve more and more. The main thing you should do to be successful is you should always think positive, study for tests, take good notes, do well on your projects, and study well on your finals. Those are the main things in being a successful student.

ACCESS is a very helpful class for freshmen who are struggling in their grammar, vocabulary, punctuations, and especially reading skills and boosting up your stamina to be a faster reader, also to understand what you are reading to be prepared to write an essay or paper on it. This class is also a study session two days a week. This way you can do your unfinished homework or study for tests or prepare for projects. But mainly this class is getting you ready for the big leagues. So you need to start at the bottom and work your way up toward success.

Well as I wrap it up, all I say to those upcoming freshmen are to do their best in school, stay out of trouble, always think positive never negative thoughts, never say never, and always believe in yourself. You've got to trust in the inside and follow your footsteps.

Sincerely,
Michael Caroline

While students in the program offer the most important insights—they are, after all, the users of the course—an article written about the program offers a more global perspective on the program and its merits. The article appeared after the first group of kids graduated. It focuses on Jessica Johnson, a junior, so as to answer the question *What do kids take from ACCESS that stays with them?* (See Figure 2.1.)

Prior to the interview for the article, I tried to sum up the components of the program, especially those that had a lasting effect, as measured by their impact and impression on kids. The diagram shown in Figure 2.2 synthesizes the four key domains of the program; while I tend to think of these domains by the names of the people (e.g., not school-to-career coordinator, but Beth Pascal), I offer them in a more generic form here so that schools trying to create their own academic success program will have a more detailed schema for the necessary ingredients when it comes to roles (i.e., the *who*, versus the *what* of curriculum, or the *how* or methods).

I will discuss the specific roles in detail later on, but for now let me emphasize one aspect: the collaborative, communal, strategic nature of the program not so much as a rigidly structured program (which implies meetings, memos, planning, etc.), but as a set of principles that inform our relationships with each other and guide the allocation of effort and resources. The positive deviance model offers some of the most useful analysis, for it highlights not only the local nature of our enterprise, but the analytical aspect as well: we seek to *discover* what works (and discontinue what does *not* make a difference) and why it works and then *design* (or adapt and adopt) the program based on those insights.

Perhaps the final word in any course is what the syllabus says. This is, in essence, the advertisement, the contract, the bill of goods offered to the student and parents. As all teachers know, a syllabus (aka course outline or prospectus) is a living, evolving document, so you should take what follows as the latest incarnation at the time of this writing.

## ACCESS: PROGRAM OVERVIEW

**Description**   *What is ACCESS?* ACCESS stands for **Ac**ademic Suc**cess**. While the school district calls this course Developmental Reading, we will never use that name because this course is much more than that. ACCESS develops the skills and capacities you need to succeed in school in general and your academic classes in particular. In addition to learning to read strategically, for example, you will also learn how to take notes, how to think more effectively, and how to participate in academic classes. This program exists to

# HOMETOWN

# Reading is right on track

## BHS program helps students to soar

### BY SABRINA CRAWFORD
*Staff Writer*

BURLINGAME – Three years ago, 17-year-old Jessica Johnson came to Burlingame High School facing all of the challenges high-schoolers face.

She had to adjust to a new place, new teachers, a new teenage social life, a rigorous course load and high-level academic demands.

But Jessica faced something else much tougher as well – severe difficulty reading.

Now, thanks to the help of a collaborative first-year reading assistance program and hands-on four-year academic support, the buoyant brunette, who speaks with confidence and ease, is on her way to college.

"I'm going to go to a junior college for two years and then

I want to transfer," she said. "I want to be a nurse."

That's music to English teacher Jim Burke's ears. Having taught the standard format reading assistance program for some time, Burke says he began to see the students – many who came in reading at elementary school levels – needed much, much more.

"I realized that reading was only one slice of the pie," said Burke.

And so, working with the BHS administration, fellow teachers, counselors and support staff, Burke developed ACCESS.

A new, collaborative, holistic approach designed to do more than help students read just a little bit better, the acronym originally stood for "Academic Confidence Creates Equality and Success for all Students." But now, Burke has simplified it to its core meaning – Academic Success.

SPECIAL TO THE INDEPENDENT
Tony Artega, left, was a member of the first class to graduate from Burlingame High School's ACCESS program.

"The heart is literacy, but the global reach is success in all subjects and the opportunity to grow in all areas," Burke said. "It's about figuring out who you are and what you have to offer and then taking that knowledge and going out into the wider community."

Recently, ACCESS celebrated five years of success with the graduation of its very first fresh-

man class – 72 percent of whom went on to college.

"These are kids who came in the furthest behind or the most in need," said BHS Principal Matt Biggar. "They'd been written off by others before and told they're not going to college."

The secret to ACCESS' success, Burke and Biggar say, is its homegrown nature, its collaborative approach and the staff's dedication to following through with students all the way to graduation and in many cases, beyond.

In addition to the intensive reading program, students learn good study habits – how to form a homework group, make daily schedules and perhaps most importantly how to think about what they want in life and the necessary steps they need to get there.

Everyone from the local fire chief to state Sen. Jackie Speier has come through to talk to stu-

dents about how to be successful not only in their schoolwork, but in life. Connections with student tutors, visits to local college campuses, job shadowing and ongoing connections with mentors round out the academic support program.

"There was a girl, Paulina, who graduated last year," Burke recalled. "We went up to CSM for a Latino literature conference, and at one point she saw the students and said, 'They look like me.' She thought people who go to college were somehow different."

Burke says it's this moment of awakening, when students – many of whom are the first in their families to go to college – realize what they can achieve, that makes his work all the more worthwhile.

"We help them see what they are capable of becoming, and that personal connection makes all the difference in the world,"

Burke said. "At some point, they just begin to know what's possible, because [in ACCESS] you're an individual and yet you're a part of something."

In this year's freshman class, there are 25 students enrolled. Overall, 165 students have been a part of the first-year academic foundation class.

As for Jessica, she's busy with six classes, volunteering as a coach for junior cheerleaders through Pop Warner and setting her sights on a future nursing career. She's already done two job shadows – which she says confirmed that healthcare is the path she wants to take.

"And I just finished reading a book in three days for fun," she adds. "Before, reading was hard for me, so I never, never read just for fun."

FIGURE 2.1.

FIGURE 2.2.    Components of the ACCESS program at Burlingame High School

help you as both a student and a person in the year ahead. Throughout the year, we will further challenge ourselves through a variety of experiences (e.g., field trips, guest speakers, special programs, and mentorships). These challenges are meant to improve both your skills and your confidence. My role as your teacher is to support you and to help your teachers in whatever ways I can to ensure that you learn how to succeed in their classes. So let me summarize what I just said by listing the key components of this program:

- School skills
- Personal and world knowledge
- Habits of mind
- Personal, academic, and social success
- Conversations
- Opportunities

**Texts**

While this course uses other texts, the core books are:

- *Reader's Handbook: A Student's Guide for Reading and Learning* (textbook)
- *Writer's Inc.: A Student Handbook of Writing and Learning* (textbook)
- *The Essentials of Speech Communication* (textbook)
- *San Francisco Chronicle* (through the Newspapers in Education Program)

**Required Supplies**

You must *immediately* (by tomorrow) obtain the following materials. They will serve as the basis for Friday's class. Please purchase:

- ❑ One 1.5-inch white three-ring binder with a plastic sleeve cover on front and back
- ❑ 100 sheets of binder paper
- ❑ Pens and pencils
- ❑ Five section dividers
- ❑ Highlighter pen
- ❑ Three-hole punch that snaps into your three-ring binder (*highly* recommended, not required)

**Reading**

Students in this course will:

- Read self-selected books every day for fifteen minutes in class.
- Learn how to read in a variety of ways (e.g., surface, close, critical).
- Develop strategies to read different types of texts: stories, poems, essays, tests, textbooks, graphics, websites, and images.
- Learn how different texts are organized.
- Read for a variety of purposes (e.g., academic, personal, informational).

- Study and learn to monitor their reading processes.
- Improve their reading speed, stamina, and confidence.

**Academic Literacy**

Students in this course will:

- Maintain an Academic Notebook (see separate guidelines for this).
- Take effective notes to improve reading comprehension, study for tests, and write.
- Learn how tests work and develop strategies to improve performance on them.
- Keep track of and complete assignments for all classes.
- Manage time to ensure they have fun *and* succeed in school.
- Participate in classes in ways that improve their standing and show respect.
- Ask for and accept help when they do not understand how to do an assignment.
- Determine which ideas and information matter most when reading or viewing.
- Research subjects of personal interest.

**Writing**

Students in this course will:

- Write coherent, thoughtful explanations of or responses to what they read.
- Learn and use the Six Trait Analytical Writing model.
- Learn how to assess and improve their own writing.
- Generate their own writing topics and questions to help them write.

**Language**

Over the course of the semester students will:

- Learn those academic terms needed to succeed in academic classes and on state tests.
- Use appropriate strategies to comprehend new/unknown words.
- Expand their vocabulary through direct, weekly study of words and roots.
- Discuss words as ideas to extend discussion of texts.

**Speaking**

Students in this course will:

- Read aloud (in various settings, but rarely in front of the whole class).

- Participate in class and group discussions about what they read and think.
- Learn how to ask for help in ways that get positive responses and useful information.
- Learn and use appropriate academic vocabulary to discuss ideas and texts.
- Prepare and deliver a series of short speeches to the class on different subjects.

**Opportunities** Throughout the course of the year, all students will participate in some or all of the following programs, experiences, or events:

- Field trips to college campuses
- Field trips to job sites around Bay Area
- Toastmasters International leadership program
- Reading Buddies at Washington Elementary School
- Guest speakers in our class

**Policies**

*Attendance*
- All school attendance policies regarding absences and tardies apply to this class.

*Food*
- *No food or drinks are allowed in our classroom.* Sometimes kids choose to hang out in my room during lunch or brunch; food and drinks are permissible during those times *so long as you clean up.*

*Seating*
- Seating is assigned according to the alphabet and an individual's learning needs.

*Distractions*
- Makeup: I will confiscate any makeup products you take out or use.
- Cell phones or other electronic devices are not allowed. I use them myself, but part of having a phone or music player means knowing when you can and cannot use it. If your phone rings, I take it and turn it in to room 52, where you can reclaim it at 3 P.M.
- Backpacks on desks: Please store them on the floor.

| **Grading** | • Your grade is based on your performance and improvement in these areas: |
|---|---|

              • Attendance
              • Classwork
              • Daily reading
              • Materials
              • Study hall
              • Contribution

**Principles**

I take the seven core principles for this class from Tom Morris, a teacher and philosopher who studied successful people's lives throughout history. He identified what he calls the Seven Cs of Success. In order for people to be successful, Morris says we must have:

1. A clear **CONCEPTION** of what we want, a vivid vision, a goal clearly imagined.
2. A strong **CONFIDENCE** that we can attain that goal.
3. A focused **CONCENTRATION** on what it takes to reach the goal.
4. A stubborn **CONSISTENCY** in pursuing our vision.
5. An emotional **COMMITMENT** to the importance of what we're doing.
6. A good **CHARACTER** to guide us and keep us on a proper course.
7. A **CAPACITY TO ENJOY** the process along the way.

These principles will offer us useful guidelines as a class and as individuals.

**Office Hours**

I do not offer scheduled office hours but instead make myself generally available before, during, and after school. Room 82 is open and available for tutoring and studying by about 7:15 (most of the time!) and available to those who wish to study during lunch and after school. Those who use the room (or the computer lab across the hall) may use all available resources (including the computers) so long as they are good citizens.

**How to Reach Me**

I encourage both parents and students to communicate any concerns, questions, or needs as they arise. The school phone number is (xxx) xxx–xxxx. Email is a blessing to us all; I encourage you to use it, but please consider the length and frequency of your messages. My email address is: jburke@englishcompanion.com; my website is www.englishcompanion.com. I promise to do my best to reply in a timely fashion.

Signing this document indicates that you and one of your parents have read and understood this document. Moreover, by signing it you agree to the policies and standards outlined herein.

Student Name and Signature  _____  Date _____

Parent Name and Signature  _____  Date _____

## Who Is in ACCESS—And How Did They Get There?

My district faces a challenge unlike most high schools: We are a high school district, which means that schools have no formal, structured coordination with the many different feeder schools in the surrounding K–8 districts from which our students come. Moreover, as an open-enrollment district, we allow students to apply to any high school they choose, regardless of where they live (within the district). Thus the incoming ninth graders at my school, for example, come from as many as eight different middle schools in five cities, from about eight districts, each with its own unique culture.

To ensure students make a successful transition into high school and our district, people from the district office go out in the spring to test the incoming eighth-grade students using the Gates-MacGinitie comprehension test (Level 7/9, Form L). Only one school, which is, ironically, my school's biggest feeder, refuses to use this test and provides instead the students' reading scores on the state standardized test taken in April. Figure 2.3 shows a memo that outlines the assessment process.

When the testing is completed, several memos go out from the district office, including one to each school (see Figure 2.4) and a second to the parents of students whose scores merit mandatory placement in the Developmental Reading class. The second memo informs parents about their child's performance and the options available to them, one of which is to enroll in a summer reading program. (See Figure 2.5.)

In early August, following the completion of summer school, the district office examines the performance of those students who enrolled in the summer reading program and sends each school an update on placement in the reading program. (See Figure 2.6.)

# SAN MATEO UNION HIGH SCHOOL DISTRICT

## MEMORANDUM

**To:**      District Reading Coordinator
             District Reading Teachers

**From:**    Director of Assessment/Professional Development

**Date:**    May 26, 2004

**Subject:** FEEDER SCHOOL AND SUMMER SCHOOL READING TESTS

Following is a summary of what was decided at the reading meeting on May 25.

### Summer School

1. The Gates-MacGinitie Level 7/9, Form L comprehension test will be administered at the end of summer school. The reading teachers at Capuchino and San
   Mateo will make copies available to the summer school teachers. I will provide
   the scantrons. Do you want my office to score the tests or do you want to provide answer keys to the summer school teachers so that they can score the
   tests? Let me know.

2. Students must score 8th grade or higher on the Gates <u>and</u> receive a grade of "A"
   or "B" for the summer school class in order to be eligible to exit from the fall
   reading class.

### Feeder School Testing

1. We will continue feeder school testing next January. There will be a problem with
   staffing for the testing which we will address next fall.

2. Feeder school English teachers will be able to recommend students out of reading only if the students' Gates score is between 6.0–6.9. Students scoring 5.9 or
   below cannot be recommended out by the English teacher.

3. The district will continue to send letters to notify parents that their students
   must enroll in reading in the fall.

4. The district will purchase a new set of Level 7/9 Gates tests for the feeder testing.

FIGURE 2.3.   Effective communication with parents, students, schools, and teachers is an
essential trait of academic success programs.

To: _____

# GUIDELINES FOR READING PLACEMENT

Attached are the scores and recommendations for reading placement for your eighth grade students and a copy of a letter that will be sent to the parents/guardians of students who are required to enroll in a reading class in ninth grade.

The placement recommendations for the developmental reading class are based on the following scores:

*Gates-MacGinitie Reading Comprehension Test, Level 5–6*

| | |
|---|---|
| Grade equivalent score 6.9 or below | reading required |
| Grade equivalent score 7.0 or higher | no reading |

*SAT9 (Spring 2002) Reading Comprehension or other standardized reading test*

| | |
|---|---|
| 35th national percentile rank or below | reading required |
| 36th national percentile rank or higher | no reading |

These are <u>preliminary</u> recommendations based solely on one score on one test. We rely on the classroom teacher to make the final recommendation as to whether a student should be required to take a developmental reading class, in addition to an English class, in high school. Note that the letter to the parent/guardian states that the student must be reading below grade level <u>and</u> must have the recommendation of the eighth grade language arts teacher.

Please make any changes, either into or out of reading, based on your knowledge of the student's classroom performance, report card grades and/or other standardized test scores. This is especially important for students who are near the borderline. All district high schools offer developmental reading classes for students who are reading below the seventh grade equivalent.

Let <u>David Hanson</u> know by <u>Tuesday, February 18</u>, about your changes to (or confirmation of) these reading placements. After your input is incorporated, a <u>final</u> copy of these placements will be sent to all high school district counseling and English departments. The high school counseling departments will enter the student's reading score and reading placement on the Recommendation Card for high school placement in English/Social Studies before sending the card to you for completion.

If you have any questions, contact the Director of Assessment at the San Mateo Union High School district Office.

FIGURE 2.4.  Establishing and communicating the guidelines is another aspect of any effective program.

# SAN MATEO UNION HIGH SCHOOL DISTRICT

Samuel Johnson, Superintendent

Date _____

To the Parent/Guardian of _____:

Your student recently took a standardized reading test at (<u>middle school</u>). The test was administered by the San Mateo Union High School District. Your student's score on the test was grade equivalent _____.

Because good reading skills are fundamental for academic success, the San Mateo Union High School District requires entering ninth grade students to enroll in a reading class if the student:

1. is reading below grade level <u>and</u>

2. has been recommended to a reading class by the eighth grade language arts teacher.

Based on these criteria, your student is required to take a reading class in September. This class is in addition to the regular English class. It receives elective credit toward high school graduation. (If your student is in Special Education, the student's enrollment in a reading class will be discussed at the Articulation Meeting in the spring.)

If you have any questions regarding your student's class schedule for September, please contact a high school counselor.

Sincerely,

Mark Avelar

Associate Superintendent Instruction

| Aragon | Hillside |
|--------|----------|
| Burlingame | Mills |
| Capuchino | San Mateo |

FIGURE 2.5.   Support from district-level administration is essential to any program's credibility and sustainability.

# SAN MATEO UNION HIGH SCHOOL DISTRICT

Director of Assessment/Professional Development

---

## MEMORANDUM

**To:**      Principals
Assistant Principals Instruction
Counseling Chairs
Developmental Reading Teachers

**From:**   Director of Assessment/Professional Development

**Date:**   August 11, 2004

**Subject:**  SUMMER READING SCORES – STUDENTS ELIGIBLE
TO DROP READING

---

Attached is an Excel file containing the reading scores and grades of each of the incoming ninth grade students enrolled in reading in summer school. There are four different worksheets:

- all students listed alphabetically

- all students listed by school

- students eligible to drop reading by alpha

- students eligible to drop reading by school

By agreement with the district reading teachers last spring, students who score at grade equivalent 8.0 or higher and who also earned an "A" or "B" for the summer school class would be eligible to drop enrollment in developmental reading for Fall 2004. These students have been marked "drop" in the last column. Please have your counseling staff contact these students and arrange to change their schedules.

In addition, students who scored at grade equivalent 9.0 or higher but who received "Cs" or lower for the class have been marked with a "?" in the last column. Your staff may want to consider allowing these students to also drop reading since their academic problems are probably not related to an inability to read.

cc: Assistant Superintendents

FIGURE 2.6.   Maintaining an effective communication loop throughout the district, something made easier by email, is a vital part of any sustainable program.

After the eighth-grade assessment, however, and prior to the summer school course, parents can refuse to have their child enrolled in the Developmental Reading course. This is, of course, a curious option, given the context of the student's grades and test scores, both of which no doubt signal some sort of academic SOS. It reminds me of a similar form we used on rare occasions when I worked in an emergency room and patients refused treatment. *Usually* people with a head full of glass, or chest pains, or, say, difficulty breathing wanted us to touch them, to take care of them, were even grateful for our offer of help; still, on occasion, for whatever personal reasons, someone would say (usually not in the nicest tone) that they didn't need our help. In the event that a student's parents refuse to enroll their child in the ACCESS program at our school—and it happens every year—they must sign a form (shown in Figure 2.7) drawn up by the district's lawyers, since, as the document says, serious consequences (e.g., not graduating) can result.

I should add that in the years since beginning the program, I have informally tracked these students, and they *all* struggle and ultimately endure greater humiliations for their lack of reading skills than they otherwise would if they enrolled in the program. I track them informally because I do not get to see a list of these kids, but I learn of them down the road when, for example, their junior or senior teachers come to me and ask if they were in my program and tell me they simply do not know how to read. When investigating, I inevitably learn that they refused to enroll in the program.

Once the school year starts, there are a few additional steps to placement that are important to mention. First, as soon as I get the class lists, I scan them to see if anything stands out. One year, for example, the enrollment of Latino students (a group I have worked hard to learn more about and help succeed) was small compared with the previous year. In light of these low numbers and our school's commitment to help them succeed, I wrote an email to the principal, the beginning of the following exchange:

```
From: Jim Burke
Date:  Fri, 20 Aug 22:34:37

Matt:
Going over the roster for ACCESS (25 students), I find what
seem to be only 2—4 Latino students. I just want to be sure
there aren't kids flying under the radar, especially as it
relates to our goals to address the needs of Latino students.

Jim

* * * * * * * * * * * * * * * * * * * * * * * * * * * * * * *
```

**San Mateo Union High School District**

---

## REQUEST TO DECLINE ENROLLMENT IN READING

A student's ability to understand what is read is an important factor in a student's academic success in high school. The San Mateo Union High School District offers a Reading class for freshmen students who

- read below grade level on a standardized reading comprehension test <u>and</u>
- have the recommendation of the eighth grade language arts teacher.

This class provides students with intensive instruction to improve their reading skills and with tutorial assistance in all their other subjects. Students exit from the Reading Class at the end of the semester in which they meet district-wide exit criteria. Students in the Reading class earn elective credits toward graduation.

Student's Name _____

Name of Standardized Reading Test _____

Score _____ (circle one: grade equivalent or national percentile rank)

Date Administered _____

To Whom It May Conern:

I have been informed that _____ qualifies for the Reading Class offered at _____ High School.

**I understand that my student will have to pass the California High School Exit Examination in order to receive a high school diploma. (_____ initialed by parent/guardian)**

I met with high school staff on _____ (date) and discussed my student's enrollment in the reading class. I do not wish to have my student enrolled in this class.

Sincerely,

_____     _____
Signature of Parent/Guardian                                    Date

Address _____

Daytime Telephone (_____) _____

_____     _____
Signature of High School Administrator/Counselor          Date

Rev. Spring 2002          white: school     yellow: district office     pink: parent/guardian

FIGURE 2.7.

To: Jim Burke
Subject: Re: Question

Jim,
I appreciate your concern and sharing this information with me. Please communicate this to Jackie [the assistant principal] and the counseling team so they can look into this. Thanks Jim.

Matt Biggar
Principal
Burlingame High School

* * * * * * * * * * * * * * * * * * * * * * * * * * * * * * *

Hi Jim:
The placement for reading support comes from the test scores and/or teacher recommendations from the students' middle schools. When we are scheduling, we follow those recommendations. I went over all of the recommendations this past summer and made sure we had everyone appropriately placed or had the Waiver forms. Many of the students who needed support were either Special Education students or ELD students. I hope the low number means that our students are reading better. Let's continue the conversation.

Jackie

In addition to examining the lists like this and reaching out to the administration, I analyze the fall reading scores in the opening weeks of school—when incoming freshmen all take the Gates-MacGinitie comprehension test—to see if we missed any kids. This amounts to obtaining the reading scores for the entire freshman class and scanning them for anyone who scored below the seventh grade. Here is a memo I sent to the administration after doing this one year:

I just finished counting up the freshmen who, according to the Gates-MacGinitie, scored at or below the seventh grade level. Here are the stats.

Ninety out of roughly 300 freshman students are identified as reading two or more grade levels below the ninth grade.

Out of those 90, 25 are currently in ACCESS. This leaves 65 kids currently enrolled in mainstream academic classes whose reading scores suggest serious obstacles to success. Lest we get carried away, it's important to remember that this test is ONE measure of many. I suggest we circulate the list (Counseling could do a quick sort in Excel) with just those kids and ask teachers to just give some general sense of whether the kid is or will soon be in trouble and needs help. I can take more kids in ACCESS no problem. I'd welcome it. Perhaps the list could have a few columns: Estimated Grade; Overall Performance; Recommend for ACCESS?

Thanks for doing what you can to help these kids. History has
its first big exam today, so I expect a number of kids to go
into deeper waters this week.

Let me know what I can do to help. I'd be glad to meet with any
kids or parents who want to know more about ACCESS.

Jim Burke

Such extra scrutiny is important given the mobile nature of our society.
Kids often enroll at the last minute, some of whom need a program like
ACCESS. Other kids miss the testing in the spring or even again in the fall.
Finally, there is the first six-week progress report, a crucial juncture for freshmen as it marks the end of the first stretch of serious work in high school and
reveals definite performance patterns. This is the last point in the first semester
when a student can be redirected into ACCESS. So long as I have spaces, I
continue to solicit students up through this time. These progress reports
become important secondary sources when checking those reading scores that
were below grade level. Sometimes it happens that a kid bombs the Gates-
MacGinitie test but then earns a 2.75 or even a 3.2 GPA on their progress
report. Who knows why they scored as they did on the test, but their overall
academic performance suggests that all is well and they do not need the course.

Before moving on to consider the content of the course, I want make a few
final observations about placement. First, while there is no question that such
programs carry with them a stigma if students are required to enroll, teachers
can help students and parents make informed decisions by talking to them,
explaining the nature of the course, and sharing the results of the program.
Counselors at my school always get the latest data about my program so they
can help kids and parents understand how the course will help; the counselors
also know that I will meet or speak with parents who have concerns about their
child being in the program. Thus a second issue is whether induction should be
voluntary or involuntary. Many academic success programs recruit students,
seeking out unrealized potential that conforms to that program's stated goals.
AVID, for example, has very strict entrance requirements that demand commitment not only to policies but to practices; it is like signing a contract for a team:
you play by their rules so long as you are on that team. ACCESS, on the other
hand, is not voluntary; if students score at or below the seventh grade, they are
in. There are, however, a few notable exceptions: English learners and special
education students are not eligible for ACCESS since they have their own programs with curriculum specifically designed to better meet their needs.

Toward the end of the first semester, several placement processes begin. First, I evaluate whether anyone currently in the program should exit at that time. I generally conceive of the program as a yearlong course. There are, however, sometimes one or two students who have made so much progress (perhaps motivated by the very desire to get out of the class) that the class no longer meets their needs. I am always proud of the progress such students have made and grateful for the example they have provided the rest of the class. Early in the second semester, I try to send these students a short note to celebrate their success and establish a new relationship with them so that I can continue to support them in their remaining years of high school. Here is a sample of such a letter:

I hope the new semester is beginning well for you. I wanted to write to congratulate you on your excellent work and progress during the first semester. It is a genuine achievement, but it too often goes uncelebrated due to the sudden end of the semester. Then we all come back—and you are gone!

Each one of you worked so hard not just for your own success but that of the program and the class, of which you were an important part. You taught me many things, all of which will help me improve the ACCESS program in the future. It's a great blessing for a teacher to watch a student like yourself make the transition into high school and challenging academic work with such speed after working so hard.

I am entirely confident of your future success here at BHS. I do want you to know, however, that in my mind I remain your teacher until you graduate. So if you need help, for a minute or a month, please come by and ask for it. We can meet before school or during lunch, after school or at brunch. And if you never need my help again, always know that I'll be happy to see you around school, that you can always drop by or hang out in the room that will always be yours.

Life is strange: I could end up being your English teacher at some point over the next couple of years and we could spend some more time working with and learning from each other.

As I said at the beginning, you should be proud of yourself. Instead of seeing my class and the ACCESS program as something you have escaped, I hope you feel it is something that helped you gain "ACCESS" to both your classes and that part of yourself that hungers for the success that I am sure will be yours. I hope you feel proud that you have "graduated" from the program. *I'm* proud of you. Good luck and keep up the hard—and good—work.

Keep in touch.

Sincerely,
Mr. Burke
jburke@englishcompanion.com

Such midyear departures, though rare, create new openings in the second semester. Thus the second part of the midyear process involves reaching out to those students not currently in the program whose first semester performance, combined with their reading scores, suggests the class would help. I reach out through two groups: teachers and counselors. I send out a note to the freshman academic teachers—primarily English and social studies—reminding them what ACCESS is and who should enroll. Then I follow up in person after a few days in case the teachers have questions or just did not get to my memo yet. This keeps the lines of communication open about kids they already have and reinforces the relationship by allowing me to help with kids that failed the first semester. The second group, equally crucial in some ways because they do the scheduling, are the counselors. About a month before the first semester ends, I send the counselors the following note:

> Dear Karen, Jean Marie, and Bill:
>
> Of course everyone's mind is on everything *but* next semester at the moment, but it seems important to initiate an inquiry through the ninth-grade teachers about potential ACCESS students for the second semester. I have plenty of room for as many kids as need to come in. Let me know what I can do to help promote the course and the kids who need it.
>
> Thanks again for everything you do to help me, the kids, and the program.
>
> Jim

These midyear kids typically benefit from the course, for it is the solution to a problem they cannot ignore: they failed key academic classes the first semester and already have earned spots in mandatory summer school. If they do the same thing spring semester, they could wind up at the continuation school, the adult school, or a second summer of summer school. They tend, therefore, to see me as an ally and give me permission to coach them right away so they don't get into the hole again. Brandon Coleman offers a glimpse into the contrast between first semester and second semester (when he transferred into ACCESS) in this reflection:

> Since I've joined this ACCESS class I've steadily improved my reading skills. At the beginning of the year I was only able to read about 50 or 60 lines in 5 minutes, now I can read about 90. The speed read in this class has helped me alot in so many ways.
>
> My increased reading skills have also helped my writing skills. For example it would take me 2–3 days to write an essay for English. Now I can write and type an essay within an hour and a half. This skill has improved the quality of my homework in some of my classes.

I have also improved my study habits, which was a very hard thing for me to do, but once I made the change I felt a lot better about my ability to do my work on time and better quality of work. I used to spend about an hour on my homework every night, now I spend an hour to an hour and a half.

Another thing that was a big improvement for me was my organizational skills, such as using my planner everyday, and having my teachers sign it so I could show my parents when I got home, and it also helped to keep me on track as far as what needed to be done, where to find it, and when it was due. I think that my organizational skills have helped me to become a better student. Organization is something I definitely need to succeed in high school, and before taking this ACCESS class was one of my biggest weaknesses.

As embarrassed as I am to say this last semester my grade point average was a 1.2, and before that it was below a 1.0, now that I'm making some progress I'm almost at a 1.8, and hopefully when I finish school this year and get my final grades I will have at least a 2.0. Next year I hope to achieve at least a 2.5 every semester which shouldn't be that hard if I continue doing what I've learned in Mr. Burke's class.

I believe that I have become a much better student as the year has progressed. I've made some good choices about studying which will hopefully carry on to next year and all the way through my senior year. Since I've joined ACCESS I believe I have become a much better student.

Brandon Coleman

Some kids come into the class in September saying that a mistake was made, that they are not supposed to be in the class. These are often kids who have successfully hidden their reading problems from not only their teachers but themselves as well. They enter the class in August feeling much like Brittni Marshall: "When I first came to your class in August I was a little slow because none of my other friends had to take ACCESS so when I went into second period, I didn't want anyone to see me go into that 'dumb' class. I was embarrassed to say that I had you for a teacher because people knew you as the 'Reading Development teacher.' So I didn't tell anyone that I had you as a teacher."

Jennifer Reyes had a similar attitude with some variations:

When I first came to your ACCESS class in August, I felt like I shouldn't be a part of this class. I didn't like the students in my class and I just thought this class was boring. I was never in the mood to do any work and I never wanted to participate in this class. I never knew what the point of this class was. I thought it was because I wasn't a good reader or if it was because I couldn't write good or spell. In my head all I could think is that this class isn't for me and that if there is a possibility of me switching classes. The main reason I had that feeling was because I thought this class was like those classes for people who needed help in many ways. Also because my friends would joke around saying that I was stupid and that no wonder I was in this class. But after coming to this class for about a week, I realized that this class would actually help me go through my freshman year easier and that it would help me out in the future.

As time has passed, I have learned to listen to such words without taking offense or otherwise seeing them as personal since, as Jennifer noted, students' attitudes change over time. After all, the kids writing such words are students I have come to know and care about; moreover, I know they have benefited from the program, as both Brittni and another student, Jeff, went on to say.

"But after a while," Brittni continued:

I realized that my work was not the best to my ability and one of the people who pointed it out to me was you. I didn't want to listen to my parents, or the other teacher that I didn't like or trust. You helped me pass most of my classes all year and no other teachers cared as much about my grades as you do. You always take time to say "Hi" in the halls and always have an extra five minutes to ask how I'm doing not just in school but life in general.

The way you teach is way different than other teachers, you don't really yell but you get the point across with out disrespecting us or embarrassing your students in front of the class like most teachers do when they get mad. You stay calm and don't burst out which is very much appreciated.

When people make fun of me for being in ACCESS I make fun of them for not being in one of your classes and not being able to know you. You're not only a great teacher but a good friend/advisor. Your advice always helps me make up my mind to do the right thing. If it weren't for you I don't think I would be trying as much as I am now. I wish I could show you good grades to show my appreciation but I don't have those to show so all I can say is thanks so . . . Thanks.

Jeff wrote:

From the first day of school at Burlingame I had no clue what your class was about. Over the course of the end of August to the beginning of September, I started to get a feel of it though. Your class is about opportunity to improve the reading skills of all of your students. In the beginning of the year I hated to read. I thought to me that it was a sin. Over the course of September I read some books that I really enjoyed. I learned that reading can be sort of fun and you can learn a lot of new words from it and also learn new information.

In the middle of the year, specifically January, I was struggling in a lot of my classes, including the most important one English, which from your class I was able to use the reading time to read my solo books. I also greatly improved my stamina by the middle of the year. I could read 20 pages in 25 minutes. As a student I was happy with my performance reading wise but grade wise I was not applying myself as a student. I soon realized that each class is to prepare you for a final that you have to take.

By June I have learned that each class has a purpose and that I am not going to just sit around and do nothing in my classes because then I cannot do any sports or stuff like that. After I got the bad grades the first semester it still didn't hit me, but by May I was really excited to do good in all of my classes and apply myself. In your class by June I have not increased my stamina it is about the same but the fact that you taught us organization skills has made me more organized and also apply myself. Thank you Mr. Burke!

So who is in ACCESS? A great bunch of freshman kids, some of whom want what I'm selling in August and others who resist or even resent it and won't check out my goods until after the first (awful) progress report, or the second. Some wait until it's too late and they've blown that first semester. Some get in there as the district planned: via the reading scores in eighth grade; others through teacher or counselor recommendations; still others at the hands of a concerned parent who found the courage in themselves and confidence in me to enroll their son or daughter in the class.

## *What We Do in ACCESS, When We Do It, and Why: A Brief Overview*

ACCESS embodies the four traits of effective school success programs outlined in the previous chapter, which I will summarize here. The ACCESS curriculum is designed to develop students':

1. *Commitment* to academic success
2. *Content* knowledge needed to complete assignments and participate in academic activities
3. *Competencies* in those areas essential to academic success in general and that teacher's class in particular
4. *Capacity* to meet the demands of various academic tasks

While many, even most, kids arrive at school understanding what school is for, ACCESS kids often do not. So much of the work in high school seems pointless, reducible to cynical questions like "When am I ever going to use *this* [e.g., algebra, writing, history, even reading] when I grow up?" Only when they understand who they are, or could be, how the world works, and that they alone must create a place for themselves in it will they see school as the solution to a problem we all face: how to have a good, which is to say satisfying and successful, life as an adult. This is at the center of the academic enterprise: the belief that education leads to a better life for the individual and, consequently, a better society for us all. As the following chapters will show, we cannot always bring the ACCESS students to the real world, so we try to bring the world to them in the classroom through a variety of avenues. Such academic and personal enrichment helps them build a bridge to the world they felt they could not enter, one they began to feel would offer them no chance for success. Emily Wagstaffe, who graduated with the first group of ACCESS students, wrote the following when I asked her to reflect on her success in high school:

> As you know I have always had trouble with certain academic subjects and getting the concept in my head. When I was placed in your ACCESS class I wasn't fully on board and worried about the upcoming speeches (in Toastmasters) we had to do. As I reach graduation, I know that without ACCESS and your help I would not have been as successful and may not have gotten into [a four-year!] college. All the opportunities in that class really changed the way I approached school and life. I just wanted to thank you for introducing and inviting me to that class. I owe some of my success to you and the ACCESS program.

Emily is right to credit only *some* of her success to ACCESS, for the real credit should go to her, something I routinely emphasize to the kids throughout the four years they are at our school. ACCESS is only a freshman class, so I have only nine months to help them get going. In the three remaining years, I have only notes and encounters in the hall during which I try to check in, connect with, and generally encourage them, reminding them to come by if they have questions or need help. Emily also identifies the key elements of the program, which I want to now introduce before discussing them in depth in subsequent chapters. These different elements are effectively outlined in a letter I wrote to the class as part of an ongoing effort to improve and better understand the class:

> Dear ACCESS Student:
>
> I need to take some time to think about the ACCESS program, its purpose, and how it is (or should be) improving your performance in your academic subjects. I see amazing progress for some; moderate improvement in most; continued struggle or outright academic failure for a few.
>     When I first taught this class four years ago, it was "just a reading class." Since then I have realized there is much more to school success than reading. So I have tried to add those experiences, lessons, and activities that would help you improve not just your reading but your ability to study, take tests, write,

and participate in class discussions. I see lots of progress, though some have improved more than others. Still, I think I can do better; I think this program can accomplish more. I know you can do better. To accomplish all this, however, I need to know how you think I can improve the program. After all, you are the most important part of the program.

Before you give me your ideas, let me explain a few of mine so you know what I have been trying to accomplish.

- *Daily reading/SSR*: We read every day so you can improve your speed, stamina, and fluency. This daily reading (aka SSR) requires that you have your own personal book so that you are reading about subjects that interest you in books that are at your level of comprehension.
- *Reading Record*: We keep track of how much you read each day and write about what you read so you (and I) can see your growth over time.
- *Speakers* come to our class so you can learn about the world for which you are preparing. They bring to us ideas about how to live and what is possible for you out there.
- *Study hall* provides time for some to go to Washington and others to work. Some use this time better than others. If we are to continue to have it, people must work better and improve their standing in other classes.
- *Academic essentials*: These include lessons about studying, reading, taking tests, taking notes, or making inferences, and so on. These are lessons from the *Reader's Handbook*.
- *Conversations*: Participating in group and class discussions is an important part of school success. Whether using discussion questions you create, or articles from the *San Francisco Chronicle* on Fridays, we have had many discussions throughout the semester. Conversations also include writing in response to what you read.
- *Opportunities*: Washington Elementary and field trips to businesses and college campuses expose you to what is possible. My goal is to show you what is out there so you will find what interests you and work to achieve it.
- *Advanced planning, goal setting, and pep talks*: I make time for these because they are what successful people do—they plan, they set goals, they seek guidance. You must know where you are going at all times; if you don't, you will get lost. "There is no such thing as luck—only successful planning." (Colin Powell)
- *Personal connections*: I make an effort to connect with people over time through notes and private conversations in class, across the hall, or when I see you around school. You all have different needs, so these notes and chats are one way I try to get to know you better so I can teach you better.

Few things work well for everyone. These are the ideas I have so far. I want to hear from you about the following:

- How does this class help you?
- What can I do to improve the course? (And why do you think that will help?)

- How could this class specifically help you do better in those classes you are failing or struggling to pass? (Explain how your ideas would help.)
- What classes (if any) are you failing or struggling to pass? Why are you having so much trouble with this class?
- What should we do more or less of? Why?
- What does school not give you the chance to learn about? How can this class support your desire to learn about that subject?

Thank you for taking time to write back this morning. This class is important because you are important. I want it to be not just a class but an experience that makes a difference in how you work, what you do, how you live. Help me be the teacher you need to be able to succeed.

Sincerely,
Mr. Burke

Figures 2.8 and 2.9 give an idea of how the program plays out over a year and during one week. I examine the different components in detail in the following chapters, but I want to conclude with an introduction of three key roles, all of which fall under the "Mentors" heading in Figure 2.2. I cannot discuss these roles without discussing the people who fill them, for so integral are they to the success of ACCESS that I cannot render them in generic terms. I refer to the service learning coordinator (Sue Glick), the school-to-career coordinator (Beth Pascal), and student tutors (Andrew Lundstrom and Sarah Coit). Both Sue and Beth have been at the school since I began the program; this ongoing relationship has given them (and us) the chance to shape their programs to better meet the needs of the students and the goals of the ACCESS program. Both Beth and Sue were originally funded through grants available through the county; their positions have since become the responsibility of the school site, which has maintained its commitment to their programs because students throughout the school so obviously benefit from both.

Sue Glick named her service learning program PAWS (People Action Work Service), which is a local homage to the Burlingame High School Panther and the infamous Paw that goes to the winner of the annual Little Big Game between BHS and our rival, San Mateo High School. Here is Sue's description of her program:

PAWS was initiated at BHS in October 1996 as part of the San Mateo Youth Service Collaborative. The Collaborative represented a coalition of schools from throughout the county working in partnership with the Volunteer Center of San Mateo County Office of Education. PAWS' purpose has been to

ACCESS Program: Year Overview

| Schedule | FALL | | | SPRING | | |
|---|---|---|---|---|---|---|
| | Grading Period 1 | Grading Period 2 | Grading Period 3 | Grading Period 1 | Grading Period 2 | Grading Period 3 |
| Assessment | **September**<br>• Gates-MacGinitie Reading Test (3d ed., Form K, Level 7/9)<br>  • Comprehension<br>  • Vocabulary<br>  • Miscue analysis | | **December**<br>• Scholastic Reading Inventory (Form A, Level HS-Alt2) | | | **May**<br>• Gates-MacGinitie Reading Test (3d ed., Form L, Level 7/9)<br>  • Comprehension<br>  • Vocabulary<br>  • Miscue analysis |
| SSR[1] | **15 minutes a day, 3–4 days a week**<br>Note: While we read for 15 minutes, the time is more like 20–25 depending on what we do as a follow-up to the actual SSR. Students always take a minute to update their Reading Records (i.e., enter the number of pages they read that day and the title of a new book if they just began one). | | | | | |
| Academic Essentials | • Reading<br>• Writing<br>• Managing<br>• Taking notes<br>• Taking tests | • Reading<br>• Writing<br>• Talking<br>• Taking tests<br>• Studying<br>• Representing<br>• Managing<br>• Arguing | • Reading<br>• Writing<br>• Talking<br>• Taking tests<br>• Studying<br>• Representing<br>• Managing<br>• Arguing | • Reading<br>• Writing<br>• Talking<br>• Taking tests<br>• Studying<br>• Managing<br>• Arguing<br>• Researching | • Reading<br>• Writing<br>• Talking<br>• Taking tests<br>• Studying<br>• Managing<br>• Arguing<br>• Researching | |
| School Smarts | Emphasized in the first month, but addressed throughout the first semester in response to various situations. | | | Not specifically discussed throughout the second semester, but referred to as needed. | | |
| Reading Buddies | Two teams (A Team and B Team) made up of four students each. | | | Two teams (A Team and B Team) made up of four students each. | | |
| Opportunities | • Guest speakers<br>• Occasional | • Guest speakers<br>• JC visit[2]<br>• Occasional | • Guest speakers<br>• Job shadow<br>• Occasional | • Guest speakers<br>• Toastmasters | • Guest speakers<br>• Toastmasters<br>• University visit<br>• Job shadow | • Guest speakers<br>• Toastmasters<br>• Occasional |
| Core Texts | • Reader's Handbook: A Student's Guide for Reading and Learning | | | • Reader's Handbook: A Student's Guide for Reading and Learning<br>• Essentials of Speech Communication | | |
| • Study Hall<br>• Tutoring<br>• Chess<br>• Conferences | Each day students can earn time for study hall or chess if they get their assignments done (to my standards). This is also the time during which they get tutoring from each other or the program's student tutors (if available). | | | Each day students can earn time for study hall or chess if they get their assignments done (to my standards). This is also the time during which they get tutoring from each other or the program's student tutors (if available). | | |

[1] SSR: sustained silent reading
[2] JC visit: junior (aka community) college visit

FIGURE 2.8.

**ACCESS Program: Week Overview**

| DAY | MONDAY | TUESDAY | WEDNESDAY | THURSDAY | FRIDAY |
|---|---|---|---|---|---|
| 20–25 min. | **SSR**<br>• Before<br>  • Purpose<br>  • Plan<br>  • Goal<br>• During<br>  • Read with a purpose<br>• After<br>  • Record<br>  • Reflect<br>  • Respond<br>    • Write<br>    • Represent<br>    • Talk | **SSR**<br>• Before<br>  • Purpose<br>  • Plan<br>  • Goal<br>• During<br>  • Read with a purpose<br>• After<br>  • Record<br>  • Reflect<br>  • Respond<br>    • Write<br>    • Represent<br>    • Talk | **SSR**<br>• Before<br>  • Purpose<br>  • Plan<br>  • Goal<br>• During<br>  • Read with a purpose<br>• After<br>  • Record<br>  • Reflect<br>  • Respond<br>    • Write<br>    • Represent<br>    • Talk | **SSR**<br>• Before<br>  • Purpose<br>  • Plan<br>  • Goal<br>• During<br>  • Read with a purpose<br>• After<br>  • Record<br>  • Reflect<br>  • Respond<br>    • Write<br>    • Represent<br>    • Talk | **Opportunities**<br>• Job shadow<br>• Guest speaker<br>• Toastmasters<br>• Conversations<br>• Study sessions (when they have a huge exam that day)<br>• College visit |
| 20–35 min. | **Instructional Focus**<br>• Introduce | **Instructional Focus**<br>• Elaborate | **Instructional Focus**<br>• Refine | **Instructional Focus**<br>• Extend | |
| 0–20 min. | **Optional/Conditional**<br>• Study hall<br>• Chess<br>• Tutoring<br>• Teacher conferences | **Optional/Conditional**<br>• Study hall<br>• Chess<br>• Tutoring<br>• Teacher conferences | **Optional/Conditional**<br>• Reading buddies<br>• Study hall<br>• Chess<br>• Tutoring<br>• Teacher conferences | **Optional/Conditional**<br>• Study hall<br>• Chess<br>• Tutoring<br>• Teacher conferences | |
| HW | No homework assigned | No homework assigned | No homework assigned | No homework assigned | No homework assigned |

FIGURE 2.9.

improve the quality of education by providing youth service opportunities. In its eight years at BHS, PAWS has:

- Implemented high quality programs to involve young people in service
- Made youth service an essential component in the education program
- Increased community awareness of the educational value of youth service
- Created a model of school-community collaboration that combines existing resources to promote youth service

Examples of projects that BHS students have participated in that reflect the above-mentioned goals are:

- *Gateways to Service Assembly/Fair*: A school-wide assembly and volunteer fair where students have a chance to sign up with more than 40 county and private agencies for volunteer work.
- *Reading Buddies*: High school students read to elementary school students and serve as positive role models for children at various elementary schools.
- *Special Olympics*: Students work with developmentally disabled children to participate in various sports, including swimming, track, and soccer.
- *After-School Tutoring*: BHS students work one-on-one with elementary school students at Homework Central, First Presbyterian Church, Mid-Peninsula Boys and Girls Club, and local elementary schools.

To ensure that the quality of education improves by providing youth service opportunities, the administration and staff are committed to the following principles:

- All stakeholders—students, educational staff, parents, and community members—must support youth service.
- The number of students participating in community service and the opportunities must increase.
- The program must integrate service into the curriculum and provide opportunity to evaluate, recognize, and address the needs of the community and the faculty.

Young people involved in service gain self-esteem, critical thinking and problem-solving skills; experience real work and their role as citizens; and are valued by adults, often for the first time. In an increasingly disjointed community, service enlivens the daily curriculum by providing young people with opportunities for building compassion and community.

Beth Pascal started the school-to-career program, which she subsequently named EXPLORE (Exploring Pathways Learning Opportunities Real Experiences). As Figure 2.2 shows, she provides essential leadership in several areas crucial to the ACCESS program's success: job shadowing, guest speakers, college visits, Toastmasters International Youth Leadership Program, and even the student tutors. Here is how Beth describes her program:

> Burlingame High School's EXPLORE program was established in March 1998. The program has formed an alliance of businesses, educators, students, labor and community organizations committed to helping all students prepare for success in rewarding careers and become productive citizens and lifelong learners.
>
> EXPLORE joins education and workforce development in a system in which meaningful, relevant learning experiences lead to advanced educational opportunities and high wage careers. EXPLORE helps students make the connection between their academics and future careers as well as college by exploring a variety of professions and gaining real world experience in the workplace.
>
> Goals and Accomplishments:
>
> - College field trips and programs: Exposed students from the underrepresented and middle quartile group to post-secondary school opportunities.
>   - *College of San Mateo*: Introduced students to the campus, vocational and transfer opportunities to four-year college.
>   - *Canada College*: Introduced students to the campus, vocational and transfer opportunities to four-year college.
>   - *Sequoia Institute*: Introduced students to vocational college.
>   - *San Francisco State University*: Brought group to Burlingame High School.
>   - *University of California, Berkeley*: Took ACCESS class for full-day field trip to UC Berkeley to learn about four-year college opportunities.
> - Coordinated individual job shadow opportunities
> - Coordinated Toastmasters International Youth Leadership Program
> - Coordinated teacher aides for BHS faculty
> - Coordinated classroom speakers
> - Coordinated other opportunities such as local Rotary Club Youth Leadership Program to find and enroll candidates to participate in this program

In order to create a sense of momentum in the ACCESS class during the first week of school, I have the administrators, including the principal, come in and introduce themselves. They field questions, give the kids some attention, and, in the process, help establish the credibility of the ACCESS program. In addition, Sue Glick, Beth Pascal, and Lori Friel (the college and scholarship coordinator, who shares an office with Beth) come in to further emphasize the network of people who are committed to the kids (see Figure 2.10).

I have one last group to introduce: the student tutors. This is an invaluable but unstable part of the program. AVID recruits tutors from neighboring uni-

FIGURE 2.10. Effective programs rely on the intelligence and commitment of many people. These three women are essential to the ACCESS program: Sue Glick (left) coordinates all service learning opportunities; Beth Pascal (middle) arranges all job shadows, guest speakers, college visits, and Toastmasters events; and Lori Friel (right) inspires interest in college and helps kids find their way to the right one while working just as hard to help them find money to pay for it all.

versities for kids in that program; I, however, don't have that kind of connection and also feel like a school is part of the community and should thus offer community service to its own people. Beth Pascal keeps her eyes open for kids who fit the bill, but we have not yet created a reliable process that ensures we always have a tutor. This is the letter I sent out first:

September 20

TO: Advanced Math and Science Students (Juniors or Seniors)
FROM: Mr. Burke
RE: Academic Support for ACCESS Students

Too often we think of community service as an activity that takes place off campus. Yet the truth is that you are a member of our community here at school; moreover, you possess skills and knowledge that can help others in our school. I am writing to ask you to help others who want to succeed but need the extra attention and guidance you can provide.

I created a program that I call ACCESS. Here is a brief description of the program and its goals:

ACCESS is for those students who want to do well in academic classes but lack the confidence or skills. ACCESS students develop habits and strategies that will ensure success in school and the world of work. ACCESS offers a network of tutors, resources, mentors, and opportunities that will prepare and inspire students for life after high school. It's a program for those who are willing to work hard today to gain access to their dreams tomorrow.

ACCESS is for those students who:

- Want to succeed in school and after graduation
- Lack the academic skills and knowledge they need to succeed in academic classes
- Need support and tutoring they are not getting through other programs
- Are willing to work hard to succeed
- Want to explore careers, gain access, and contribute to their community
- Want to be prepared to begin work or go to college when they graduate
- Want to learn and work within a small, supportive community of students

ACCESS meets during first and second periods. Students have begun the year well, but are now beginning to run up against increasingly difficult work in math and science.

My hope is that a group of students will be interested and able to contribute a limited but regular amount of time each week on Tuesdays and/or Thursdays. On Fridays we have speakers; otherwise I would be happy to change things around to make other days available. I think it is important that the time be scheduled, however, so the students know they can count on getting the support they need. You would need to come to my class (room 82) for approximately twenty minutes one or two days a week, depending on your and your teacher's needs.

These are great kids, every one of them. They are eager to learn from you. If you are interested and available, please come by to talk with me to learn more. You might not plan to be a teacher tomorrow, but that shouldn't keep you from being one *today.* Hope to see you soon.

Jim Burke

This approach did not work, perhaps for what now seem obvious reasons. When you need help, you need to go up to one person and say, "You would be great and I need you to do this." Of course, you say it with a bit more grace, but no less force. I had a few kids who wanted to do it, but they were elite kids who had so many obligations that they couldn't make it to my class consistently. So the ACCESS kids ended up feeling left behind after establishing initially productive and satisfying relationships with the tutors. Instead, I have now begun to seek out (through Beth, who has an eye for such kids) individual kids (usually seniors) who have a period available during the ACCESS program.

I solved the problem in two different ways. One was to give interested kids, like Andrew, an added incentive to participate. Andrew is a great kid, the kind of kid who was on the principal selection committee with me when he was a freshman. Andrew is the kind of kid who at fourteen thought nothing of challenging assertions the superintendent made about different candidates or holding forth on the merits of a particular candidate. When he was a junior, he wanted to work with the ACCESS kids but also needed something more to engage himself. So Andrew became involved in Humanities–IS (independent studies), which I describe in the following letter to Amherst College, where Andrew applied and was quickly accepted:

Amherst College
P.O. Box 5000
Amherst, MA 02002-5000

To Whom It May Concern:

I am writing to explain what "Humanities–IS" means on Andrew Lundstrom's transcript. He is applying to your school for the coming year. This is not a recommendation letter, though for the record, I only extend the Humanities–IS opportunity to kids I respect.

Briefly, by way of background, I created the Humanities–IS course for individual kids who wish to challenge themselves at the highest levels intellectually. High school rarely offers kids the chance to study a subject in depth for an extended period of time as colleges, especially one like Amherst College, encourage or even require them to. Over the years, I have seen kids investigate a remarkable range of subjects, all of which culminate in a one-on-one conversation about what they learned over the course of the semester.

Andrew's experience was unique in that he divided the time between the Humanities–IS program he created for himself and my ACCESS program. ACCESS stands for Academic Success and is a program for incoming freshmen with reading difficulties and general academic needs. Andrew sought me out and asked if he could work with the kids in my program as a way to contribute to the school community.

Throughout the spring semester of 2004, Andrew studied the modern conflict in the Middle East, specifically focusing on the writings and ideas of Thomas Friedman. Andrew was inspired to learn more about the Middle East and Friedman's ideas after hearing him speak in the fall of 2003. His Humanities–IS program thus amounted to reading Friedman's books and columns, all of which he synthesized with what he learned from his own daily reading of newspapers. At the heart of the Humanities–IS course is the notion that students should generate a focus question or some purpose to their study; this amounts to a problem they want to examine and, through their studies, learn more about and ultimately try to solve (even if only intellectually). They must work independently at all times and seek guidance from those who understand the subject.

As for the ACCESS program, Andrew came each day to tutor and mentor ninth-grade students who struggled to learn basic algebra and to pass English and Modern World History. He worked closely and patiently with them to help them understand not only what the right answer was but how they could reach it. He was, I must say, a gifted tutor, one blessed with abundant patience and genuine goodwill. He taught them not only how to solve math problems but how to study for tests and take better notes. He helped them learn how to survive high school.

Please contact me if you have any further questions.

Sincerely,
Jim Burke
ACCESS Coordinator/AP English Teacher

Andrew was great with the kids, especially the boys. He was just what we needed and the experience gave him the chance to explore his own interests while helping kids in the community of his own school. Imagine what it is to have the attention of one of the school's top students, who says hi to you around school and helps you do your math.

The second, more reliable way to obtain such tutors is through the school's teachers aide program. Sarah Coit, a confident but quiet senior, also one of the top students, who would graduate and pursue a degree in chemistry at the University of California at San Diego, was the most effective tutor we have found so far. I have had others who were nearly as good: Alice Lee, another quiet, brilliant girl, related well to the kids. These tutors seem to all have shared a certain quiet confidence that was seasoned with some compassion but not pity or judgment, all of which allowed them to get along well with the kids. The girls' down-to-earth temperament did not intimidate or otherwise adversely affect the kids who needed help, something they are reluctant to admit they need to people they do not know or trust.

When her year was up, Sarah sat down to reflect on the year with the kids, telling me what she got from the experience and how I might improve it. Here is her letter:

Dear Mr. Burke:

I wanted to thank you for giving me the opportunity to be a part of your ACCESS class. I have benefited a lot from this opportunity. I have had the chance to read again for pleasure and have read some of the interesting books that you have suggested. You have planted an idea in my head that has changed the way that I read books now. You told me that sometimes you like to read science books and apply the ideas to the classroom. I find that idea very interesting and I find myself thinking about how ideas in a book apply to other elements in my life. I have enjoyed listening to the speakers on Fridays and feel that I was very lucky to have the chance to hear the inspiring words of many of the speakers. The thing that I am most thankful for has been meeting and working with the students in your class. I have been inspired by their dedication to improving their skills and grades. I have felt their frustration and have been honored to share in their triumphs. The students in this class are the heart of Burlingame High School and have been a big part of my senior year here at Burlingame High School.

I feel that the program is very successful and I do have a few suggestions on how to keep the program successful. I enjoy working in the computer room across the hall but sometimes there are too many people in the room and it becomes hard for me and the person that I am helping to think. Although one positive aspect of the computer room is that people feel comfortable in the room and it becomes a forum for everyone to talk. A lot of the time the talk does have to do with math and why people are having trouble and how other people are coping with math. I feel that I have gotten to know a lot of the students better because we can talk in the computer room. I have also tutored in the library this year and I found that was a nice change. In the library things are much quieter and I felt like I got more tutoring in that day. I suggest that the week should be divided between the library and the computer room. Students who really need help could come into the library and get one-on-one tutoring one day and the next day the tutor could be in the computer room so the tutor can check in with everyone.

Some of the material that I think a tutor needs to be successful are resource books. It would be helpful if the math department could loan a textbook to your class so the tutor could refresh their memory and use it when students forget their textbooks. I like the book I used in your class this year, it was a reference book for geometry I forget the title [*Algebra to Go*, published by Great Source]. I also think it would be useful if students had a sheet of paper that they used to track their test and quiz grades. I feel that Brandon, Paulina, and Danielle all exemplify what the program is all about. Brandon is probably the most dedicated student that I have ever met. He came prepared everyday with problems that he needed help on. Not only did he get help from me but he also went after school to his math teacher and also to an outside tutor. He had a hard time this year with tests but the material was hard. He needed someone to help him memorize equations and learn how to apply the equations. Paulina is a girl who exemplifies another aspect of the program. I saw her a lot when I first started tutoring. She got off on the right track and for the rest of this year she checked in with me and occasionally needed help on a few problems. Danielle is a student who would come in and do a few problems of her homework with me and if everything was going ok she would finish the homework later at home and work on something else in the period.

I feel that I benefited from the students in your class more than they benefited from me. I would like to share with you some of my favorite memories from this experience. I was talking one day to the ACCESS kids about my last basketball game and how they were going to honor the seniors on the team one day in the computer room. We all started talking about basketball and I forgot that I had mentioned that that night was my last basketball game. That night I saw about eight kids from the ACCESS class all sitting together cheering for me. I was so surprised that they came and I was so honored. They made my last basketball game very special. Another memory that I will cherish is looking at cars on the internet with Christian. I told him that I really wanted to find a purple Mustang. He helped me look on the internet and we determined that they don't exist. I am really glad that I have had the chance to meet Christian; I think that he is a great guy. My favorite memory of this year is when Danielle got a 20 out of 20 on one of her quizzes. She was so excited and I was so happy for her. There is another memory that I will always remember and that is the music in the computer room. I can't say that I did not like the music and I remember looking up from a math problem and seeing the MTV grind breaking out. It always looked like a dance was about to break out in that room. These students have taught me to love life and not to be too stressed by school and that sometimes a person just has to get up and dance. Thank you again for inviting me to be a part of the ACCESS class.

Sincerely,
Sarah Coit

# THREE
## *Curriculum*

### *What We Do: A Day in the Class*

The kids shuffle past the gray metal bookcase that holds their binders and *Reader's Handbook*s in a sloppy but stable disorder. They seem to arrive at the same time, like a swarm, but the truth is some—Chris and Joel, sometimes Rebecca—arrive by 7:30, using that half hour before school to settle in, check their email, get some work done, or just chat (about how much Joel sold his X-Box equipment for, or the flat Chris got on his bike, or the grief Rebecca's sister caused her the previous night). As we begin, others straggle into our first period class, predictably late: Henry, Anthony, the Murphy twins, and Martin, of course. Even Spencer is with us today, something we can't always count on (thirty-two absences this semester!).

As they settle in (prior to the bell), I move around the room, shaking kids' hands, passing them notes I've written, asking the Reading Buddies if they remembered that they are supposed to go to Washington Elementary School the next day (and be there by 8:30, dressed appropriately). I swoop down on another kid who's munchin' on a big bag of Cheetos and tell him he'll get them back at the period's end. I cry out to put all the food and drinks away. If this were a theater, the lights would be flicking on and off now, the show about to begin. This is the period—just before the bell rings—during which I can check in with individual kids, ask them how they did on the Health test the previous day, give them a push about English, monitor their progress in Algebra since the past progress report, three weeks ago. With twenty-five freshmen in the class, eighteen of whom are boys, there is a lot of energy in the room and a wide range of kids to monitor.

And so we begin, as we do most days, by going through the ritual of planning ahead, "getting our head in the game," and getting out the necessary gear

("Thomas, would you *ever* show up at football practice without your helmet?" I ask when I hear him ask someone for a pencil). I remind them that we have a speaker on Friday, and I'll tell them more on Thursday. Antonio insists on knowing who it is, "What do they do?" he wants to know. Then Andy and Krish chime in, urging me to tell them about it, distracting themselves and the rest of us from the task, so I guide us back, saying calmly, "That is for another day. We need to get ready to read." I ask them to make sure they have their Reading Records and SSR books out. As they fish out their goods, I remind them that there are three more weeks in the semester, that every assignment in every class counts, saying with some force that they must *not* give themselves permission to slack off. We are about to begin SSR when I notice Jeff, usually a serious distractor, absorbed by something in his lap, which I immediately realize is a cell phone on which he is reading a text message sent from a buddy on the other side of campus. Without making a big deal of it or embarrassing him, I just hold out my hand and tell him quietly he can get it at the end of the day in the dean's office; then I calmly reiterate what we have discussed lately: you have to learn to manage your attention, to keep your head in the game you are playing at the moment. He doesn't give me any trouble, no attitude; I pocket the phone and we move on.

"Get out your SSR books and your RRs [Reading Records], guys," I say as I pull out my digital organizer and set up the timer on it. It's set for 15:25 minutes, as always. "On the back of your Reading Record, jot down the day's PQ [purpose question] for your book so you have some kind of goal in mind. Also, pay attention to how many pages you read the day before and do your best to read more than that." I reach for my book, too: *Mountains Beyond Mountains,* by Tracy Kidder. And then we read, all of us, for fifteen minutes. No doing homework. No reading a novel for English. And I *always* read with them, sitting up front. The most that I will do, often without lifting my head, is point to Andy to get back to reading if my peripheral vision shows he is tuning out, or reach over and tap Victor's desk or Chris' book if they are getting sidetracked, as can happen.

During today's reading, which goes well, the following distractions happen: four boys crack their knuckles at different times; three kids fan the pages of their books to sound like playing cards in bike spokes; two cell phones vibrate; one kid fumbles in his pocket for a mint in a metallic tin; six kids tap their feet; two boys drum on things; and of course one kid farts, which, interestingly enough, becomes the most impressive test of their improved concentration for no one responds even though I know they all heard it. Twice the door swings open: once for the attendance person and again for the girl that brings appointment reminders from the counseling office. And Chris, who used to tinker with various things, now has a stress ball, which I suggested he get so he could silently work it while reading, meeting his need to do *something* while reading (his fifth book of the semester). Yet they read, and by this point, three months into it, they seem to clearly enjoy it, settling into the quiet time, reading a book they have chosen, for no other reason than to enjoy it.

When my timer chirps, we know the time is up and we return to our Reading Record (see Figure 3.16, page 98) to enter in the information from today's performance. "Make sure you go onto the back and try to answer your PQ also," I remind them, adding as always, "and look at today's performance and compare it with yesterday and the other days this week. If you read more or fewer pages, ask yourself why. If you tried something different that helped you read faster or understand better, pay attention to that and do it again tomorrow. Also, the PQ is not just for SSR. When you go to Health next period, or sit down to read your Contemporary World Studies textbook tonight, create a PQ for yourself based on the headings or the title." All of this—the reading, filling in the form, answering the question—takes about twenty minutes. I push hard, keep them focused.

Now it's time to begin the day's main course: introducing the unit "Life Studies." *Time* magazine has published a series of books that feature the one hundred most influential people—entertainers, leaders, visionaries, artists, and so on. Articles in the books average two pages and are written by distinguished people. Thus you get Bill Gates, for example, writing the article about the Wright Brothers, explaining what made them unique as people and inventors as he discusses how their invention changed our world. Nonfiction expository prose within the genre of biography, however, has certain conventions that one must know to read such texts successfully. To prepare them to read these and other biographical writings, as well as to extend their academic essentials, we use the *Reader's Handbook* (Burke 2002).

"OK, I want everyone to get out a sheet of binder paper and turn your *Reader's Handbook* to page 193, which talks about reading biographies." While they do this, I write "Biography" on the board, circling "Bio." I ask them if they know what *bio* means. A few kids raise their hands and offer misguided responses like "science" and "human." No one really knows, but we have established an atmosphere in the class that encourages this participation and ensures that they won't be embarrassed if they say anything "wrong." They are learning to participate in academic discussions, something kids in my honors English classes seem to have been born knowing how to do.

"Joel, you are taking biology, right?" I point to the biology textbook at his feet. He nods, worried I will call on him instead of just including him as I have so far. I write "ology" on the board under "graphy." We are talking about language as a way of getting into the topic, using the discussion to practice . . . discussion. I tell them (and write on the board) that *bio* means "life." "If *ology* means 'study of,'" I press on, "what is *biology* then?" A chorus gives back the right answer. I extend it to reinforce the idea: "If *psych* is 'mind,' what does *psychology* mean?" Again, they respond on cue with the correct answer.

"What about *graph*?" I query, to which Alice answers, "that means drawing." She is thinking about how they draw out (i.e., graph) things in Algebra. I answer with a question: "How many of you have ever had someone autograph something?" A bunch of hands go up. A bunch of guys take off on a conversational digression about different athletes they've asked to sign things. They start calling out names, dismissing one athlete as "useless" and praising another as "awesome." I raise my hands and voice like a coach trying to get them back to the huddle. "You have to learn not to let yourselves wander like that," I remind them, drawing attention to successful academic behavior. I'm about to move ahead when Anthony calls out, "Hey, d'you hear Barry Bonds got busted for doing steroids?" A new chorus of voices rises up, but I immediately quell it, saying with some force, "That's for later, guys. It has nothing to do with what we are doing now."

"*Graph* means 'to write,'" I finally explain. "And *auto* means 'self.' For example, *automobile* means to move yourself. So *autograph* means—what?" I ask this both to include them and to get *them* to think (instead of just watch me think).

After someone correctly answers my question, we return to "Biography" on the board. "So what does *bio* + *graphy* mean, then?" At this point, they understand it and say, "Writing your own story." "What if you add *auto* to the front?" I push. We go back and forth until we arrive at the idea of writing about one's own life. So in a few minutes we have discussed language and the larger concept of lives worth studying.

Instead of jumping straight into the book, I ask them to generate a list of five people they think are so important or interesting that it would be worth studying them. About six kids jump to it and start listing; some of these are what I call accelerated performers and others are steady performers, but not all of them. As those kids set to work, others pelt me with questions, trying to figure out what I mean, what the boundaries are: "People we know?" "What do you mean?" and so on, interspersed with the inevitable "I don't get it." All this is as it should be and is, in fact, a sign of good work: they are asking questions, standing up for themselves, demanding that the teacher make clear what they must do. So I clarify with some examples, adding that if they cannot think of specific names, they could list generic positions (e.g., president, inventor, etc.) or people they don't care about but know would be worth studying. I just want them to work on generating ideas, creating categories into which they must organize information, criteria they can use to evaluate the importance of any given person.

They have a sense of what I want now, and so all go to it while I circulate, asking questions, suggesting certain categories I think a student might find helpful based on their interests. Random questions still pop up: "Do they have to be alive?" "What if no one knows them except me?" I consistently praise these questions, saying, "That's a good question, Trevor," and then explain my answer. As it becomes clear that some have finished their lists, I interrupt to tell them what to do next, a step that is risky in such a class because if you do it too soon, the strugglers feel defeated (too far behind *again!*), but if you wait too long, the kids who have it done get discouraged and begin to check out.

"After you have your list, go through and evaluate the names and choose the *one* name that interests you most, that you think would be the most interesting to study or is the most important person on your list. Then write for a few minutes about what makes that person so important. Use the different strategies we have learned: ask the reporter's questions, make inferences, draw conclusions. You have about five minutes to get this all done."

When they are finished with this activity—which I'm doing to establish a connection to what they care about, to see what they know, to get them thinking about the subject—we turn our attention to the *Reader's Handbook*. Every student has their own copy of this book so they can annotate it, write in it, and eventually take it home to keep as a resource in the years ahead. The idea for giving them their own copy came from watching ESL students create a relationship with their dictionaries, those well-thumbed godsends that helped them solve so many academic problems. I hope that the *Reader's Handbook* might work the same way. Kids immediately become more purposeful, active readers when they can annotate or otherwise underline portions of a text.

"I want you to read that first page there, the one that introduces what a biography is. When you read, I want you to underline what you must know or do when reading a biography. Then at the bottom of the page, I want you to jot down some questions you would ask if you were writing a biography about the person you just chose to write about from your list." I move around while they read (see Figure 3.1). Some highlight, others use a pencil, some a pen, though I

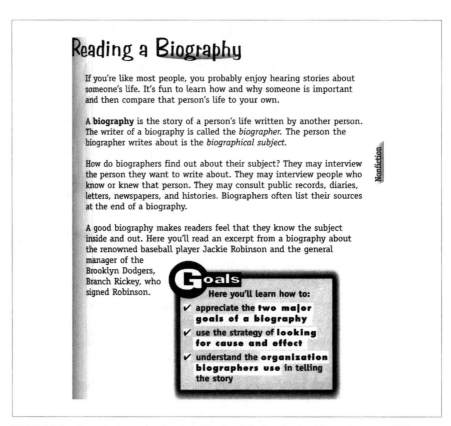

## Reading a Biography

If you're like most people, you probably enjoy hearing stories about someone's life. It's fun to learn how and why someone is important and then compare that person's life to your own.

A **biography** is the story of a person's life written by another person. The writer of a biography is called the *biographer*. The person the biographer writes about is the *biographical subject*.

How do biographers find out about their subject? They may interview the person they want to write about. They may interview people who know or knew that person. They may consult public records, diaries, letters, newspapers, and histories. Biographers often list their sources at the end of a biography.

A good biography makes readers feel that they know the subject inside and out. Here you'll read an excerpt from a biography about the renowned baseball player Jackie Robinson and the general manager of the Brooklyn Dodgers, Branch Rickey, who signed Robinson.

**Goals**

Here you'll learn how to:

✔ appreciate the **two major goals of a biography**

✔ use the strategy of **looking for cause and effect**

✔ understand the **organization biographers use** in telling the story

Nonfiction

FIGURE 3.1.   Sample from the *Reader's Handbook* by Jim Burke (Great Source: 2002).

discourage the use of pens to annotate; for that matter, I urge them to use pencils over highlighters because you can not only underline but comment in the margin with a pencil, whereas a highlighter can only indicate something is important.

When they finish, I push them onto the next two pages, which explain the importance of setting a purpose when reading and how to do that when reading a biography (see Figure 3.2). Once more, they must underline the key words or phrases that will help them formulate a PQ (purpose question). The book offers two sample questions it thinks are adequate; I ask them to add more, to generate a few more questions that would be useful when reading a biography. The kids come up with great questions:

• What did this person do that was so unique?
• What obstacles did they face and overcome to become successful?

Nonfiction

## Before Reading

A good biographer has two goals in mind when writing:

■ tell an interesting story

■ create a "portrait," or impression, of the biographical subject so that readers can understand what he or she is or was really like

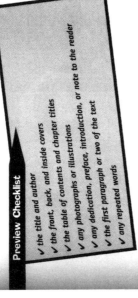

### A Set a Purpose

Imagine yourself looking over the biography shelves at your library. What drives you to choose one book over another? Most likely it's your curiosity about the biographical subject. Two questions that may come to mind as you thumb through the pages of a biography are:

*What kind of life has he or she had?*

*What was he or she really like?*

These two questions apply to any biography you read—whether for a school assignment or for pleasure. Finding answers to these two questions can be your purpose for reading.

**Setting a Purpose**

■ **What kind of life has this person had?**

■ **What was he or she really like?**

## B Preview

Before you begin your preview of the book about Jackie Robinson, consider what you already know. Who was Jackie Robinson? What did he do that made him famous? What stories have you heard about him? Keep this information—called "prior knowledge"—in mind as you preview.

If the biographical subject is completely new to you, your preview takes on added importance. It will be your first introduction to someone that you will get to know very well. When you preview, pay attention to the items on this checklist:

**Preview Checklist**

✓ *the title and author*
✓ *the front, back, and inside covers*
✓ *the table of contents and chapter titles*
✓ *any photographs or illustrations*
✓ *any dedication, preface, introduction, or note to the reader*
✓ *the first paragraph or two of the text*
✓ *any repeated words*

Now preview the covers and table of contents of John C. Chalberg's biography *Rickey & Robinson.* Use sticky notes or a highlighter to keep track of important details.

FIGURE 3.2. Sample from the *Reader's Handbook* by Jim Burke (Great Source: 2002).

- How did people feel about this person at that time?
- What made this person so unique—like, what talents or qualities did they have?
- How did they get to be who they were?

During such exchanges I praise them, responding to each question with questions that clarify or extend their thinking. I never call on a kid whose hand is not up unless I have learned, while circulating (which is one of the reasons I *do* circulate) that some kid has a great question to share. Then I know I can call on those students and ensure their success, offering them lots of public praise for their excellent contribution. Sometimes, during such generating sessions, I pull back and try to connect what they are doing to other classes, telling them that this (e.g., comparing and contrasting, asking questions, making inferences) is exactly what they must do in their English class or Health class: raise their hand, ask questions, contribute comments. By doing this, I explain, "You help that teacher succeed and they appreciate it and see you as a valuable member of the class and a student who wants to be taken seriously. Remember: Smart isn't what you *are* but what you *do*."

We are moving along, twenty-five kids thinking about important lives, working their academic muscles, demystifying the means by which kids succeed in school. When kids—Andy, Joel, Chris, or Victor, who all sit right up front for easy access and extra guidance—drift off, I can move in to clarify or coax them back, usually without a word, just a look, a tap on the book so they don't feel singled out.

A brief word about the *Reader's Handbook* (Burke 2002) before I move on. It is organized around the reading process (as described in the book), and each chapter describes how to apply the reading process to a different type of text. So, for example, the chapter on reading biographies will show the reader how to set a purpose, preview the text, and make a plan when reading a biography. Each stage, such as previewing the text, is clearly organized into a short section that uses a sample text to show the reader how, for example, to preview a biography. Thus students, when reading this chapter, practice each step while reading excerpts from a book about Jackie Robinson and Branch Rickey.

"I want you to read the next three pages, which include the front and back covers of this biography about Robinson and Branch, as well as the table of contents and the first page. When you read, underline the words that would help you answer the question, *Why is this person so important that we should study his life?* Also, when you finish, I want you to jot down (on your binder paper) what you know (or think you know) about this book and these two men."

A few minutes later (the pages are not long and are well suited to such in-class reading) we talk about what they know and have learned. I push them at times with questions to clarify or extend their thinking, asking them why they think such a piece of information is important, forcing them to explain, to analyze and evaluate, to elaborate on their thinking. At this point, with not much time left in the class, I want to move toward some closure for the day so we can pick up in a cohesive way the next day. I draw a cluster on the board with "Life Study" in the middle. On one branch, I draw a subcluster with "Who" in the middle, then "When," "What," "Where," "How," and "So?" growing out of it (see Figure 3.3).

I then reinforce our ongoing discussion of which strategies work best in which circumstances. Reporter's questions (aka the five Ws and an H) are ideal for biographies, I tell them. Then I write an additional subcluster with "Jackie Robinson" in the middle, and we use those same questions to sum up what they learned about him from the preview. As we do this, I make the point, as I often do, that in only five minutes they can gather a lot information by previewing. "Think about how much better you read if you preview the text," I say. Or this: "The next time you think to yourself, 'Oh, man, I don't want to read that text-book tonight. It's so dull!' tell yourself, 'OK, let's see what I can do in fifteen minutes.' Then you can preview the chapter, and you will certainly know more

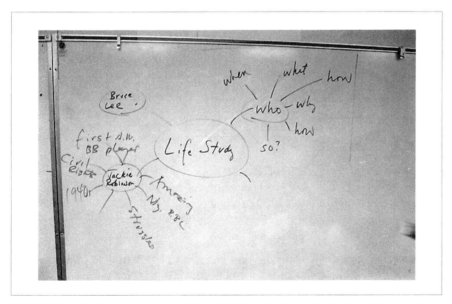

FIGURE 3.3. I make extensive use of the whiteboard and overhead, using different colors when I can, to help them see and thus better understand what we are learning.

in fifteen minutes of previewing than you would have known if you didn't look at it at all."

Such skill reminders are not the entire lesson, however. I am always trying to fit in the personal, and so I continue, saying, "You have to do this, take that time to at least preview the text, though of course I expect you to read the whole thing. You don't think, 'I'm doing this for Mrs. R.' No! You do this because you are worth the investment, because every thing you learn is like a deposit into some account that increases your own value. The more you know, the more you can do, the more valuable you are. What does every speaker we have talk about when they come in here? The things they learned to do that make them a valuable member of the department, the team, the community. Things that no one else learned how to do or could do as well. But it begins with seeing yourself as worth the investment, as valuable, worth the time. Is there anyone in here who doesn't think they are worth *at least* fifteen minutes? Of course not. So when you go home tonight, and you get out that history textbook, or that health article, you think about what we did today, how we did it. You think about previewing that text before, coming up with a PQ for that article about the leading causes of cancer; then you will read it better because you will have a destination in mind: you will be reading to answer the question, *What are the leading causes of cancer?*"

With one minute left, they gather their stuff, move toward the shelf to return their binders, having put today's work in there so they can work on it again the next day. As they move around, I check in with a few kids, asking Danny if his ankle is healed enough to play football yet, telling Krish I heard a teacher say he was doing great stuff. I have just time enough to jot down and hand off the following note to Martin, a Latino boy with a black eye who has made great strides lately:

Martin,

You have made such great progress since the beginning of the semester. Today you worked well and asked good questions. All this work is paying off as your grades come up. Keep the faith. I'm proud of you.

Mr. Burke

I call him over to give him the card but also to check in with him about the black eye. "Some kid punched me in PE," he explains. "Did you hit him back?" I ask. He tells me he didn't, so I shake his hand and say, "I'm so proud of you. That's exactly what that speaker was talking about last week when she talked about managing ourselves, not letting others bring us down to their level. I really respect that you didn't get into that stuff. Now get out there and have a great day." He began the year with a tough face, the face of a young man who was learning not to trust the world that had taken his father from him, that put him in a school where he had few friends and put him in classes that seemed too hard. Now after three months, he smiles more than he frowns, comes on time more than he comes late, and works all the time because he sees it paying off.

The bell rings, and as they leave, I call out, "Have a great day; thanks for your great work today! See you tomorrow!" And they call back "Good-bye," "Take care," or "Have a good day." In their wake come the burly, mature, jaded senior AP English students I teach next period, whom I care about and work just as hard to teach, whose examples and whose success help me better understand what I am trying to accomplish with my ACCESS students.

In the next few days we will follow up that first encounter with "Life Studies" in different ways. But some things will remain the same: SSR, PQs, reminders, reflection on process, connections between whatever we do and other classes, encouragement, praise, challenging questions to clarify and extend, finger tapping, text messaging, kids coming late, and, of course, Cheetos. The next day is similar but different, beginning with Victor coming in all jumpy, slugging on a huge can of some energy drink, asking me if I knew that this particular drink had "bull sperm in it." "That's what my friend said. It gives you strength and energy," he says. I can tell him only that I have a hard time imagining how they can get enough bull sperm to put some in all those cans and that unless it is somewhere on the list of ingredients, it isn't in there. I don't make fun of him, but I give him a wink and encourage him to read the label and to drink less sugary stuff and eat less candy because the sugar makes it that much harder to concentrate. The next day Victor comes in and proudly shows me that he listened and has now changed over from that energy drink and candy to the biggest bottle of Gatorade and the biggest bag of Doritos I have ever seen. It's progress—I think. And in truth, it is: Victor is trying harder every day, paying attention to what works, what gets praise, and he is getting there, moving along that continuum, coming in each morning to tell me what he got on his Health quiz, what his English teacher said the day before, that he got all his homework done.

## Why We Do What We Do: Revisiting the Research

An ACCESS class, as with many such academic success (AS) classes, can drift, get lost, or just plain come apart if you don't know where you are going or how you will get there. Instead of using dozens of fancy techniques and strategies, I find it best to follow a few key conclusions from research done in similar settings with similar kids. These instructional principles allow me to be more flexible when I encounter unexpected turbulence or a sudden storm of confusion. While the core research findings focus on reading, I apply them to instruction in general, for both affect each other in the interplay of the curriculum.

Many needs are specific to adolescent students, something the National Council of Teachers of English recognizes in its position statement about adolescent literacy. It offers the following summary of research on adolescent literacy:

1. That literacy is a dynamic interaction of the social and cognitive realms, with textual understandings growing from students' knowledge of their worlds to knowledge of the external world (Langer, 2002). All students need to go beyond the study of discrete skills and strategies to understand how those skills and strategies are integrated with life experiences. Langer et al. found that literacy programs that successfully teach at-risk students emphasize connections between students' lives, prior knowledge, and texts, and emphasize student conversations to make those connections.

2. That the majority of inexperienced adolescent readers need opportunities and instructional support to read many and diverse types of texts in order to gain experience, build fluency, and develop a range as readers (Greenleaf, Schoenbach, Cziko, and Mueller, 2001; Kuhn and Stahl, 2000). Through extensive reading of a range of texts, supported by strategy lessons and discussions, readers become familiar with written language structures and text features, develop their vocabularies, and read for meaning more efficiently and effectively. Conversations about their reading that focus on the strategies they use and their language knowledge help adolescents build confidence in their reading and become better readers (Goodman and Marek, 1996).

3. That most adolescents do not need further instruction in phonics or decoding skills (Ivey and Baker, 2004). Research summarized in the National Reading Panel report noted that the benefits of phonics instruction are strongest in first grade, with diminished results for students in subsequent grades. Phonics instruction has not been seen to improve reading comprehension for older students (National Reading Panel, 2000). In cases where older students need help to construct meaning with text, instruction should be targeted and embedded in authentic reading experiences.

4. That utilizing a model of reading instruction focused on basic skills can lead to the mislabeling of some secondary readers as "struggling readers" and "non-readers" because they lack extensive reading experience, depend on dif-

ferent prior knowledge, and/or comprehend differently or in more complex ways. A large percentage of secondary readers who are so mislabeled are students of color and/or students from lower socio-economic backgrounds. Abundant research suggests that the isolated skill instruction they receive may perpetuate low literacy achievement rather than improve their competence and engagement in complex reading tasks (Allington, 2001; Alvermann and Moore, 1991; Brown, 1991; Hiebert, 1991; Hull and Rose, 1989; Knapp andTurnbull, 1991; Sizer, 1992). In addition, prescriptive, skills-based reading instruction mislocates the problem as the students' failure to learn, rather than the institution's failure to teach reading as the complex mental and social activity it is (Greenleaf, Schoenbach, Cziko, and Mueller, 2001).

5. That effective literacy programs move students to deeper understandings of texts and increase their ability to generate ideas and knowledge for their own uses (Newmann, King, and Rigdon, 1997).

6. That assessment should focus on underlying knowledge in the larger curriculum and on strategies for thinking during literacy acts (Darling-Hammond and Falk, 1997; Langer, 2000; Smith, 1991). Likewise, preparation for assessment (from ongoing classroom measures to high stakes tests) should focus on the critical components above. (May 2004)

Improved comprehension lies at the heart of much of the reading instruction in ACCESS, with a special focus on teaching students to use strategies with different texts in different situations. Block, Gambrell, and Pressley (2002) offer the following features of effective strategy instruction:

- Teachers taught students a small repertoire of comprehension strategies.
- They instructed students in how to use the strategies.
- Students practiced the strategies.
- Students modeled and explained strategy use for one another.
- Teachers conveyed to students information about when and where to use strategies.
- Teachers often used strategy vocabulary (clarification, summaries, and so on).
- Flexibility in students' use of strategies was apparent.
- Teachers continually sent the message that student thinking mattered. (10)

It is Judith Langer's research that has proven most useful. Langer conducted a study of "beat the odds schools" whose students did much better than their demographic information would have predicted. After studying these schools for five years, Langer identified six features that accounted for these schools' consistent success:

FEATURE ONE: STUDENTS LEARN SKILLS AND KNOWLEDGE
IN MULTIPLE LESSON TYPES.

- Providing overt, targeted instruction and review as models for peer and self-evaluation
- Teaching skills, mechanics, or vocabulary that can be used during *integrated* activities such as literature discussions
- Using all three kinds of instruction to scaffold ways to think and discuss (e.g., summarizing, justifying answers, and making connections)

FEATURE TWO: TEACHERS INTEGRATE TEST
PREPARATIONS INTO INSTRUCTION.

- Analyze the demands of a test
- Identify connections to the standards and goals
- Design and align curriculum to meet the demands of the test
- Develop instructional strategies that enable students to build the necessary skills
- Ensure that skills are learned across the year and across grades
- Make overt connections between and among instructional strategies, tests, and current learning
- Develop and implement model lessons that integrate test preparation into the curriculum

FEATURE THREE: TEACHERS MAKE CONNECTIONS ACROSS
INSTRUCTION, CURRICULUM, GRADES, AND LIFE.

- Making overt connections between and across the curriculum, students' lives, literature, and literacy
- Planning lessons that connect with each other, with test demands, and with students' growing knowledge and skills
- Developing goals and strategies that meet students' needs and are intrinsically connected to the larger curriculum
- Weaving even unexpected intrusions into integrated experiences for students

## FEATURE FOUR: STUDENTS LEARN STRATEGIES FOR DOING THE WORK.

- Providing rubrics that students review, use, and even develop
- Designing models and guides that lead students to understand how to approach each task
- Supplying prompts that support thinking

## FEATURE FIVE: STUDENTS ARE EXPECTED TO BE GENERATIVE THINKERS.

- Exploring texts from many points of view (e.g., social, historical, ethical, political, personal)
- Extending literary understanding beyond initial interpretations
- Researching and discussing issues generated by literary texts and by student concerns
- Extending research questions beyond their original focus
- Developing ideas in writing that go beyond the superficial
- Writing from different points of view
- Designing follow-up lessons that cause students to move beyond their initial thinking

## FEATURE SIX: CLASSROOMS FOSTER COGNITIVE COLLABORATION.

- Students work in small and large groups to
  - Share their ideas and responses to literary texts, questions, etc.
  - Question and challenge each other's ideas and responses
  - Create new responses
- Teachers provide support during discussions and group work by
  - Moving from group to group
  - Modeling questions and comments that will cause deeper discussion and analysis
  - Encouraging questions and challenges that cause students to think more deeply (2002)

In addition to Langer's six key features of effective literacy instruction, Marzano, Pickering, and Pollock (2001) conducted an extensive survey of research on general instructional principles that are effective. Outlined in *Classroom*

*Instruction That Works*, these nine aspects of instruction also guide my instructional design and decisions. The essential nine are:

1. Identifying similarities and differences
2. Summarizing and note taking
3. Reinforcing effort and providing recognition
4. Homework and practice
5. Nonlinguistic representations
6. Cooperative learning
7. Setting objectives and providing feedback
8. Generating and testing hypotheses
9. Cues, questions, and advance organizers

All these principles—identified by Marzano and colleagues, Langer, and the others—inform the opening sequence of my program in one way or another, giving me guidance during planning, during the class, or after class ends and I wonder why certain things did or did not work. The primary framework for the ACCESS curriculum, known as the Academic Essentials, derives from careful analysis of what students must know and be able to do in all academic classes to succeed.

## The Academic Essentials: An Overview

Some years ago Mike Rose, author of *Lives on the Boundary* (1989), analyzed what kids in college needed to know to succeed. After sitting in different classes at UCLA for a year, he reduced this set of essential skills down to six (after initially coming up with four):

- Define
- Summarize
- Serialize
- Classify
- Compare
- Analyze

Being able to list these skills fascinated me: after all, if we know what they are, we can teach them and help kids achieve greater success. Yet something didn't seem quite right. I examined the assignments I gave my students in English and compared them with others from the core academic subjects. I routinely monitored the stacks of assignments in the photocopy room, sometimes sneaking a copy of an Economics or a Health assignment; other times, I studied what ACCESS students did for other classes. In the end, I arrived at the Academic Essentials, a list that combines key skills (reading, writing, talking, taking notes, and taking tests) with fundamental cognitive abilities (generating, evaluating, analyzing, organizing, and synthesizing) that high school students, in any academic class, must be able to not just do but *use* with fluency in a variety of settings and on a range of assignments. I have arranged them in a matrix (see Figure 3.4) to indicate the extent to which students must often use more than one and sometimes all five of the cognitive abilities, for example, when writing an essay.

The Academic Essentials provide the instructional framework for the course by reminding me what to emphasize on any given lesson. Like the Four Cs of Academic Success, which serve as more of a conceptual than instructional framework, the Academic Essentials force me to evaluate any instructional task by asking, "Which of the Academic Essentials does this assignment or activity address? Which of the Four Cs does this assignment address?" And if I can see no clear and effective connection between the Academic Essentials, the Four Cs, and a task I was going to have students do, I reconfigure it to better meet that end. In this way instruction becomes more deliberate, making a ten-minute conversation an opportunity to teach them how to participate in an academic subject, or the day's silent reading assignment an occasion to generate, evaluate, and synthesize. To better focus on these fundamental aspects—the Academic Essentials and the Four Cs, along with the core habits of mind—I created a lesson plan template that includes them all so that each day I can check to see which ones I am touching on and find others I might also hit if I revise the assignment a bit (see Figure 3.5).

But what does all this look like, you wonder? What do I *do*—or, more importantly, what do the *students* do in the class? It's impossible to include the year's curriculum here; instead, I include a detailed sequence that represents what we do and how we work in the ACCESS class.

## *What We Do: Samples of Curriculum*

### Reflecting on Performances and Processes

Whether they win or lose Friday night, the football team always watches the game film Saturday to study what worked and what did not. Effective performance and steady improvement stem from conscious efforts to reflect on the results and process by which one achieves these results in any area, whether it be

# The Academic Essentials Matrix

| SKILLS | Generate: Questions, Hypotheses, Claims, Explanations, Examples | Evaluate: Importance, Effectiveness, Relevance, Validity, Accuracy | Analyze: Cause/effect, Meaning, Implications, Logic, Consequences | Organize: Events, Information, Process, Ideas, Emphasis | Synthesize: Information, Events, Ideas, Sources, Perspectives |
|---|---|---|---|---|---|
| **Read** • Fiction • Information • Argument • Poetry | | | | | |
| **Write** • Reader response • Narrative • Expository • Argument | | | | | |
| **Talk** • Discussion • Speech • Presentation | | | | | |
| **Take Notes** • Expository • Research • Literary • Textbook | | | | | |
| **Take Tests** • Multiple choice • Essay • Short answer • Standardized | | | | | |

*(Column group heading: ABILITIES)*

## Explanation of the Academic Essentials (AE) Matrix

The AE matrix gives structure, depth, and sequencing to my lessons. For example, when I decide which of the **skills** (reading, writing, talking, taking notes, or taking tests) I need to focus on next, I then use the **abilities** lists to organize and improve that instruction. If we are reading an article on the topic of personal success, for example, I might have students **generate** a list of factors they think contribute to such success. I might then have students, to increase their processing of the information, **evaluate** which *three* factors from their list are the most important, then **analyze** how they contribute to success. The matrix challenges me to achieve more but in a structured sequence; thus I might have students **organize** their three essential factors from most to least important or in some other logical order. Finally, to integrate the different skills, I would have students **synthesize** by first writing a well-organized paragraph and then, if time allows, discussing it with each other or the class. In addition, I would ask myself (before, during, and after this instructional sequence) what other skills—writing, talking, taking notes, taking tests—I could or should integrate. In this way, the AE matrix ensures my instruction is designed to achieve maximum effectiveness in ways that promote learning and academic success.

FIGURE 3.4.   A full-size, downloadable version of this form is available on the ACCESSing School page of the Heinemann website, at www.heinemann.com.

*May be copied for classroom use. ACCESSing School by Jim Burke (Heinemann, Portsmouth, NH), © 2005.*

| | |
|---|---|
| $C^1$ | $C^2$ |
| $C^3$ | $C^4$ |

**Academic Essentials**

- Read
- Write
- Talk
- Take notes
- Take tests

- Generate
- Evaluate
- Analyze
- Organize
- Synthesize

| Class | Subject[1] |
|---|---|
| **Period** / **Date** | **Subject[2]** |

| Personal Curriculum | Public Curriculum |
|---|---|

**Notes**

_____    _____
_____    _____
_____    _____
_____    _____

**Before**

- What do they already know?
- What do they need to learn?
- What instructional technique is best?
- What is their motivation for doing this?
- What is the Big Idea this relates to?
- What is the best instructional set up?
- Do they know what a successful performance of this task looks like?
- How will you know they achieved the desired outcome?
- Are there other ways students can demonstrate understanding or mastery?

**During**

- Is the instructional technique and/or academic strategy effective?
- Who is struggling and why? How can you help them?
- Are students making the expected progress toward the state's goals?
- How can you have them further manipulate the material to improve comprehension, fluency, and memory?

**After**

- What do you want them to do now?
- How can they demonstrate their understanding and ability?
- Did they reach the instructional goal?
- If not, what should you reteach and by what method to ensure improved learning, fluency, and memory?
- How can they extend what they learned here to improve fluency and memory?
- What do they need to do or learn next—and how does that relate to what they learned through this lesson?

_____
_____
_____
_____
_____

FIGURE 3.5.   Lesson plan templates like this help me achieve greater instructional consistency by providing structure and guidance when planning and teaching. (A full-size, downloadable version of this form is available on the *ACCESSing School* page of the Heinemann website, at www.heinemann.com.)

Curriculum

football or tennis, writing or reading. Known as *metacognition*, this process plays an important role in the ACCESS curriculum. We reflect on our process to better understand *what* we do and *how* we do it; thus during silent reading, kids often use the bookmark in Figure 3.11 to examine the process that leads to their successful or incomplete understanding of the book. We reflect during and after many assignments, integrating metacognitive observations into the assignment itself; however, we also reflect each week and month, at the end of each semester, and at the end of the year. The premise is simple: unless you know which actions result in a successful performance—on a test, while reading, in a class—you will be unable to repeat that success reliably; thus your success will be an accident, the chance result of the right questions asked the right way. Ah, but you won't *know* they are perfect unless you stop to consider the effect they had.

The opportunity to reflect creates an important conversation between the students and the teacher, the students and the text, and the students and themselves. This conversation has both practical and personal aspects to it. On the practical level, kids need to consider what strategies they used on the test and what effect the strategies had on the outcome. Recognizing that the technique of eliminating impossible and improbable answers *did* help, the students come to understand that they should do this again; after further consideration, the students realize that it might be even more effective if they not only eliminate but "check (the question again) before they choose" what they consider to be the correct answer. To the extent that such reflection becomes a mental habit, students can then study their own game, always trying to notice what they did and asking what effect it had on their performance. Embedded within the habit of reflection is the important principle that one can always improve, that there are steps one can take to read faster and understand more. In ACCESS, however, the reflection is also personal, for they are trying to improve themselves as both students and people. Thus we look at academic as well as personal successes, asking how the student accomplished each—or why they didn't.

Figure 3.6 shows an example of a Personal Progress Report, which we complete at the end of each week (or, if something on Friday prevents that, on Monday). I use this to draw attention to and reinforce the importance of various behaviors that lead to success in academic classes.

Later on in the year, usually at the beginning of the second semester, we use a different form: the Weekly Record. This version emphasizes goal setting as well as strategic and argumentative thinking, both essential to success in any field. I want the kids to become wiser about the world and themselves, also, so I

**PERSONAL PROGRESS REPORT**

Complete the following evaluation of your performance so far this semester. The more honest you are, the more you will benefit from this activity. Please be as specific as possible.

*(handwritten top right)* √+ I'm very impressed by all that you are doing, Marina.

| Class: History | | Teacher: Rhorbach | Grade: D+ |
|---|---|---|---|
| **Habits of Success** | | **What Helped/What Hurt/What Was Hard?** | |
| 1. Completed all assignments? | Y/Ⓝ | What helped was doing | |
| 2. Did my best on *all* work? | Y/Ⓝ | my homework, what hurt | |
| 3. Turned it all in? | Y/Ⓝ | was not turning in my | |
| 4. Arrived *on time* to class every day? | Ⓨ/N | art notebook. But I'm | |
| 5. Had materials *every* day? | Ⓨ/N | gunna do good on my | |
| 6. Participated in class discussion? | Ⓨ/N | next test and i'm already | |
| 7. Talked to my teacher at least once? | Ⓨ/N | getting prepared & taking | |
| 8. Wrote *all* assignments down in planner? | Ⓨ/N | notes) | |
| 9. Took a risk in class? | Ⓨ/N | | |
| 10. Came to class *every* day (no absences)? | Y/Ⓝ | | |

*(handwritten note on #1-2: homework in the art notebook)*

| Class: P.E | | Teacher: Mr. Phil | Grade: C |
|---|---|---|---|
| **Habits of Success** | | **What Helped/What Hurt/What Was Hard?** | |
| 1. Completed all assignments? | Y/N | I run as fast as i can. | |
| 2. Did my best on *all* work? | Y/N | I talk to him a lot, try | |
| 3. Turned it all in? | Y/N | my best when we play | |
| 4. Arrived *on time* to class every day? | Ⓨ/N | volleyball. I put in a lot | |
| 5. Had materials *every* day? | Ⓨ/N | of effort and he knows | |
| 6. Participated in class discussion? | Ⓨ/N | it. | |
| 7. Talked to my teacher at least once? | Ⓨ/N | | |
| 8. Wrote *all* assignments down in planner? | Y/N | | |
| 9. Took a risk in class? | Ⓨ/N | | |
| 10. Came to class *every* day (no absences)? | Ⓨ/N | | |

*(handwritten note right: but now I have a B. great)*
*(handwritten note #2: doesn't apply)*

| Class: English | | Teacher: Caret | Grade: C |
|---|---|---|---|
| **Habits of Success** | | **What Helped/What Hurt/What Was Hard?** | |
| 1. Completed all assignments? | Ⓨ/N | I love this class, I | |
| 2. Did my best on *all* work? | Ⓨ/N | got my self to like her | |
| 3. Turned it all in? | Ⓨ/N | class. I'm taking a quiz | |
| 4. Arrived *on time* to class every day? | Ⓨ/N | today and i've been studying | |
| 5. Had materials *every* day? | Ⓨ/N | really hard it's 20 points | |
| 6. Participated in class discussion? | Ⓨ/N | I think i'll do good and | |
| 7. Talked to my teacher at least once? | Ⓨ/N | that will really raise my | |
| 8. Wrote *all* assignments down in planner? | Y/N | grade. | |
| 9. Took a risk in class? | Ⓨ/N | | |
| 10. Came to class *every* day (no absences)? | Ⓨ/N | | |

*(handwritten note right: now! B great)*

turned in CSM perm. slip

| Successes | Disappointments |
|---|---|
| English — everything has been a success! I'm getting involved. I'm doing: McKinly Haunted house, Leadership skills workshop, and reading buddies! I'm going to ask mrs. Glick if i can get more volunteer work! | • not doing my art notebook • low test and Quiz grade in Zeller • I want to hurry up and finish the book "CUT". I took a test on 2 books i've read and that will help my grade! |

FIGURE 3.6. The back side of Marina's Personal Progress Report. (The front shows three "class" boxes.)

ask them to think about what they learned that week about themselves, people, or the world. Such reflections, so long as the kid is making a sincere effort, provide an opportunity to examine their actions and, when appropriate, celebrate the results of those actions. (See Figure 3.7.)

FIGURE 3.7.  Mitchell's Weekly Record.

At other times we must focus more specifically on their grades, helping them understand not only why they have the grades they do but how they can improve them. We focus on strategies and goal setting throughout the year, applying it to the daily assignments when appropriate, such as silent reading, and to the long term for more global success. In the Progress Report: Strategic Planning worksheet (see Figure 3.8), for example, you see Sergio entering into a conversation with himself (and, indirectly, with the teacher of each class as well as with me) about the consequences of his decisions and then coming up with specific plans to achieve the grade he *wants*.

You will notice that not all of his items in the strategic plan boxes are action items; saying that he is not doing well in history "because recently [tests have] been getting really hard" provides a crucial opportunity for us to discuss the

**Progress Report: Strategic Planning**                          Name: *Sergio*

Note    Progress reports are in. Some of you are proud and happy; others are angry, worried, or depressed. Regardless of how you feel, the only question today and in the weeks ahead is: What are you willing to do to achieve the success you want? Success for you might mean raising that B+ in English to an A-; for others it means pushing that F up to a D so you pass your Algebra or Modern World History class. This page is designed to help you make a game plan that will lead to the success you want.

| Class | The Grade You *Have* | Strategic Evaluation<br>• How do you feel about this grade—and why?<br>• Why do you have this grade in this class at this point?<br>• Whom have you asked for help?<br>• What have you done to try to improve your performance in this class? | The Grade You *Want* | Strategic Plan:<br>• What you are willing to do to achieve your goal?<br>• Who can and will help you achieve this goal?<br>• What is your biggest obstacle and how you will overcome that in order to achieve your goal?<br>• How will you reward yourself if you achieve this goal? |
|---|---|---|---|---|
| 1. Modern Language Arts | C+ | I feel disappointed with my grade because I know I could of done better if I would of yourself finished things on time - I have a c- because I turned in important assignments late. Nobody I haven't asked for help. Turn in things on time | B- | Be prepared and turn in things on time. I think that people took helped is enough already and that its the responsibility for my own actions and I should do it myself. I get distracted easily when I'm doing things on topics that I love are. |
| 2. Modern World History | F | Extremely disappointed because I know I could do better because I've been doing All my work and getting decent scores and still I see no progress | D+ or C-? | I think that my biggest obstacle is to keep on doing good on tests because recently they've been getting really hard |
| 3. Aces | A | Really happy with this grade because I know that I've really worked for this grade and I earned it. | A | I want to keep this grade so I will continue to work hard for the remainder of the semester |

FIGURE 3.8.   Sergio's Strategic Planning Progress Report.

language of responsibility. What I try to do, when it is appropriate and useful, is cull from such worksheets language that invites further reflection:

ACCESS: LANGUAGE OF RESPONSIBILITY

1. I didn't achieve my goal because I did all but one homework assignment.
2. It's hard for me to do all my homework because I'm always busy and I always have so much to do.
3. I didn't reach my goal because there was too much work.
4. I achieved my goal by scheduling the time when I would do my homework.
5. I achieved my goal by writing everything down in my planner and checking it off as I did it.
6. I didn't achieve my goal because I didn't give it my best effort.
7. I didn't achieve my goal because football wore me out and I was too tired to do it.
8. I achieved my goal because I took a nap after practice to get my energy back and then worked hard and got everything done.
9. I didn't achieve my goal because I couldn't concentrate on my work with the computer on and people calling me on the phone.
10. I achieved my goal this week by asking the teacher to explain what I did not understand before I left the class at the end of the period.

I will put this list on the overhead and we will take time to go through it, discussing items point by point. When someone wants to argue, "But it's true, Mr. Burke! She just doesn't like me!" I can use that to start a conversation about their logic, pointing out that whether a teacher likes you has nothing to do with whether you got the answer on the history quiz wrong. By looking at the language they use, reflecting on the implications of saying, "I can't take tests," versus "Tests are hard for me, so I need to learn some new techniques that will help me do better," they come to realize how mental the game of success is.

Over the course of the year the kids change. My job, among others, is to be like the meteorologist who watches satellite weather patterns so I can see signs of approaching trouble. So if I begin to sense, often from overheard conversations before class, that the kids need to regroup, we might have a conversation about mistakes they have made and how they can learn from and avoid them. The purpose, as always, is to get them to pay attention to their decisions, their actions, and the consequences of those actions. (See Figure 3.9.)

Conversation: Learning from Mistakes          Name: _Louis_____

| What I Did (Mistake I made) | What happened (Consequences) | Repeat? | # |
|---|---|---|---|
| • Did not turn in homework assignment. | Lost points; lowered my grade. | Yes | 8 |
| • Came to class late. | Disrupted class; upset teacher; missed pop quiz; lowered my grade; got detention. | | |
| ★ Did not turn or do homework | lost point, lower my grade didn't know what was going on. | Yes | 8 |
| Didn't have a pencil or pen | teacher got mad. | Yes | 1 |
| Came late to class | disrupted the teacher, lower my grade. | Yes | 3 |
| talked in class | disrupted the teacher | Yrs | 8 |
| didn't dress for football ball | got the coach mad | yes | 3 |
| didn't try my hardest one homework or football | lower my grade, lowered my quiz grade | Yes | 5 |
| forget to study for a test or quiz | lower quiz grade, lower grade | Yes | 7 |
| Not drawing my hardest for art. | not coming out how I want it, drawing is not good. | Yes | 1 |
| Good Decisions | | | |
| I help out my friend in art class, | help me feel good. | yes | 2 |
| come home and do hw | help my grade, raised my grade | Yes | |
| Using homework planner | know what my hw homework is. | allthe time | |
| ★ did my homework instead of playing games | rase my grade | Yes | 5 |

FIGURE 3.9.   Louis' work here shows a student thinking about how decisions—both good and bad—lead to certain consequences.

While not included here, the back side of the Learning from Mistakes assignment includes Portia Nelson's poem "Autobiography in Five Short Chapters," a poem that narrates five different stages of learning to make better decisions. After they finish the worksheet, I ask them to read the poem, which has five enumerated stanzas, and choose the stage that best describes their current level of performance. Then, to incorporate writing, they write a paragraph about decision making, drawing from their answers on the worksheet and the details from Nelson's poem, on which they wrote notes about *why* they are stuck, say, at level three. Here is Louis Hernandez's paragraph:

> In the first semester I made good and bad decisions along the way. Some of the bad decisions I have made were not doing my homework, coming to class late, not turning in my homework, and not paying attention in class. I try not to do those things, but it's a habit for me. I try not to make it a habit but it doesn't work out. My grades have lowered because of that habit and also my quiz and test grades. Some good things I have done lately include write my homework down in my planner, do my work at home, listen in class, try not to come late, not do my homework in front of the television, and do my homework instead of playing games.

When we get to the end of the semester, we use the Argument Organizer to practice more of the Academic Essentials (see Figure 3.10). As you can see with this, as well as the previous reflective assignments, academic thinking is at the core: the kids are generating, evaluating, analyzing, organizing, and synthesizing, often while using more than one skill (e.g., talking *and* writing). At semester's end, I ask students to reflect on their progress in the class and argue what their grade should be. This requires them to generate possible categories, evaluate which ones are most appropriate, and then generate details within those categories after analyzing their performance over the course of the semester. In the process, they learn the structure of argument—that is, they must acknowledge another side to their argument and then respond to it—while reinforcing their ability to organize and synthesize information by writing a well-organized paragraph. While I do not include Nicolle's paragraph here, you can see from her organizer in Figure 3.10 how easy it would be for her to write it, as she has her claim, her evidence, and her counterpoints all worked out.

Before moving into the primary curriculum, I want to point out a few things. First, these different reflective activities are *instructional* activities: I use them to introduce, extend, and reinforce the Academic Essentials. I treat them as distinct teaching moments that give me occasion not just to give mentoring talks about working "smarter, not harder" but to think at the overhead or on

**Argument Organizer: Reading, Writing, Speaking**          Name: Nicolle

**Claim**

Claim — What do you want people to know, do, think, or believe?

I deserve an A in access

**Reason(s)**

Reason(s) — A sentence or two explaining *why* you are making this claim.

I think I deserve this grade because I always try my best in this class with all my work and studying all.

**Evidence**

Evidence — Facts, Figures, Statistics, Quotations from the text, Expert analysis

| Evidence | Evidence | Evidence |
|---|---|---|
| Contribution — I have given a lot of contribution at Washington, because I play with the kids and make them laugh when they are down. I always enjoy going there and talking to them. I would like to go there more often if possible. | Studying — I study as much as possible for any test. — Use as much time to study — Need to build up study habit and spend more time on it when needed. | Reading — I am a better reader than I was in middle school — I read alot more than I use too. — My comprehension has improved during the year. — Strategies are always good so you have them when you read 1 dif. book |

**Acknowledge and Respond**

Acknowledge and Respond — Discuss, address, and respond to alternatives, criticisms, and objections.

| Acknowledge | Respond |
|---|---|
| While I have improved I still need to participate more. I participate when I know if the answer is 100% right, but then I don't raise my hand. So I need to participate more | Despite these obstacles I am improving more in reading and participation I think I deserve an A in this Access class because I always try my best |

© Jim Burke 2003. May reproduce for classroom use only. www.englishcompanion.com

FIGURE 3.10. Nicolle reflects on her performance while using argumentative thinking to make the case for the A she worked so hard to earn.

the whiteboard about how to write, generate, evaluate, and so on. If I have them, I will put up examples that former students or I created so the kids can see what a successful performance looks like. We process the information and the techniques, discussing what we did and why. Schoenbach and her colleagues write of metacognition:

> Gaining metacognitive awareness is a necessary step to gaining control of one's mental activity. Consciousness of their own thinking processes allows learners to "reflectively turn around on their own thought and action and analyze how and why their thinking achieved certain ends or failed to achieve others."

Moreover, knowledge of one's own thinking is like other kinds of knowledge in that it grows through experience (that is through the metacognitive activity itself) and becomes more automatic with practice. (1999, 29)

In order to develop metacognition, Schoenbach and her colleagues suggest that students:

- Notice what is happening in [their] mind in a variety of everyday situations
- Identify various thinking processes [they] engage in a variety of everyday situations
- Notice where [their] attention is when [they] read
- Identify all the different processes going on while [they] read
- Choose what thinking activities to engage in; direct and control [their] reading process accordingly (29)

Now let us look at a sample sequence of the primary curriculum so that you can get a sense of what we do when we are not busy reflecting; after all, one must do *something* before one can have anything on which to reflect.

### Silent Reading: A Sample Sequence

While many see sustained silent reading as sacred territory, I see it as the perfect opportunity to accomplish a variety of goals. After all, the students are reading books they choose, about subjects that interest them, so motivation is not the problem it might be if I were choosing the core text and telling them all to read it. This almost daily ritual (we read three to four days a week, and always for exactly fifteen minutes) allows them to read books appropriate to their level. It provides them a daily opportunity to quiet down and reflect through their reading on life. It begins and accelerates the process of developing an identity as a reader, the importance of which cannot be overstated, as they all enter the class not only hating reading but believing they cannot do it well. Over time, however, many of the kids come to feel like Russell: "I also want to thank you for having fifteen minutes every morning to read. Before that I didn't like reading because I never gave it a chance, but since I have started reading in your class, I read in my free time, too."

I feel compelled to use the silent reading to achieve more than an interest in reading and an identity of themselves as readers. For one, SSR (aka silent reading or drop everything and read [DEAR]) has come under increasing scrutiny from school boards and administrations who think that it is a waste of instructional time because it's something they should be doing at home. Though my techniques are not a response to this pressure, they nonetheless provide a strong rationale for why I should be allowed to do it in school—and why others should, too. Returning briefly to the Four Cs of Academic Success and the Academic Essentials, daily silent reading provides an ideal opportunity to improve:

- Commitment (to reading, to their identity as readers)
- Content (through what they learn as they read)
- Competencies (through reading and the activities we do to build skills)
- Capacity (by reading increasingly difficult books and thus developing their fluency, speed, and stamina)

It also gives me a natural context in which to work on essential skills (reading, writing, talking, taking notes, and taking tests) and core abilities (generating, evaluating, analyzing, organizing, and synthesizing).

Before they begin reading, we might do one of a variety of activities depending on my curricular goal. While this is not a complete list, *before* reading, we might:

- Generate a PQ (purpose question), which requires them to think about their book and come up with a question about what will happen (i.e., make a prediction) based on what they know about the book, the characters, the plot.
- Make a prediction about what will happen based on all that we know and then explain why we think that will happen (i.e., make an inference).
- Make a plan about which note-taking technique to use while reading that day based on whatever goal we are trying to achieve (e.g., synthesizing, making conclusions, evaluating importance).

So before they read, if there is a tool or technique to introduce or remind them to use, we *quickly* go over that. This might mean modeling it; it might involve giving them a sheet (e.g., a Paraphrase Prep, discussed in further detail later) or reminding them to use a tool such as one of the bookmarks I give them at different points. Figure 3.11 shows a sample bookmark.

When they use a bookmark, they write responses in the "Reading Notes" section of their binder. Such bookmarks give students the chance to choose the topic or prompt that matters most to them, that will help them most, or that

**Reading: Think About It!**

**Thinking about *how* you read**

- I was distracted by . . .
- I started to think about . . .
- I got stuck when . . .
- I was confused/focused today because . . .
- One strategy I used to help me read this better was . . .
- When I got distracted I tried to refocus myself by . . .
- These word(s) or phrases were new/interesting to me . . . I think they mean . . .
- When reading I should . . .
- When I read today I realized that . . .
- I had a hard time understanding . . .
- I'll read better next time if I . . .

**Thinking about *what* you read**

- Why does the character/author . . .
- Why doesn't the character/author . . .
- What surprised me most was . . .
- I predict that . . .
- This author's writing style is . . .
- I noticed that the author uses . . .
- The main character wants/is . . .
- If I could, I'd ask the author/character . . .
- The most interesting event/idea in this book is . . .
- I realized . . .
- The main conflict/idea in this book is . . .
- I wonder why . . .
- One theme that keeps coming up is . . .
- I found the following quote interesting . . .
- I _____ this book because . . .

**Elaborating on what you think**

- I think _____ because . . .
- A good example of _____ is . . .
- This reminded me of _____ because . . .
- This was important because . . .
- One thing that surprised me was _____ because I always thought . . .
- The author is saying that . . .

FIGURE 3.11. Sample bookmark from *Reading Reminders: Tools, Tips, and Techniques,* © 2000 by Jim Burke (Boynton/Cook: Portsmouth, NH).

they feel will allow them to write most effectively that day. The bookmark also uses prompts to develop the academic language they need to write about and discuss—in short, to *think* about—the texts they read. It also challenges them to think about not only what they read but *how* they read it, thus incorporating metacognitive reflection on their process and performance as readers. Tools such as this bookmark also serve another purpose: they articulate for students how much is really going on when they read, showing them what effective readers do and that they can do things to become a better reader. This last point is important: Far too many kids, reflecting the larger American society, subscribe to the notion that ability trumps effort. In other words, they think you either can or can't do something—draw, do math, write, or read—so there is no reason to try. The bookmarks are useful throughout the year, but the one I include here is especially important in the first quarter as they begin to study their own process as readers and thereby come to better know their own mind through such reflection. Later on, I might bring out other, more specialized bookmarks they can use.

During that same first quarter, I try to develop new cognitive habits—for example, reading actively by asking specific types or sets of questions such as the reporter's questions—so they can learn to evaluate which information is most important. Evaluating importance is an essential ability to master quickly so they can apply it to their reading in other classes; without it, they are unable to prepare for tests, take notes, or take tests because all information seems equally important—or, to some, *un*important. When introducing a new tool or strategy to help them, for example, evaluate importance, I follow a process similar to the one that follows.

First, I decide on the skill they need to focus on; I try not to have them do too many things simultaneously, especially if those actions are complex. Evaluating importance is a demanding task, one that will be undermined if I have them juggle a few other actions at the same time. So I must select the right tool for the job; in this case, that means using the Paraphrase Prep Tool. Note the word *Prep*: When I first started working with paraphrasing, it demanded that students do too much simultaneously. To extend my juggling metaphor: they kept dropping balls. So I broke it down. This is what it means to scaffold an activity and develop higher-level abilities instead of dumbing down the curriculum. I don't expect less from my ACCESS students than I do from any other kid; I just accept that I might have to find some alternative routes or bring along additional tools to get to the same place. Note that the Paraphrase Prep Tool provides student examples to refer to and forces students to generate (names, examples), to evaluate (which events, people, actions, are most important), analyze (why the character or the author did something), organize (into three categories), and synthesize (by using the ideas on this page to help them write a paragraph). Moreover, this one tool can require them to use all the different Academic Essentials—reading, writing, talking, note taking, and test taking—if I want it to.

After I introduce the tool that first day, they read, use the tool, and turn them in. I take them all home that night, evaluate them for general understanding of both their book and the technique (paraphrasing), and then choose one student paper that I can use the next day as a model. (For the sake of continuity, I am going to use the work of one student, Bruna Palmeira, throughout this sequence to show one student's progress—see Figure 3.12).

As part of the assignment, Bruna uses these notes to write the following paraphrase of her SSR book, *Esperanza Rising*, a wonderful young adult novel by Pam Munoz Ryan:

> Esperanza and her mom is going to US with their old servant (a married couple and their son). They are going because sence Esperanza's dad died, Tio Luis wants to marry Esperanza's mom, be a governador and become rich with all the land and the house that Esperanza's dad left. So now they are trying to escape from Tio Luis because he is mean.

The next day, I copy Bruna's example to a transparency and put it up on the overhead. Thus before they begin reading that day and using the Paraphrase Prep Tool again (they use it until they reach some level of mastery), I take time to explain what Bruna did that makes hers so effective. I make a point of using different kids' work as exemplars so that everyone gets the spotlight over time. Using student work to demonstrate success proves effective, for the others' work is dramatically better the next day: they write more, with greater precision and more insight. On the first day, Victor, who was reading *The Giver*, struggled to understand what I was asking him to do; it was too many things to do at the same time for him. But after seeing what a successful performance looked like, he was able to do the sheet shown in Figure 3.13.

As we move away from one skill—paraphrasing, for example—we use other tools to study and develop the other Academic Essentials. No other essential troubles ACCESS students more than test taking. To address this need, I created the Test Creator (see Figure 3.14) as an unobtrusive means of integrating test taking into the curriculum. This tool allows us to have a conversation

# Paraphrase Prep Tool

**Name** Bruna      **Period** 1° 9/2

**Directions**    As you read, watch for key actions or moments in the story when a person does, realizes, or feels something that matters. You should only put down *major* events; these, along with their description and analysis, will prepare you to write an effective paraphrase. Be prepared to explain *why* you think this event is *so* important that it should be included. Try always to use active, specific verbs (e.g., *asked, betrayed, decided,* and so on) in the What column. Sylvia Ubau's two examples show obviously important events and provide effective explanations. Use these notes to then write a concise paraphrase.

*v+ This is excellent Bruna.*

TITLE: Esperanza Rising

| WHO | WHAT DO THEY DO? | WHY DO THEY DO IT? |
|---|---|---|
| Keisha (This is important because it causes...) | ~~breaks-up with Andy when he was in serious pain. She didn't show him any compassion when he was depressed.~~ | ~~Keisha said that she could not tolerate Andy's crying, weeping, and sorrow for his lost friend any more.~~ |
| Andy | ~~committed suicide at the age of 17 with his dad's shotgun.~~ | ~~Andy couldn't survive his feelings. He couldn't accept that no one was willing to help him when he reached out during his depression.~~ |
| Athens | ~~tried and condemned the philosopher Socrates.~~ | ~~Leaders within Athens believed his teachings undermined their authority and the stability of the social order.~~ |
| Tío Luis | He burned down Esperanza's family house. | He did it because then Esperanza's mom wouldn't have where to live so she would marry him, since her husband died. |
| Esperanza | Esperanza and her mom and a couple with a son is going to USA. | Because they had no where to go or work and they need to runaway from Tío Luis. |
| Esperanza's Mom | She is doing crochets in the car. | Because even though they didn't have a house or a place to live, they could use when the get to US and/or sale. |

*(In left margin: "Sample Bodies")*

FIGURE 3.12.    Bruna's initial exemplar, which I used to help others improve.

Curriculum

# Paraphrase Prep Tool

**Directions**　As you read, watch for key actions or moments in the story when a person does, realizes, or feels something that matters. You should only put down *major* events; these, along with their description and analysis, will prepare you to write an effective paraphrase. Be prepared to explain *why* you think this event is *so* important that it should be included. Try always to use active, specific verbs (e.g., *asked*, *betrayed*, *decided*, and so on) in the What column. Sylvia Ubau's two examples show obviously important events and provide effective explanations. Use these notes to then write a concise paraphrase.

*Excellent progress, Victor.*

**TITLE:**

| WHO | WHAT DO THEY DO? | WHY DO THEY DO IT? |
|---|---|---|
| ~~Keisha~~ (This is important ~~because it is unclear...~~) | ~~broke-up with Andy when he was in serious pain. She didn't show him any compassion when he was depressed.~~ | ~~Keisha said that she could not tolerate Andy's crying, weeping, and sorrow for his lost friend any more.~~ |
| ~~Andy~~ | ~~committed suicide at the age of 17 with his dad's shotgun.~~ | ~~Andy couldn't survive his feelings. He couldn't accept that no one was willing to help him when he reached out during his depression.~~ |
| ~~Athens~~ | ~~tried and condemned the philosopher Socrates.~~ | ~~Leaders within Athens believed his teachings undermined their authority and the stability of the social order.~~ |
| "Giver" | The Giver nodded and told Jonas to lay down. he said it was time because the Giver said he can not shield Jonas for ever | resien boaing that Jonas was turning to the twelv age groupe where the twelv move on. |
| "Giver" "memory" | Jonas wants the Same dreem of Sliding down the sleed on the snowey hill with the wind in his face and the thrill of dueing something and lyshing to the wild life | Because Jonasas world dose not have color, nature it is flat no one drives cars and there is no wind rain or Snow or aro plains |

*(Left margin: "Sample Entries")*

FIGURE 3.13.　Victor's Paraphrase Prep Tool.

## TEST CREATOR

Name: _____

Period: _____     Date: _____

| Question Type | Example | Notes |
|---|---|---|
| **Vocabulary** | Which of the following best defines *resolute* in the sentence "The President was *resolute* in his efforts to . . ." | • Find word<br>• Define it<br>• Explain it |
| **Factual** | How long did the Wright Brothers' first plane stay in the air? | Find the answer *in the* text, *on* the page. |
| **Analytical** | How—and why—does the character change by the end of the story? | Find the answer *between the lines;* make an inference. |
| **Essay** | Choose one invention from the Industrial Revolution that continues to benefit us today. Discuss three ways in which this invention has made life easier or better for people. Be sure to provide examples. | Draw from source to illustrate and support what you are saying about the subject. |

| | |
|---|---|
| Question Type | Factual |
| Question | Why did George and Lenny leave their last job? |
| Answer | Because Lenny was accused of raping a woman so they had to get out of town. |
| Evaluate (1–10) | 10 |
| Explain | This is a *very* important question because it gives us essential information about both men and foreshadows later events in the story. |

**Question Type**

**Question**



**Answer**



**Evaluate (1–10)**



**Explain**



FIGURE 3.14.   A full-size, downloadable version of this form is available on the *ACCESSing School* page of the Heinemann website, at www.heinemann.com.

Curriculum

about not only test questions but other important issues—fact and opinion, cause and effect—while at the same time allowing them to keep working on their ability to evaluate (e.g., which of all the details in this text is so important that the teacher would likely put a question about it on the test?). We can use the Test Creator quickly but effectively with whatever they are reading.

One of the reasons I always read with them during silent reading (aside from setting the standard and providing an example) is to be able to model in real time when we use certain techniques. So while they read their books, I read mine (in the following example, Howard Gardner's *Changing Minds*). When they finish reading, I slap a transparency on the overhead and give them an example based on what I read. I always try to come up with examples that are both helpful and engaging so that they can realize that there is so much out there to learn and think about. Figure 3.15 shows my sample factual questions, followed by the list we generated when discussing how to tell a fact when you see one.

When they finish reading that day, they turn to the "Records" section of their reading notebook, where they find their Reading Record. They quickly fill in the number of pages they read that day. As they do this, I say different things each day that reinforce the importance of self-study, such as "Now you need to

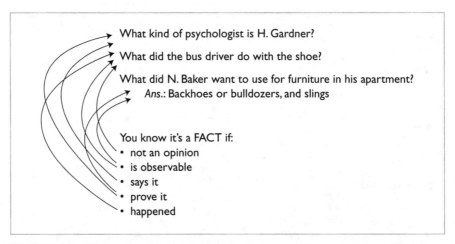

FIGURE 3.15. This overhead (which I would handwrite in a classroom setting) shows how I model generating sample factual questions. Then, down below, we discuss (and I make notes about) how to determine if something is a fact. The arrows (which do not match specific questions) are my way of directing students' attention, sort of visually narrating what I am doing as I demonstrate and explain not only *what* I am doing, but *how* and *why* I am doing it.

pay attention to how you did today compared with yesterday. If you read more or fewer pages today than yesterday, you need to think about that. Did you sleep more last night and read more today? Then maybe you need to pay attention to the fact that how much you sleep affects your performance. Or if you read slowly, maybe you need to remind yourself that when beginning a new book you have to learn a lot of new stuff about the setting, situation, characters, and so on, so it slows you down." On Friday, they reflect on their performance that week. Figure 3.16 shows Krish Singh's Reading Record after the first month.

What the kids do with silent reading is embodied in the reading process (Figure 3.23), which I discuss in the next section, where I describe what we do in ACCESS for the "main course" once we finish our silent reading and any related assignments.

## Core Curriculum: The Reading Process and the Academic Essentials

The curriculum in ACCESS is a conversation with the text, the author, the teacher, and, of course, the students themselves. We begin that conversation about where they are as readers by asking first where they *were*. Students use the Reading Scale to evaluate their performance, attitude, and identity as they relate to reading when the kids were in middle school. Figure 3.17 shows Victor's example.

It is late September, perhaps early October (about five weeks into the semester) when we begin this unit. While it might seem a bit late, it's important to use those first few weeks to do some intense, accelerated work with a few Academic Essentials (such as I discussed in the previous section) that will help them get up and running in their core academic classes. Then we can begin to go into new territory, exploring not just the world of reading but the readers themselves and the processes they use to navigate their way through the world of texts. You will notice, as you look at Victor's paragraph in the margin (see Figure 3.17), that we embed the Academic Essentials at every possible opportunity. In this assignment, Victor organizes and synthesizes through writing his observations about his experience as a reader. You will also notice, if you look at his paragraph, that he employs various comparative structures, including the opening subordinate clause; this is no accident but the result of modeling and encouraging them to use some sentence structures to develop their academic language and organize their ideas. I put up on the board a few beginning phrases to help them get started and to better understand the nature of the writing they were to do.

Before we delve deeper into what they must do if they are to read well, I try to build a bridge between what they do well (in any domain) and what they do not. When I was their age, I was getting terrible grades in school but was one of

**Weekly/Monthly Reading Record**  Name: KRISH

Date: 09/28/04                Period 1

**Week of:** 9/27 - 9/30    THE CONTENDER / THE OUTSIDERS

| Pages | Days of the Week | | | | | Total Pages: 59 | Daily Average: ~~~~ 11 |
|---|---|---|---|---|---|---|---|
| | M | T | W | Th | Fri | ~~~~ "THE Contender" | Title(s) |
| 20 | | | | | | the outsiders | |
| 15 | | | | | | " | |
| 10 | | | | | | " | |
| 5 | | | | | | " | |
| 0 | | | | | | " | |

**Reading Reflection** - My reading is now getting to be faster. One day I had a well rested day and it was wonderful. I also started my second book and my attitude is starting to change. And every day I slowly started getting into them.

**Week of:** 10/3    "THE OUTSIDERS"

| Pages | Days of the Week | | | | | Total Pages: 68 | Daily Average: 13 pages |
|---|---|---|---|---|---|---|---|
| | M | T | W | Th | Fri | | Title(s) |
| 20 | | | | | S | "THE OUTSIDERS" | |
| 15 | | | | | P | " | |
| 10 | | | | | C | " | |
| 5 | | | | | a | " | |
| 0 | | | | | KER | | |

**Reading Reflection** My daily Averages is slowly starting to get longer and longer. I also think my speed is catching and going up. I also start to understand what I'm reading and what the author is talking about. I also feel emotions and find my own voice, tone and mood.

**Week of:** 3/10    outsiders

| Pages | Days of the Week | | | | | Total Pages: 60 | Daily Average: 15 pages |
|---|---|---|---|---|---|---|---|
| | M | T | W | Th | Fri | | Title(s) |
| 20 | | | | | | "The Outsiders" | |
| 15 | | | | | | " | |
| 10 | | | | | | " | |
| 5 | | | | | | " | |
| 0 | | | | | | " | |

**Reading Reflection** Throughout this week I kept my pace and read higher than my expectation my average is still starting to rise. This week my average rose by 3 pages I kept my pace more or less but I always stopped and think but now I can think while reading and understand.

**Week of:** 10/23

| Pages | Days of the Week | | | | | Total Pages: 75 | Daily Average: 15 |
|---|---|---|---|---|---|---|---|
| | M | T | W | Th | Fri | | Title(s) |
| 20 | | | | | | THE OUTSIDERS | |
| 15 | | | | | | " | |
| 10 | | | | | | " | |
| 5 | | | | | | | |
| 0 | | | | | | TAMING THE STAR RUNNER | |

**Reading Reflection** Slowly my reading went up for one day but then went down the next. I think it went down because it was friday also I had a sub and was not as focused as I was the other days. My average stade the same which I didn't like so next week I will try harder and push myself up and try to put my pages longer. Also on friday I started a new book on friday.

Monthly total - 837
Average - 15

FIGURE 3.16.    This is Krish's Reading Record, which I put up on the overhead and used to help others improve their work on the same assignment. I often try, on such an occasion, to use a boy's work, if possible, to promote their identity as students and readers.

Victor

while last year I was a under levil reader I never fit in on reading out loved in school I was The kid who would stope down in his desk and hide But this year I am a more self confident reader. I used to find the smallest Book or text because I would get scard when I would read big long pages, it would intimidate me, But I now know that I can read long pages, Just take little chunks at a time. Another area in which I've changed is my speed Because ~ usto read really ~~slow~~ Because I thought the faster I red it the faster I would finish. But now I read slow and under stand it better

**Inexperienced Reader (1)**
☐ Limited experience as a reader.
☐ Generally chooses to read easy, brief texts.
☐ Has difficulty with any unfamiliar material.
☑ Needs a great deal of support with the assigned reading.
☐ Rarely chooses to read for pleasure.

**Less Experienced Reader (2)**
☐ Is developing fluency as a reader and reading certain kinds of material with confidence.
☑ Usually chooses short books with simple narrative shapes.
☐ Reading for pleasure often includes comics and special interest magazines.
☐ Needs help with the reading demands of the class, especially complex literary, reference, and informational texts.

**Moderately Experienced Reader (3)**
☐ Feels at home with books.
☐ Is developing stamina as a reader.
☐ Is able to read for longer periods and cope with more demanding texts, including novels and poetry.
☐ Willing to reflect on reading and often uses reading in his/her own learning.
☐ Selects books independently and can read juvenile fiction and nonfiction.
☐ Can use information books and materials for straightforward reference purposes.
☑ Still needs help with unfamiliar material.

**Experienced Reader (4)**
☐ Is a self-motivated, confident, experienced reader who may pursue particular interests through reading.
☐ Capable of tackling some demanding texts.
☐ Can cope well with the reading required in all classes.
☐ Reads thoughtfully and appreciates shades of meaning.
☑ Capable of locating and drawing on a variety of sources in order to research a topic independently.

**Exceptionally Experienced Reader (5)**
☐ Is an enthusiastic and reflective reader who has strong, established tastes in fiction and/or nonfiction.
☐ Enjoys pursuing reading interests independently.
☐ Can handle a wide range and variety of texts, including some adult material.
☐ Recognizes that different kinds of texts evoke different reading stances.
☑ Is able to evaluate evidence drawn from a variety of information sources.
☐ Is developing a critical awareness as a reader.

FIGURE 3.17. In order to maximize cognitive processing and cultivate the habit of reflection (while simultaneously working on writing), I have the kids use the details from the Reading Scale to write a well-organized paragraph.

the top tennis players in California. Again, such inquiries have other benefits: they celebrate students' strengths; they help students build bridges between what they do well and what they're learning to do better. In the following example, Christian considers his success as a skateboarder, his primary identity and one that teachers don't often make room for in the curriculum. Note that such writing also integrates several Academic Essentials, given the structure of the assignment: he must generate a claim and examples, evaluating which one is most effective; he must analyze just what it is that he does when he skates; and he must organize these details into a cohesive paragraph that will prepare him to participate in the subsequent class discussion. Here is Christian's paragraph:

> I am pretty good at skateboarding. I learned how to do it when I was in fifth grade. I still skateboard today in ninth grade. I've learned a lot of new tricks during those past four years. I can do a lot of crazy stuff like jumping off six foot ledges and jumping off a roof. I've also had a lot of sprained ankles and wrists, and have broken three of my toes on my left foot and sprained my foot at the same time. One trick that I tried to land took me one month to land and now I'm pretty good at it. It's called a kick flip. I'm so good at it now that I could kick flip off a six foot ledge or a stair case. I wanted to skate because I thought it would be fun and it is and a lot of my friends skateboard with me.

Such personal reflections, while providing useful opportunities to discuss aspects of effective writing, serve as a prelude to a more sustained inquiry about what good readers do and what the students themselves do when reading. To help them think through their reading process, I have them first draw what they do. They can do this in a variety of ways. I show them examples from previous students: some are done as cartoons, others as flow charts, still others like Bruna's (see Figure 3.18).

When they finish drawing what happens in their head, they must write an explanation of what the diagram shows. This activity—both the drawing and the writing—incorporates the metacognitive aspect of learning; it draws their attention to what they do and thus begins a conversation within themselves about how they can improve.

Once they finish exploring their reading processes, we read from the *Reader's Handbook: A Student Guide for Reading and Learning* (Burke 2002), which begins by offering the following schema for the reading process:

BEFORE

1. Set a purpose.
2. Preview the text.
3. Make a plan: Choose a strategy or technique most appropriate to the text.

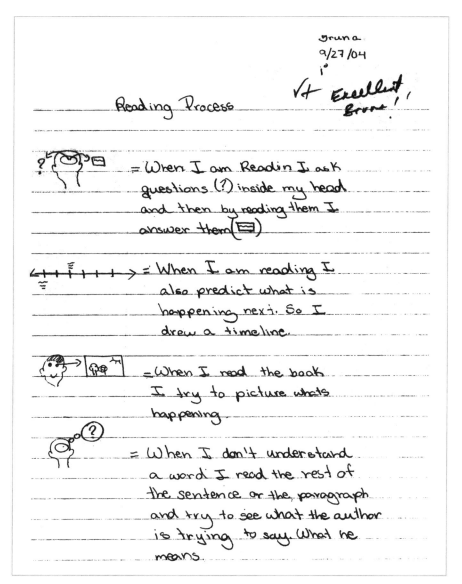

FIGURE 3.18. Bruna illustrates what she does during her own reading process to make sense of what she reads.

DURING

4. Read with your purpose in mind.
5. Connect what you do or read to other subjects you have studied and to your own interests and experiences.

AFTER

6. Pause and reflect on what was important, what you learned, and what you still do not understand.
7. Read to clarify, connect, or examine more closely (e.g., for a different purpose).
8. Remember what you read and learned so you can apply it or demonstrate your understanding of it (e.g., on an exam, in an essay, during a class discussion).

Before I continue, it is important to note that these steps apply equally to both the student and the teacher. The teacher must decide upon the purpose for reading any text. The same text can be read for many purposes. Thus for instruction to be coherent and effective, the text should be aligned with the larger goals and standards in the course. Before the students ever make a plan, the teacher should have considered which of the different possible strategies was best to use on this assignment and prepared the students to use that tool or technique. In the following example, which comes as the next step in the instructional sequence, students read the chapter on the reading process in the *Reader's Handbook*. Having previewed the text and considered what my instructional purpose was, I made a plan, to have them work on taking notes as part of this assignment. As the example in Figure 3.19 shows, students had to use a combination of outline notes and a T-chart. This approach created a useful context for me to extend our discussion about taking notes (one of the Academic Essentials) and to reinforce lessons about evaluating importance and organizing information. But in this context I wanted to achieve more: I wanted them to make substantial connections to their other classes. So I had them take outline notes on the left side about what to do during the reading process and generate examples on the right about what each stage looks like in two separate academic classes. In Bruna's example (see Figure 3.19), she looks at English and Health, providing examples of what it looks like to set a purpose when reading her Health textbook or a short story like "The Necklace" in English.

Bruna's notes are typical, not exceptional, for I take some time to directly teach this assignment, gradually releasing them to complete the assignment on their own once they have shown they understand how to read, take notes, and think in these structured ways. I begin by having them draw a line down the page, which I model for them at the overhead. Then I have them write down "Before," as you see on Bruna's example. We read through the first section of the book, discussing what use we can make of the headings and subheadings

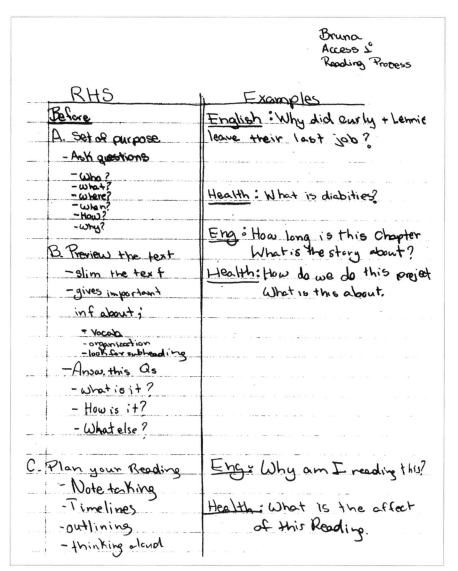

FIGURE 3.19. Using a T-chart strategy, Bruna takes notes as she reads about the reading process in the *Reader's Handbook*.

when taking notes. I emphasize writing as little as necessary but as much as they need to take effective but efficient notes. Then when I have finished showing them how to do the first one, we jump over to the other side of the chart and generate (collaboratively, out loud) examples from their classes till we find a few examples that serve our purpose. Assured that almost everyone has an initial grasp, I turn them loose to read the next section and complete both sides of the notes; then I circulate to offer help to those few who still need it.

The structure of the reading process (as outlined in the *Reader's Handbook*) provides a touchstone for the remainder of the year, giving us a common vocabulary we can use to discuss what they should do, when and how they should do it—and *why*. It also lends a framework—that is, what they should do before, during, and after they read—that they can use and remember, which can become habitual as they work in my class and others, which is a crucial point, for I accomplish nothing if I do not teach them strategies they can use outside my class to succeed in core academic classes.

It seems appropriate to mention several things about the *Reader's Handbook* before going on. First, I am the lead author of the book, a point I make for the sake of full disclosure. The book develops students' "textual intelligence" (Burke 2002) by teaching them how different types of texts work and should be read. Each student gets a copy of the book, which costs about eighteen dollars; this allows them to annotate it and, I hope, establish a relationship with the book the way ESL students do with their dictionaries, using them as a trusted guide to get through a foreign landscape that, over time, becomes more familiar. I also use the *Reader's Handbook* because it is not a remedial book; in fact, I used portions of it in both my advanced classes and my ACCESS classes as I wrote it to make sure it helped students at all levels. The sample texts represent the types and levels of difficulty of texts kids in high school read; thus the book supports accelerated instruction, teaching kids how to do what their teachers assign. Finally, it is ideal for use in the classroom given the constraints of fifty-five (or so) minutes per class. The kids leave them in class, though those who wish can check out an extra copy to keep at home for the year. In June, they take the *Reader's Handbook* home to keep and use for their remaining years.

Now that the kids have finished reading the chapter on the reading process and have taken notes on it, it's time to use those notes, to pause and reflect through writing. By doing this, I embed writing instruction and discussion in the curriculum; so, using their notes, they prepare to write a well-organized synthesis of the reading process. Before they jump into the writing, however, I want them to manipulate the information more, work on organizing their ideas. They use the Main Idea Organizer, a tool I use frequently throughout the year in many ways, to craft a working claim that summarizes what they learned (i.e., "Remember" from the last step of the reading process) while preparing them to write (see Figure 3.20). Although this process would be too scaffolded for proficient students, it provides ACCESS students the structure they need to

**Main Idea Organizer: Reading, Writing, Watching, Listening**    Name: Bruna

| Subject — What are you or the author writing about? | Subject — Reading Process | |
|---|---|---|

| Main Idea — What are you (or the author) saying *about* the subject? (i.e., what is the *point* you or the author want to make?) | Main Idea — The reading process has three stages: before, during and after. | |
|---|---|---|

| Details • Examples • Stories • Quotations • Explanations | Detail — Before | Detail — During | Detail — After |
|---|---|---|---|
| | Set a purpose<br>– ask questions<br>– What is "Charming Billy" about.<br>– What do arteries do?<br>Preview the text.<br>– look at the subheadings<br>– skim the text.<br>– How long is this chapter?<br>– How do we do this project?<br>Plan your Reading<br>– Notetaking<br>– outlining<br>– thinking aloud<br>– Why am I reading this?<br>– What is the affect of this Reading? | Read with a Purpose<br>– Revisit your original purpose<br>– Keep an eye on what you are reading.<br>– Why does she want to earn money? (Weather)<br>– Why do a lot of people lose obisity?<br>Connect<br>– make a connection on what you read.<br>– think about it<br>– Is it because she wants to buy presents?<br>– Is it because they eat too much junk food. | Pause and Reflect<br>– Reread.<br>– Pause and think.<br>– What is she going to do next?<br>– I don't think people should eat junk food.<br>Reread<br>– Read more than one time.<br>– get information related to what you read.<br>– So, she sold her hair because she wanted to be her husband gift<br>– They have to eat b/ they can't stop<br>Remember<br>– make summary<br>– Everything happen because she wanted to buy a gift.<br>– They eat because |

FIGURE 3.20.    Bruna uses the Main Idea Organizer to synthesize her ideas and prepare to write.

increase their fluency. The more they process or manipulate ideas in different ways, the better they understand, remember, and use those ideas and skills.

Though they are ready to write, I want to use the instructional context to accomplish more than just a quick end-of-the-period paragraph. So I bring in the parsed outline (which I created at home the previous night) shown in Figure 3.21, giving them a paper copy and using a color-coded version on the overhead for added visual illustration of my ideas. I want them to see how ideas in a text have three key components—focus, organization, and development. While I stand at the overhead and get them started, thinking out loud about what I wrote and why, they copy down my opening from the overhead, which I leave up for the entire period in case they need to refer to it as they work.

The reading process has three main stages: before, during, and after.

Before someone even begins to read, they can do several things to improve their performance.

First, they can set a purpose for themselves.

Asking questions is one way to do this.

In English, for example, you might ask, "Why did Lennie and Curly run away from their last job?"

Or before you begin reading a chapter on cell division in Biology, you might ask yourself, "Why (or *how*) do cells divide?"

Before reading, you can also preview the text to find out . . .

In English, you might preview the chapter to figure out how long it will take you.

In Health, you might skim the chapter headings, subheadings, and bold words to get a quick sense of what the chapter is about.

One last thing you can do before reading is make a plan.

This means . . .

In English, . . .

In History, on the other hand, you might . . .

Once you actually begin reading, there are things you can do during the reading. You can read with a purpose. For example,

FIGURE 3.21. I use different colors on my computer to indicate levels and emphasize the organization. This combination of visual cues—arrangement and color—helps kids see how ideas relate to and build on each other when writing.

After they get started—through a process much like that described earlier for the reading process notes—and I make sure they understand the process and the content, I give them the rest of the period to finish and let them continue writing at home if they need to. This gives them strong incentive to "work hard, work well, work fast," as I often say, telling them that this (i.e., being quick, efficient) is one of the many ways successful students must be able to work. Such support, such deliberate instruction prepares them for the culminating performance (the writing) that also acts as a sort of informal assessment of their understanding of the material. Figure 3.22 shows an excerpt from Bruna's essay, which she wrote with the help of her notes and organizers.

This writing assignment brings one portion of the process to a close, but I try to do more with less, taking advantage of the opportunity to work patiently, until the kids get it and can use it to help them in this class and others. Instead of calling it quits, we continue and study another Academic Essential: test tak-

> The reading process has three stages: before, during and after. The first stage is the one you do before reading anything. The first part is set a purpose. You should ask questions. For example on you English class you can ask, "What is Charming Billy about?" The second part is Preview the text. To preview the text by looking the subheadings and also slim the text. You can also preview the text on your English class by asking yourself, "How long is this chapter?". Or on your Health class, "On what will this help me on my future?". Then you have the last part that is Planning your reading. When you are planing your reading you notetaking, out ling, and thinking aloud. You might ask yourself these questions before planing your reading; "Why is there a picture of a little boy crying?" that's what you might ask for you English class.
>
> The second stage is During your reading. It has two parts. The first part is Read with Purpose. When you are reading you should keep an eye on what you are reading, and revisit your original purpose. For example on your English class you might ask, "Why does she want

FIGURE 3.22. An excerpt from Bruna's description of her writing process. The previous steps prepared her for a successful performance.

ing. We use a short multiple-choice test provided by the publisher of the *Reader's Handbook* to evaluate what they know and, more importantly, to focus on test taking. Figure 3.23 shows the "test."

Hardly a scary test, yet tests of any sort intimidate most ACCESS students, giving them, as they see it, another opportunity to fail or to confirm others'

## The Reading Process

**1.** Which item below is NOT a step of the reading process?
   a. Plan
   b. Preview
   c. Draft
   d. Connect

**2.** Which is a characteristic of previewing?
   a. Reading the supporting details
   b. Browsing the index
   c. Planning a reading strategy
   d. Quickly skimming the material

**3.** Comparing a reading to your own life is doing which of the following?
   a. Connecting
   b. Previewing
   c. Setting a Purpose
   d. Rereading

**4.** What is true of rereading?
   a. Rereading clarifies confusing parts of the reading.
   b. Rereading always requires a new reading purpose.
   c. Rereading involves memorizing key passages.
   d. Rereading is part of the previewing step.

**5.** How can you remember the material you have read?
   a. Read the material only once.
   b. Read in a noisy environment.
   c. Personalize the material and make it your own.
   d. Reread all of the material word for word.

FIGURE 3.23.   Reading process quiz that accompanies the *Reader's Handbook.*

opinions of their (perceived) incompetence. However, they take this test in a different way than they would tests in most of their classes. They are graded not on their answers but on their method of taking the test (i.e., whether or not they use the strategies I teach them). They must do the following:

- Underline key words in the question stem (e.g., in number one, the word *not,* or on some other quiz, a word like *mainly* or *most*)
- Put a dot next to any that are *possible* correct answers

- Cross out any answers that are *not* possible and, in the margins, explain *why* they are not viable
- Indicate the correct answer and explain why that is the correct answer
- Identify any possible tricks in the answers (as they read through *all* the answers)
- Note any questions that stumped them and reflect on what made those particular questions so difficult to answer
- Compare their answers with each other's, stopping to discuss and figure out any discrepancies, until they reach consensus on the correct answer

When they finish the last step, I put a copy of the same page up on the overhead and we discuss the individual answers. This fosters what some call test wiseness but which I think of as textual intelligence. The point is not to correct the test but rather to correct their understanding of how tests work, to consider what techniques help them and why, so they can use these in other classes to leap over what have been such hurdles to them for so long. ACCESS students are plagued by a sense of doubt when it comes to testing, and this is by far the most difficult but crucial aspect of the curriculum, for without some ability to take tests, they cannot pass certain classes, cannot pass the state exit exam, and, when applying for college, cannot do well on the SAT. Moreover, many fields require applicants to take tests as part of the entry or certification process; I don't want tests to be an obstacle. My father, who dropped out of high school after the tenth grade, took a job with the state printing office and advanced to the highest level by the end of his career, providing well for our family by virtue of his ability to take tests, which, in those days, were the primary means of ascent. As Langer (2002) argues, however, test-taking instruction must be integrated into the larger curriculum; you cannot teach such skills effectively without some context. Moreover, tests are their own type of text and so must be considered alongside all the others, by analyzing their conventions and the different genres (multiple choice, essay, short answer, matching, and so on).

I bring this sample sequence to a close with one last assignment: the annotated bibliography students must complete at the end of each semester. Here they total the books and pages they have read; my hope is that they will feel some sense of achievement. This is exactly what Amanda Mason felt when she tallied her pages to find that she had read a few thousand pages in a semester, something she had never imaged she could do. This achievement was all the more important in light of the fact that she had failed nearly all her classes. A difficult life outside of school made books, once she began reading, a sanctuary for her throughout much of her freshman year (see Figure 3.24).

## Annotated Bibliography

**Cabot, Meg. *All-American Girl*. New York: Harper Trophy. 2002. Novel. 398 pages. \*\*\*\***

> This is a great book for a normal person that thinks their life sucks. This is a story of a normal girl, who is the middle child. Her older sister is the most popular girl at school, her younger sister is a genius. Not to mention she is in love with her older sister's boyfriend, who is a rebel like her. This is a great book with many surprises.

**Canfield, Jack, Mark Victor Hansen, Kimberly Kirberger. *Chicken Soup for the Teenage Soul*. Nonfiction. New York: Scholastic. 2000. \*\*\*\*\* 345 pages.**

> I can't start to tell you how great I thought this book was. It is so realistic because the stories are written by young teens like me. The stories were very touching and touched my heart personally. This is a great book for people that like funny, sad, love, or stories about growing up. I gave this book a five out of five because it touched me.

FIGURE 3.24. Amanda gathers up her books and notes so she can write her annotated bibliography. This was an important event, for it brought to her attention (and mine) that she had read more than anyone else in the class over the course of the year.

I end this chapter on curriculum with a final note about Amanda, her reading, and the inevitable limits of any curriculum. Amanda is a girl whose heart is as big as it is full of anger and bitterness. I struggle to know what to do with a kid like her, how to help her find her way through the forest of her own confusion. I know I made her cry a few times, each time in response to my efforts to show I cared, something she didn't seem to know how to respond to and couldn't understand. When the progress reports were due, I wrestled with myself about her grade, for while she did no work to speak of, she actively participated in class discussions, often making some of the best contributions, and read more than anyone else. I chose the punitive route, hoping that the F (or was it a D?) might shock her into doing her work, but it had the exact opposite effect and caused some serious damage to the trust that had been sprouting up between us. I cannot remember her exact words at this point, but they amounted to something like this: "You cannot use grades to punish people. It's not fair. I come to this class and read more than anyone else. It's a reading class, isn't it?! So how can you fail me!?" I responded with the following handwritten note a few days later:

> Dear Amanda,
>
> I've continued to think about what you said to me when we talked about grades last week. I always listen to what you say.
>
> I got it all wrong on that last progress report and I apologize for that. I don't want you feeling punished. I'm too proud of all your reading and your progress as a reader. I hope you will forgive me and give me a chance. I also want you to get the forms signed so you can go to Washington when I need substitutes for the kindergartners and so you can be a regular over there next semester. You'd be great with those little kids.
>
> The best part about making mistakes is all that you learn from them. I made one with you and I learned very important lessons. I'm so glad you are back with us. Thanks for listening to me, Amanda.
>
> Mr. Burke

This was near the end of the first semester. Had I not renegotiated my relationship with Amanda, she might not have gone to Washington the following semester, might not have felt able to get up in front of the class and give her speeches in Toastmasters or ask some of the best questions when we went to visit UC Berkeley in the spring; nor would she have been likely to accept the nomination of her peers and serve as president of Toastmasters the next semester. I mention this to emphasize that the curriculum for any program like ACCESS, while made of skills, must never be reduced to skills, must never forsake the relationship between the teacher and the student that is so essential to their progress and ultimate success as people. Thus the curriculum of this program makes the students my most important teachers; their words, their experiences, their mistakes become my curriculum as we work together to gain access not just to school but to life.

# FOUR
# *Opportunities*

It's late October and Taylor is worried we are all "gonna get jumped." I assure him that people at college don't "jump" one another. I have just told them that our field trip to visit the community college the next day will include kids from a few other schools in the district, one of which is our school's rival. Taylor looks skeptical but lets it go for now. As for Taylor, I'm just glad he will get to go at all. Two months earlier, I gave each kid the permission slip so they could get their teachers' and parents' permission. Some naturally brought it in the next day. A second reminder was all that another group needed; those kids came in two days later ready and eager to visit the college. And then the rest of the permission slips trickled in for four weeks, one here, two there, until only Taylor remained. I tried everything. Beth Pascal, who arranges these visits, picked up where I left off, going so far as to have Taylor call and leave a phone message for himself on his own answering machine. I enlisted the help of his twin brother, Thomas, who had given me his signed slip within a few weeks.

Finally the day arrives. Everyone is on time and ready to go except Taylor, who is not there because he did not get his permission slip signed. As we cross the vast lawn before Burlingame High School to board the bright yellow school bus, we hear Taylor running after us, see him waving his permission slip, a sly grin on his face as if to say, "See, I had it in the bag all along. I knew I could get this thing taken care of." And so we are off, the kids gathered in the back of the bus, nervous, excited, serious, while Beth and I sit up front and imagine the day ahead and discuss all that she did to make it happen.

I think of days like this as occasions to which the kids must rise. The first time I ever took kids to a college campus was when I brought four Latina girls to a Latina Literature Conference, only one of whom—Paulina—was in my ACCESS program at the time. When we arrived on the campus that day, Paulina, whose family had come from Central America, said with an involuntary gasp, "The students look just like me!" This remark woke me up to the fact that such experiences had benefits other than mere enrichment. They helped students learn about the world, placed them in situations that allowed them to see themselves (by seeing people *like* themselves) in those places, doing those things. So Beth Pascal and I began scheduling a range of opportunities that challenged and educated the kids in ACCESS. These opportunities usually occur in the classroom, but on rare occasions—college visits and job shadows—the kids get out of class and off campus. We prefer to bring the world to the classroom, though; that way they learn about the world without missing class and experiencing the very trouble (i.e., academic failure) we are trying to prevent.

What *are* the opportunities? I have alluded to some already, but here is a summary of the experiences, which have evolved into rites of passage in the course:

- College visits (two and four year)
- Guest speakers
- Toastmasters International Youth Leadership Program
- Job shadowing
- Reading Buddies
- Unique opportunities such as local youth leadership programs, conferences for young women in business (to which high school students are invited), and special events such as the Rotary Community Luncheon

The first thing we do in September is find out who the kids are, what they are interested in, so Beth and I can keep our eyes open for speakers and events that would relate to their interests. To get this information, we give them the interest survey shown in Figure 4.1

We complete this survey the first week, something that creates a sense of momentum and immediately conveys the idea that this program is for *them* and that we will listen to what they have to say, an experience most ACCESS kids have not had in school.

## College Visits

While the guest speakers are a wonderful, crucial part of the program, it is the college visit that often makes the biggest impression on the kids. It is an encounter not only with the larger world but with something inside them that asks where their life is heading and how they expect to get there. Stepping onto a college campus clearly establishes that to get anywhere in today's world, you have to go to college.

## ACCESS Student Interest Survey

We will use this survey to identify possible job-shadowing opportunities, interesting guest speakers, and college visits over the course of the coming year. Please answer all questions that apply to you. The more information we have about you and your interests, the better we can meet your needs.

### Contact Information

Name: _____ Age: _____

Middle School: _____

City: _____

Phone: _____ (home/parent's work)

### Academic Interests (check all that apply)

- ❏ Math
- ❏ Engineering/drafting
- ❏ Health
- ❏ Drawing
- ❏ Ceramics
- ❏ Industrial arts (wood/metals)

- ❏ Cooking
- ❏ Business
- ❏ World languages
- ❏ Science
- ❏ Technology/computers
- ❏ Video production

- ❏ Drama
- ❏ Music
- ❏ History
- ❏ Government/politics

Provide more specific information down here. For example, list which *area* of science.

_____

_____

### Extracurricular Interests

- ❏ Cheerleading
- ❏ Dance
- ❏ Drama

- ❏ Journalism
- ❏ Leadership (class office)
- ❏ Music (band, choir)

- ❏ Sports management
- ❏ Video production
- ❏ Yearbook

Provide more specific information down here. For example, list *which* sports you like to play.

_____

_____

### General Interests

Area of Interest          Explanation (provide more specific details about your interest)

- ❏ Animals
- ❏ Art
- ❏ Building things
- ❏ Caring for people
- ❏ Cars
- ❏ Community service
- ❏ Designing things
- ❏ Family
- ❏ Fashion
- ❏ Fixing things
- ❏ Food cooking
- ❏ Helping people
- ❏ Making things
- ❏ Military
- ❏ Movies
- ❏ Music
- ❏ Nature/outdoors
- ❏ Religion
- ❏ Sports

NOTE: If you need more space to tell us about your interests, just write on the back. Thanks!

FIGURE 4.1.  A full-size, downloadable version of this form is available on the *ACCESSing School* page of the Heinemann website, at www.heinemann.com.

Beth Pascal begins preparing for and arranging the fall two-year college visit months in advance. She contacts the College of San Mateo (CSM), a local community college, to find out when they are offering visiting days. Working with her contact at the college, she solicits information about available programs and assembles sign-up sheets so kids can prioritize which programs they visit. Here's a typical note from her contact regarding the planning process:

Beth:

The following programs have confirmed that they will participate in the student tours:

Cosmetology

Dental Assisting

Welding

Multimedia

Administration of Justice

Fire Technology

Electronics

I understand that Nursing is only available for a walk through of the facility and will confirm that next week. I know this program is very popular so we will try to do something. At the least, we can provide students with written program information. We may also have CAD and Engineering participate. We should have a firm list early next week.

Thanks,
Gloria
Outreach Coordinator

When kids come from a family in which no one has ever attended college—one such as my own—they are limited to what they have seen in the movies and heard around school. They do not know how it works, what college is for, how to get there, or why they should try. Like Paulina, the girl I mentioned earlier, most of the kids think that college students look and are somehow different from themselves. No one in my family had ever attended college; my friends, on the other hand, came from families whose parents were doctors, lawyers, business owners, and so on. My father, who dropped out of high school, was a smart man in a different era, one in which a man could advance by will and intelligence if he applied himself.

I take the kids up to the campus primarily to reinforce the academic identity I have been working hard to help them forge in their mind. When they

FIGURE 4.2. At the College of San Mateo visit, Louis Hernandez (in the foreground) reads through the orientation packet, along with Taylor Murphy (middle), and Martin Trejo (left).

walk on that campus, as Paulina did that day, I want them to see that people like themselves *do* go to college. As I write this, ACCESS is in its fifth year; thus Paulina graduated the previous year. As we concluded our trip to the College of San Mateo this year, we crossed the campus at a leisurely pace. I saw a number of kids I knew, some of them former ACCESS students. I had hoped to see some ACCESS kids there so I could introduce them to this year's group. What I saw, however, was more than I could have hoped for: nearing the very spot (I'm not making this up) where four years ago Paulina had stood and made her comment about college kids, I heard a young woman's voice calling my name from across the campus. I turned around and saw Paulina running toward us, her arms out wide, her smile as wide as the day was long. When I got home that night, I found an email from her in my mailbox:

Dear Mr. Burke,

So Mr. Burke . . . how are you? What's new? I really like CSM, but I miss high school. I never thought I would say that, but I do. Burlingame really does offer students a lot of things. For one, I now regret not taking advantage of the job shadowing program and the teachers are so much better at Burlingame. In the math class that I'm taking now, I'm learning the same things that Mr. Willard taught us, but he made it so much easier and the teachers don't really care about their students like you did. Oh I also just started working at Winners in the mall and I might start to work two days a week at a private doctor's office in San Mateo. I think that's about everything that's happening in my life at the moment.

Sincerely,
Paulina Gavilanez

When we returned to school the next day, I had them reflect on the day at CSM. As usual, I took this occasion as an opportunity to work on their thinking and writing skills. So instead of having them jump into a rambling free-write, I put a Main Idea Organizer on the overhead, shined it on the whiteboard, and used it to facilitate our discussion and prepare them to write. We used this tool to generate the categories into which we could organize information about the experience. Figure 4.3 shows Henri Langilangi's, which he and others then used to write about the day.

Having prepared them to write, I then wanted them to write for an authentic audience, thus challenging them to ratchet up their attention to details and correctness. So I had them use the ideas we generated (and added to through a follow-up discussion about the day) to help them write a letter to Beth. This letter serves several purposes. One, they are using and developing skills within the authentic context of the class and writing to a real person. Two, it creates a conversation about manners, social customs, and obligations. They have no idea that this four-hour experience is the culmination of three months of work. Writing the letter and reflecting on the day gives them the chance to thank Beth and to realize, again, how committed the program is to them. Through such experiences the kids come to see Beth as an essential ally, someone to whom they can turn for guidance long after they leave my program.

Here are a few sample letters from kids talking about what they learned and thought about their day at CSM:

Dear Mrs. Pascal:

I learned a lot from my experience at CSM. I had a lot of fun being on a college campus. It was different than I thought it was going to be. There were not as many people as I thought there would be. I like how they let us go into some classrooms. In one of the classes there was a fire truck. We got the chance to sit in it. Part of the campus was under construction. One of our

**Main Idea Organizer: Reading, Writing, Watching, Listening**   Name: Henry

| Subject | Subject |
|---|---|
| What are you or the author writing about? | CSM/College visit |

| Main Idea | Main Idea |
|---|---|
| What are you or (the author) saying *about* the subject? (i.e., what is the *point* you or the author want to make?) | - visit personal choices <br> - looked around at electronic stuff <br> - saw new things. |

| Details | Detail | Detail | Detail |
|---|---|---|---|
| • Examples <br> • Stories <br> • Quotations <br> • Explanations <br><br> Physical | Campus <br> 1. Big buildings <br> 2. Smoking people <br> 3. Grass <br> 4. Barbaques <br> 5. Benches <br> 6. Food bars <br> 7. Nice view <br> 8. Under construction <br> 9. Old / New buildings <br> 10. ugly <br> atmosphere 11. smell like Hospital | Class Room <br> 1. key board <br> 2. computers <br> 3. students <br> 4. posters <br> 5. chairs <br> 6. windows <br> 7. ceiling <br> 8. Desk <br> 9. Dell | People <br> Students <br> 1. doing babaques <br> 2. Smoking <br> 3. fighting <br> 4. dress cool <br> 5. <br><br> Teachers/Professors <br> 1. Many teachers <br> 2. dress well <br> 3. Talk alot |

© Jim Burke 2004. May reproduce for classroom use only. www.englishcompanion.com

FIGURE 4.3. Henry's Main Idea Organizer, which he used to prepare to write a follow-up letter to Beth Pascal.

leaders said they are building a three story building just for science classes, which is perfect for me because I want to become a marine biologist. Without this experience, I would not know that I could learn to become a marine biologist at this college. I appreciate this a lot, and I hope that we can go on a lot of different field trips such as this year. Thank you very much.

Sincerely,
Thomas Murphy

Dear Mrs. Pascal:

I had a great time at CSM on the field trip we took yesterday. There were a few things that I noticed about the school campus. There were kids smoking, which to me shows that they have more freedom than we have. There were a lot of people there that were just normal people. I also noticed that the campus was huge. While we visited the classrooms I also realized a couple things.

The welding class looked just like a real shop, and I thought that was kinda cool. When I signed up for welding I never would have thought we were actually going to get to weld, but we did. This showed that we were treated like adults in my view. She had complete and total trust in us and granted us complete access to the shop. I thought the teacher was really cool because she completely trusted us. I like the teacher's teaching method, too, because it was better and more fun to learn how to weld first hand. The teacher was really nice and I would love to take another trip to CSM.

Sincerely,
Trevor Press


Dear Mrs. Pascal,

My visit to CSM was very fun. I saw many new things. The campus was huge, and also had a great view. The class I visited was in the cosmetology department. It was very interesting to watch the students cut the people's hair and give them all different types of styles. Some of the students were even working on dummies, which I thought was pretty funny. After the cosmetology department, I visited dental assisting. That wasn't something I was so interested in, because I would hate to work in someone else's mouth. So I'd have to say the cosmetology department was my favorite. The classrooms were very different than what I usually see. There weren't so many students in each classroom. Which I guess made the class better for the students. Overall, going to the college, and seeing all these new things taught me a lot. It also got me thinking of what college I want to go to. Thank you for putting your time in to getting us to go to CSM.

Sincerely,
Zovig Azizian


Mrs. Pascal:

I just want to say thank you for putting this all together for us. I had a blast. I got to weld by my self and everyone there was just like me they were average people. I thought that people who went to colage were difrent all stuck up and onley talked about there future but they were what I did not expect of colage people. I am going back to CSM on Saturday with the welding teacher to learn how to weld two peaces of metal togther and my dad is very very proud of me. Thank you for al you have done for me and my classmates.

Sincerely,
Victor

I knew the day was successful when I got an email from Victor's mother the next day:

> First off, Mr. Burke, I want to THANK YOU for all the positive input you give to Victor. You are the first teacher who really seems to care about his well being. He enjoys coming to your class and reading. (I never thought I would hear him say he likes to read.) It is really a struggle for him. I also want to Thank You for showing him the CSM campus yesterday. WOW! He is so excited to go to college and do welding. I am so happy that someone really cares about his progress and is willing to help us instead of fight with me and tell me all the negatives. You are to be commended for all your Great efforts. You ARE making a difference in his life now and for the future . . . God Bless You . . . Thanks A Million . . . Keep up the Great work . . .
>
> Appreciative mom,
> Vicky Maroosis

I could call myself content after the two-year college visit, but I'm eager to kindle a larger fire in those kids who will need to attend a four-year university, as Thomas and Taylor must do to become marine biologists and Chris must do if he is to become an architect. In the spring, we visit a four-year college. The article shown in Figure 4.4, written by a local reporter who followed along for the day, tells the story of our day at UC Berkeley.

Again, I had the kids, as I always do, reflect on the day to see what they learned, how we could improve the experience in the future. Selvana Awadallah wrote the reflection shown in Figure 4.5.

Even Simone, who began to speak to me only after the first semester, conceded that UC Berkeley was "pretty okay." She continued: "It wasn't the best college, but it was nice."

## Guest Speakers

On the rare occasions when we have not been able to arrange for college visits, we have, as the saying goes, brought the mountain to Muhammad by having people visit our classroom and give a presentation about college. We have such guest speakers all year long, typically on Fridays. They come from vocational colleges, fire and police departments, small businesses, and the community of interesting people around us. We have had doctors and basketball coaches, the founder of the American Museum of Musical Theater, state senator Jackie Speier, a SWAT commander, and the superior county judge of adolescent affairs (who has, on some occasions, met my students in her court before coming to my class).

Boutique&Villager

# THE INDEPENDENT

### The Voice of Burlingame and Hillsborough for 44 years

45th Year, No. 29                                                                 Saturday, April 10, 2004

DOUG OAKLEY

Burlingame High School teacher Jim Burke talks to freshman students in the Academic Success program about the day's visit to UC Berkeley designed to foster goals of attending college.

# The college dream

## High school visit to UC Berkeley gives students vision of future

BY DWANA SIMONE BAIN
*Staff Writer*

BERKELEY — It is a breezy Berkeley day and numbers of freshman students are wandering about the University of California campus. One group of freshmen stands out from the crowd. They seem a little younger than the Berkeley crowd, because they are. They are freshmen in high school — and it is never too early to plan. So reasons Beth Pascal, the School to Career Coordinator at Burlingame High School.

On an early Tuesday morning, a group of about 40 students boarded a school bus bound for the university, embarking on a day tour to include advice from college students and admissions experts about the future at a university.

The visit to Berkeley is one of a series of

DOUG OAKLEY

Freshmen at Burlingame High School get ready for a field trip to UC Berkeley.

higher learning educational experiences that Pascal has brought to the students this year.

The tour includes 10 students from the AVID program at San Mateo High School, a program that challenges academically average students through advanced classes.

Most of the students are freshmen from the

Access class at Burlingame High School, a program dedicated to helping students achieve academic success. Teacher Jim Burke — who started the program four years ago — believes a student can create his or her own destiny, beginning with a student's confidence in what can be accomplished.

Burke knows that not all the students will attend Berkeley. Maybe not all will go to college. But if just one student decides to go to college as a result of the experience, "It is worth the cost of the trip," he said.

The students left Burlingame at 8:30 a.m., arriving in Berkeley before 10 a.m., where they split into two groups, and tour guides offer a long walking tour of campus. Tour guide Nicole Roberts, a graduating senior, led the students around, telling anecdotes about the school's history. Ted "the Unabomber" Kaczynski once taught at the school. And Tater Tots were invented here. Of course, the school is better known for its excellent academics. Roberts offered tips about getting accepted. Many of the entering Berkeley freshmen have a 4.2 GPA, so advanced placement classes are valuable. So are the college entry essays. California takes a particular interest in essays, she said.

The tour wound past Haas Pavillion where the school's Division 1 sports teams play, past the Moffitt Library and the University Library with its four million volumes of books. The students noted the striking contrast between the campus and their comparatively tiny high schools. "The classrooms, the environment, all of it is different," said Rafael Trinidad, 17.

Pascal is not surprised by the students' surprise. "A lot of these kids have never even been on a college campus," she said.

**FIGURE 4.4.**

Burlingame High School students talk to their teacher about the upcoming visit to a college campus.

DOUG OAKLEY

# COLLEGE: Campus visit for freshmen

The idea for the field trip came from a People magazine story Pascal read about a year ago in which a Texas teacher who took students with disadvantaged backgrounds on tours of college campuses. About 65 percent of his students continued on to college — even Ivy League schools. "I decided this year that I was going to try to expose them to many types of opportunities," Pascal said. The students already visited the Sequoia Institute, a vocational school. They visited College of San Mateo, a community college. A representative from San Francisco State University visited the school. "I'm culminating it with a UC experience," she said.

Before the day ends, students get a chance to eat college style. One swipe of the complimentary meal card and the teens could choose from anything in the new circular cafeteria, from a vegan plate to sausage pizza. Donuts and ice cream topped off the meal.

It settled their stomachs long enough to listen to a speech about requirements for entering freshmen and transfer students. A graph is distributed showing the lifetime earnings' difference between high school and college graduates, nearly $1 million. It is incentive, Berkeley officials say, to get serious about school and a college degree.

"The visualization is probably going to start now," said Itati Flores, the school's transfer coordinator. "If it hasn't already, hopefully it will begin today."

Trinidad, for one, can visualize himself at Berkeley. While he thought about Berkeley before the tour, the experience made him more interested in attending the school. "I see the emotions that the students have towards the school," he said. "It makes me more anxious to go to a university, especially, Berkeley."

Several other students said they were encouraged by the trip. Freshman Caitlyn Bowl-

ing said she appreciated the direct advice about getting into a good university. "It's not as hard as most of us thought it was going to be," she said.

Gustavo Montiero, 17, also appreciates the advice. He wants to go to Westmont College, a Christian liberal arts school in Santa Barbara. Now he knows what it will take to get there.

So does Jeremy Madrigal, 15. After moving here from Mexico about four years ago, Madrigal has been studying English, which takes much of his school day. However, he plans to major in chemistry, even if it takes him another year of high school to finish the prerequisites. He has definite plans for college. "You always want to do better than others," he explained. "Here's your opportunity."

E-mail:
dbain@smindependent.com

FIGURE 4.4. *Continued.*

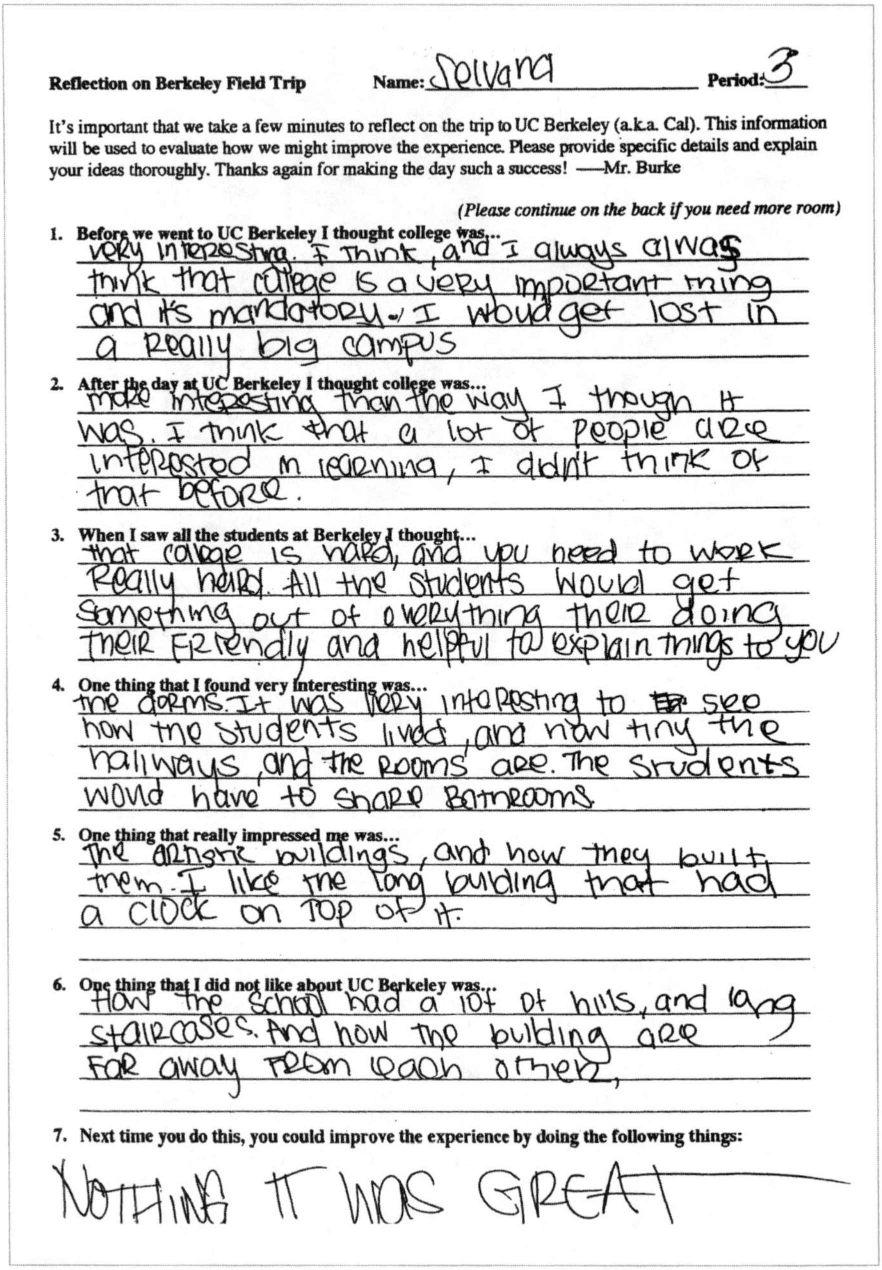

**Reflection on Berkeley Field Trip**     Name: _Selvana_     Period: _3_

It's important that we take a few minutes to reflect on the trip to UC Berkeley (a.k.a. Cal). This information will be used to evaluate how we might improve the experience. Please provide specific details and explain your ideas thoroughly. Thanks again for making the day such a success! ——Mr. Burke

*(Please continue on the back if you need more room)*

1. **Before we went to UC Berkeley I thought college was...**
   very interesting. I think, and I always always think that college is a very important thing and it's mandatory. I would get lost in a really big campus

2. **After the day at UC Berkeley I thought college was...**
   more interesting than the way I though it was. I think that a lot of people are interested in learning, I didn't think of that before.

3. **When I saw all the students at Berkeley I thought...**
   that college is hard, and you need to work really hard. All the students would get something out of everything their doing their friendly and helpful to explain things to you

4. **One thing that I found very interesting was...**
   the dorms. It was very interesting to see how the students lived, and how tiny the hallways and the rooms are. The students would have to share bathrooms

5. **One thing that really impressed me was...**
   The artistic buildings, and how they built them. I like the long building that had a clock on top of it.

6. **One thing that I did not like about UC Berkeley was...**
   How the school had a lot of hills, and long staircases. And how the building are far away from each other,

7. **Next time you do this, you could improve the experience by doing the following things:**

   NOTHING IT WAS GREAT

FIGURE 4.5.   Selvana's reflection on the day we spent at University of California at Berkeley.

The following email shows how Beth Pascal approaches people to get them to speak. In the email, she asks Lauren Kucera, founder of Co-Action, a national antiracism organization located near our school, to speak to the class.

Lauren,

As per our conversation, I would like to book you to speak to Jim Burke's ACCESS class. This class is entirely made up of 9th graders who have been academically unsuccessful throughout their academic lives. Mr. Burke's goal is to motivate and empower these students. In my opinion, your presentation about respecting others would fit nicely into his goals of getting the students to understand themselves and others and devote less time to put-downs in order to give themselves the opportunity to concentrate on what is really important and that is constructive learning.

I would appreciate it if you could provide me with a few dates that you would be available to visit us at BHS and I will coordinate it with Jim Burke.

I look forward to hearing from you!

Beth Pascal
EXPLORE Program Coordinator

The guest speakers program creates a weekly opportunity for a meaningful encounter with someone interesting who can tell students something about the world. They are not always so glamorous as Francine Ward (see Figure 4.6) and Senator Jackie Speier. Still, I am constantly amazed by the willingness of busy, important people to accept our invitation to come in and speak to the kids. Despite public frustrations with or attitudes toward youth culture, the fact is that adults worry about today's teenagers and are eager to do what they can to help. We use these occasions to work on our thinking and discussion skills. In Figure 4.7, Lidia Santiago wrote down the things that stood out in Francine Ward's talk; then, to extend that thinking, she huddled up with a few others to create a Venn diagram to compare Francine Ward's ideas with those other speakers had offered in their own talks. Though we ran out of time that day, I could have extended this activity to include a paragraph that would have given me a chance to teach Lidia how to write a compare-and-contrast piece.

But we also use these occasions to learn about the world and ourselves. Here, for example, is a list of the topics from which we could choose when we invited a speaker from the Fashion Institute of Design and Merchandising:

- The Economics or the Apparel Industry
- Fashionable First Families

# Students learn lessons on "esteemable acts"

## BHS group gives lesson in achieving dreams

**BY DWANA SIMONE BAIN**
*Independent Newspapers*

BURLINGAME — Her personal motto is "Self-esteem comes through esteemable acts."

And Francine Ward repeated it often as she addressed an invitation-only teenage audience at Burlingame High School on Oct. 20.

"Esteemable Acts," is the title of Ward's debut book, published in January.

Ward does not have the "standard" qualifications to write a self-help book, but she says she has the qualifications that matter — she walked away from addiction and despair toward fulfilling her dreams.

"The most horrible place you can think of, that's where I came from," Ward said.

Once a homeless high-school dropout, a substance abuser and a call girl — Ward is now an attorney, author and motivational speaker.

"My hope is that something I might say might resonate with one or two of you," she told the group of about 100 students.

"Even though your teachers brought you, I believe that we are all here by divine appointment."

Ward, a striking, smooth-skinned 50-year-old with high cheekbones, told the students that she used to go to bed at night wishing she could be someone else. "As far back as I can remember, I hated who I was," said Ward, who was born in Atlanta and grew up poor with a single mother in the South Bronx.

As a young girl, Ward escaped with books and old movies. When books and movies no longer gave Ward the solace she sought, she turned to other substances. "At the age of 14 I picked up drugs and alcohol

DOUG OAKLEY

Francine Ward speaks to Burlingame High School students about self esteem on Monday Oct. 20, 2003. Ward is author of "Esteemable Acts, 10 Actions for Building Real Self Esteem."

and I didn't put them down until I was 26 years old."

At 26 she was hit by a car. Her left leg twisted behind her head, the bone was sticking through her skin and doctors thought she would never walk again.

The accident was "a wake-up call" Ward said. She was so intoxicated, she did not notice the car coming. "When they found me on the street, they thought I was dead," she said.

Quitting drugs was Ward's first esteemable act. Her next was having the courage to dream. As a child, Ward believed "dreams were for other people."

"I used to have people tell me 'who do you think you are?'" Ward remembers. "If people tell you often enough that you can't do something, for most of us, you believe it."

After Ward got sober, she returned to school. She got her GED, later going to college and eventually graduating from Georgetown University Law Center. In her early 40s, the woman that doctors thought would never walk again decided to run a marathon. She ran two.

Around the same time, Ward began thinking about writing a book. But even with all Ward's accomplishments, the book seemed to her an impossible goal.

"I thought, 'I can't,'" Ward said. "Those were my favorite words, 'I can't' and 'never.'"

Many people are afraid to take risks," Ward said. "We teach each other and we teach our children that the worst thing that could happen to us is that we should fail."

To establish that such reasoning is fallacy, Ward gave examples from her own life, like

failing her driver's license test and her first attempts at the bar. "I failed the bar over and over and over again," she said. "I got up, I dusted myself off and I did it again, and again and again. Some of us have dreams and some of us aren't willing to let a little failure stop us."

Ward's book was rejected 16 times. Then she signed a six-figure deal with Random House.

Esteemable acts. It's a phrase Ward learned years ago from a friend — one she calls her first mentor.

Now Ward embraces the opportunity to serve as a mentor to others. "I feel grateful that I get to tell my story," she told the students. "It's important to me to show up wherever I'm invited to tell the story."

*E-mail: dbain@smindependent*

FIGURE 4.6.

Lidia
1.) NEVER give up ✓
2.) a rough life
3) puting yourself out there
4.) having others help you
5) Change as in life style, personality etc...
6) It's never too late to make a difference.
7.) She doesn't do drugs anymore.
8.) take the step to say no.
9.) Don't be afraid to take a risk
10.) Do your work

NEVER GIVE UP — This is something very important to because it's something in my life that I have trouble with in many ways like when I try something knew and I don't really understand it I just wanna give up, but I guess even though I have trouble with something I should never give up and try my best.

STRUGGLED TO GET TO THE TOP — To me this means that every one starts from a low point in there life and then threw time they get to the top and accomplish there goal.

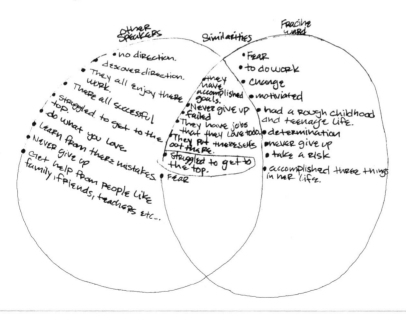

FIGURE 4.7.    Lidia's notes in response to speaker Francine Ward's visit.

- The History of Modern American Dress
- The Psychological Impressions of Dress
- Marketing Yourself in the Electronic Age
- The Business of Fashion
- Applied Art Projects: Exercises in Design
- Discovering Your Creative Abilities
- Latin American Costumes and Cultures
- A Style All Their Own: The French
- Fashions of the Biblical Era

Figure 4.8 shows the institute's home page, where students can learn more about what the school offers.

FIGURE 4.8.   Colleges like the Fashion Institute of Design and Merchandising are usually happy to have the chance to send people out to classes. It's good business for them and a powerful experience for the kids.

Here is Marina's written response to critic Joe Marchi's talk (which I must note I thoroughly enjoyed, too, for many of the same reasons Marina lists in the following commentary):

> I really enjoyed Mr. Marky's talk. His life seemed so exciting and filled with fun and interesting stuff. He was really blessed throughout his life. What he does for his job seems like a lot of fun and he loves doing it, which is very cool. So overall, I *loved* this speaker and he was so awesome because he sent a *good* message to our class. If you love something go after it and you will love your job! Never leave "What if?" as a question in your life.

Marine wrote this response after filling out the sheet in Figure 4.9.

## *Toastmasters International Youth Leadership Program*

When it comes to public speaking, most people would rather be in the casket than standing before an audience delivering the eulogy. Public speaking is regularly listed as the number one fear in the United States. It is easy to imagine how kids coming into a program like ACCESS feel about standing up in front of a class and speaking for three minutes about a subject. Yet it is precisely this experience of having to stand and deliver that challenges them to dig down inside themselves to find not only something worth saying but the courage to say it. There is a real danger to public speaking, one that calls to the speaker's mind all the anxieties and insecurities that prey on us, telling us how boring we are, how stupid we are, how little we have to say that is of any importance. Such fears explain the typical response when I walk into the class at the beginning of the second semester and announce that they are going to complete the Toastmasters International Youth Leadership Program: "*No* way, Mr. Burke. I am *not* giving speeches!" My response is always the same: "I would not ask you to do something if I didn't know you could do it."

When they settle down, I ask them to tell me what they think. I do this by giving them a copy of an article about the program (see Figure 4.10) to read and asking them to respond to the article and the program. Here is what a few kids said one year:

> I think this Toastmasters program might be interesting because my public speaking skills aren't all that great and I want to improve on them so I will know what to talk about in a speech or something related. (Carlos Tello)

**Name:** Marina Williams    **Date:** Oct. 19, 04  **Period:** 1°

√+
great response —

**ACCESS: GUEST SPEAKER NOTES**

1. What is the speaker's name: Joe Marky

2. What organization or business does the speaker represent? ~~musical~~ Play Critic

3. What is the speaker's area of expertise? ~~ooooooo~~ Info. about plays & musicals

4. What is the *subject* of the speaker's talk? following your dreams

5. List three questions you would like to ask the speaker about this subject?

 1. Have you ever tried to sing? — Yes, and he was terrible.

 2. Have you ever auditioned for a play? — Yes, he got no calls back.

 3. What else did you do in highschool? — unanswered —

6. Write down two comments the speaker make that interested you or seemed very important

 1. Follow your dreams, or at least try it because if you don't your never gonna know, what could have happened.

 2. People react to enthusiam, It's important to be enthusiastic.

7. List some *key words* that came up during the speaker's presentation:

| teacher | Carrers | highschool | enthusiam |
| television | college | musical plays | react |
| Art | Interest | | |

8. What was the speaker's *main point* about this subject? That if you follow your goal in life you can end up doing it.

9. What questions (if any) did the speaker leave unanswered for you or the class? (Answer on back) What else happened in highschool

10. Write a brief response to the speaker and the subject the he or she discussed. (Write on back)

I thought this speaker had a great life, and it seemed filled with fun and Interesting stuff. He was really blessed throughout his life. What his does for his job seems like a lot of fun and he loves doing it, is very cool. So, overall i loved this speaker and he was so awesome because he sent a good message to our class. If you love something go after it and you'll love your Job!! Never leave ... What If ... as a question in your life.

FIGURE 4.9.    Giving kids something to do while speakers present teaches them to listen and take notes but also gives them a purpose and something to keep them busy.

## PENINSULA PEOPLE & OPINIONS

# Messages from the heart

### Leadership program teaches self-confidence through public speaking

By DWANA SIMONE BAIN
*Independent Newspapers*

BURLINGAME — A student poises himself at the podium to speak. Calmly and clearly, he tells the crowd of his experiences volunteering and mentoring at Washington Elementary School.

He speaks proudly of how his bilingual ability helped him work with the younger, Spanish-speaking children. "I hope the kids got something out of it," he closes, "because I did."

On either side of the crowded room are the boy's own mentors in public speaking. English teacher Jim Burke and Toastmaster Elsie Robertson smile as they watch this sophomore delivering his final speech of the Youth Leadership Program, Toastmasters International.

Several teens stood up before a crowd of teachers and community members on a recent Friday afternoon, speaking with little shyness or hesitation.

It was tough to tell that only weeks earlier, many of them were nervous about public speaking.

"I'm so very proud of all of them because they've really come a long way," said Robertson, who coordinated the program. "The first speeches were quite painful — like going to the dentist — and now you can barely shut them up," she said with a smile.

Guest speaker Dave Katz, a tutor with Ace Homework Help, offered the students a 10-step lesson on ambition. Among the tips, "Break through your fears," Katz said. "I have witnessed people in here that couldn't put three words in a row, and now they're up at this podium doing extremely well."

This is the second year the leadership program — sponsored by the San Mateo Toastmasters Club 191 and facilitated by Robertson — has been held at Burlingame High School.

School to Career Site Coordinator Beth Pascal first explored the idea of Toastmasters on campus for a public speaking course. However, Pascal was told the program works best with smaller groups.

"I started thinking about Jim [Burke's] class," she said. The 17 student Toastmasters are part of Burke's Access program, which is designed to help students live up to the potential they display. Burke selects students that show great potential, though their grades might not reflect their abilities.

The students largely run the leadership sessions, Pascal said. "It just empowers the kids because they're the ones who are in control of the day." The students elect a president and officers twice during the eight-week course.

During the course, students prepared at least two speeches each. They took turns evaluating each other's speeches for delivery, effectiveness of opening content, and closing. Students also participated in "table topics," speaking extemporaneously on selected subjects.

Each week, students voted for a "best speaker" and "best evaluator."

Abiding by Toastmasters guidelines, speeches and evaluations were carefully timed, with those exceeding the allowed time limit disqualified from winning. Each week, the winners received a ribbon. Those who scored the most points in the course overall were awarded a special certificate at the course's culmination Dec. 13.

"It was interesting to watch the progression from the very first meeting with the students to the culmination of the program, and see the growth that occurred," Pascal said. "You could see how they felt more empowered and their self-esteem had really been effected."

Building the students' confidence was an important goal of the leadership course.

Jesse Cardoza told students and his teachers how much the class had helped him.

**TOASTMASTERS:** *page 9A*

---

FIGURE 4.10.    continues on next page

# TOASTMASTERS: Teens speak out

**SUSAN CALDWELL**

Lei Fesaitu gave a speech about the island she came from — Rotuma.

*Continued from 7A*

For the first time this year, the program closed with a guest speaker, Katz.

In his speech about ambition, Katz offered a final tip to the teens. "Never, never, never, never, never let anybody stop you."

It is a message Burke hopes his students heed.

Toastmasters is not just about giving speeches on Friday, Burke told the teens. It is about the youths representing themselves to the world. "You've given yourself permission to reach to achieve something, not just today, but tomorrow."

The 17 sophomores in this semester's Youth Leadership Program are learning important lessons, said Burke, who interviews potential students before admitting them into his class.

Through the Access program, Burke tries to provide his students with a range of experiences, including job shadowing and field trips to college campuses. He wants the students to see why it's important to go to school, Burke said. "They get a sense of what the world wants from them. They realize that they can be successful."

The message Burke aims to deliver to students is, "You've been chosen because people see things in you that you can't always see in yourself."

Burke puts the students in harm's way of experiences that will help them in the long term. Through the

lessons learned through Burke and the leadership program, one of his students — a shy girl — mustered the courage to audition for a dance team.

The students also learn a large lesson in perseverance by watching Robertson, Burke said.

"The encounter with people like her makes a big imprint on the kids."

After falling and shattering her knee midway through the course, Robertson's first concern was that she would not make the next meeting.

Despite her disability, Robertson continued providing agendas and material for her classes. Burke took over some of Robertson's duties for the second half of the course.

Robertson said she wanted to ensure the program continued smoothly. "You need to have continuity," she said. "If you stop in the middle, you never get them back again."

Robertson returned to see the teens' final speeches and to award the certificates.

The program is an inspiration to students like Jesse Cardoza, who joined Burke's Access class last year. "Ever since then, my grades have gone up," he said.

Trusting in Burke's advice, Cardoza took the Toastmasters course. As a rapper, Cardoza had no fear of public speaking, "I just never knew how to direct what to say in front of a crowd," he said.

Through the program, Cardoza learned to speak from the heart and say what he feels. The experience was so good, Cardoza plans to repeat the program. "Mr. Burke is always open to letting us come back," he said. "I'm going to take it again."

*Dwana Simone Bain can be reached at 652-6732 or via e-mail at dbain@smindependent.com.*

**FIGURE 4.10.** *Continued.*

As far as speaking goes, I don't do well in front of a big group or a class. I start stuttering and lose my train of thought. But all my friends tell me I should be a psychologist or motivational speaker. If Toastmasters can help me improve my speaking skills and get rid of my stuttering, I'm all for it. But I don't want to embarrass myself if it's not going to help me improve. (Kaitlyn Bowling)

I think that this article is inspiring because seeing a student achieve and succeed all the way makes me want to work harder to achieve my goal. I think this program is beneficial in different ways. (Sylvia Ubau)

I think this is cool. It's a good way to make people feel confident about talking in a different way. How come they give a ribbon to the winners every week? Don't you think that would put some people down? I'm glad you guys did all this for students. It really shows how much you care. (Michael Calkins)

As usual, Beth Pascal is the one who brought the Toastmasters program into my class (see Figure 4.10). She heard about it through some adults who participate in the regional meetings. The idea behind the organization and program is simple: overcoming fears in order to become an effective public speaker gives kids confidence in a variety of situations that leads to success in the classroom, the workplace, and society at large. I put it differently: learning that we can do what we did not think we could transforms us, teaches us something about ourselves and what we can accomplish. The program first belonged to the sophomore ACCESS program I attempted to get off the ground. When that class failed to thrive for various reasons, what remained clear were the benefits of the Toastmasters program. When we returned to school the following year with a freshman-only program, I decided to transplant the two things that had worked best from the sophomore class into the freshman class: guest speakers and the Toastmasters program.

In subsequent years, the program has continued to have a lasting effect on the kids who participate in it. Szarlene Lazaro, for example, who made remarkable progress in her growth as a reader and a person, wrote the following note as a senior after having transferred to a neighboring school when her parents moved:

Hi Mr. Burke, it's me, Szarlene Lazaro. I was in your ACCESS class. How are you doing? As for me, I'm doing great here at Mills High School. I just wanted to get some information from you about the Toastmasters Program we did back when I was in the ACCESS program (when we would talk in front of the class). I remembered that I won first place and I wanted to include that on my application for a scholarship. I can't believe that we are seniors . . . Also, I wanted to ask you if I should include that Reading Buddies work that we did at Washington Elementary School on my college application? Thank you for taking your time. Hope to hear from you soon. I miss everyone from BHS!

Sincerely,
Szarlene Lazaro

In Figure 4.11, freshman Michael Calkins stands to deliver his final speech at the culminating event. In the background of the bottom picture, Sam Johnson, our district superintendent, stands as an honored guest. Later, along with the city's mayor and our principal, Mr. Johnson addressed the students, telling them how impressed he was by their achievement as speakers and students. On this particular occasion, several students gave final speeches, but it was Michael Calkins' speech that we all remember from that day. Here's what he said:

### A NEW LIFE

I was about nine years old when my grandfather came to my soccer game. My grandpa came up to me, put his hand on my shoulder, and said, "Try your best." Try your best and right then I knew he cared. So I went out there and gave it my all. And we won.

My grandfather passed away a week and a half ago. The shock still hasn't hit me. I'm waiting for one of those days to come, when I wake up and try to call my grandpa for a ride. That's when it'll come.

As my grandpa was lying in his hospital bed, I held his hand and told him how much he meant to me. My grandpa has taught me a lot. One of the most important things he taught was to not give up, to *never* give up. I will live by that for the rest of my life. The saying I always remembered of his would be, "If you have to sneak, you're doing something wrong." Vern L. Calkins, also known as Grandpa, lived a great life.

At the final meeting we celebrate their success and recognize their progress. On that last day, we gather to hear a few select speeches such as Michael's; we also come together to thank Beth Pascal for coordinating the experience as well as Elsie Robertson, our Distinguished Toastmaster, who has also become, by program's end, a treasured mentor who pushed and praised (in her lilting Scottish accent) the kids for ten weeks. At the last meeting, I also take time to give a brief speech of my own to bring some closure to the program:

I think these students are sitting here wondering what the big deal is. This is the case with people who do things that impress others: it's just what they do—no big deal. And yet it is, for they have given themselves permission to reach for and to achieve something not just today but in the coming years.

Three years after starting the ACCESS program here at Burlingame, what I know is this: the kids who put themselves out there, who run for office, who

LANELLE L. DURAN

# Empowering speech

Top, Michael Calkin, 15, gives a speech to his fellow Toastmasters club members at Burlingame High School April 26, as members applaud after his speech.

FIGURE 4.11.

play for teams, who help others, who challenge themselves to do things they said they could not—like speaking in public—these kids accomplish more and find greater satisfaction in life and school.

Toastmasters asks these students to rise to the occasion such days as this provide. So has Mrs. Robertson: none of us wanted to disappoint her. The approval and respect of such honorable adults means more than money: it's something you must earn.

Toastmasters is not just about giving speeches every Friday, though the students have done that, and done it successfully. It is about presenting yourself to the world through your words, your gestures, your presence—your style. It's because of experiences like Toastmasters that some of these kids can walk into Washington Elementary School two days a week and be mentors to kids half their age and speak with confidence to the adults who work there. It is experiences like Toastmasters that allow them to visit colleges like CSM and go out on job-shadow experiences at radio stations and hotels—and represent themselves with dignity and confidence. It is experiences like Toastmasters that give these students the confidence to ask teachers for help and to contribute to class discussions; they learn that they do have ideas worth sharing, that they . . . have something to say.

When these students wonder why we gather today to celebrate them, to bear witness to their success, it is because they do what is as simple as it is hard: try to commit themselves each day to being better students and more successful individuals. They try to do, each in their own way, what Mrs. Robertson has done for them and Beth Pascal has done for us all by bringing us together so that we may learn, as we did today, from kids about not their world, but our world, the one we build together on days like this.

Kids who entered high school with challenges develop confidence in themselves through such experiences. This confidence fuels their subsequent efforts at Burlingame, a reality made visible by the number of kids who enter into the school's Video Production class after sophomore year. Every morning my class (along with everyone else) watches the school's "BTV News" program, which is produced and performed entirely by students. Every year ACCESS students show up on screen as anchors, sports reporters, and reporters (see Figure 4.12); others work behind the scenes as camera operators, producers, computer graphics specialists, and so on. It is hard to imagine this being possible without them having first learned how to speak in the Toastmasters program.

### Job Shadowing

While Beth Pascal creates many opportunities specifically for the ACCESS students, others are open to everyone at the school. One such experience is job

FIGURE 4.12. Many kids from ACCESS have become involved in the school's video production program ("BTV News"). Some, like Marcy, work on screen; others prefer the production side, though they often make videos, which appear on the morning news periodically.

shadowing, which gives kids a chance to investigate a particular career for a day. Students have spent the day with veterinarians, marine biologists, sports agents, television producers, hotel chefs, mechanics, and computer programmers, to name just a few. Here is Chris Sanford's description of the day he spent visiting the computer gaming company Electronic Arts:

> The job shadow is very cool. I went to Electronic Arts [EA]. I took the tour of EA. It was so cool. They took us through the main building and showed us their awards and the way they used to make games, then showed us how they make them now. They signed a contract with football coach John Madden. They also have a gym with weights and an NBA size basketball court. I met the director of one of the James Bond games, and the producer, too. They have lots of demo games around the place and a giant cafeteria and free video games to play. After lunch, we went to the store and got games for half price. Then we took the bus back to school.

As with the other opportunities, job shadowing sends the kids out into the world, giving them a chance to explore but also to test themselves against the world and what it expects. The girl who says she wants to be a vet but earns only Cs and Ds on her report card is forced to realize that either her expectations or her behavior must change if she is to get into such a competitive and demanding field. Some, on the other hand, realize that the truth is different than they thought; for example, Jasmin, a freshman who wanted to be a vet because she "just loved animals," came back from spending the day with a vet only to announce that she no longer planned to pursue that line of work after realizing that they had to touch "blood and poop all day!" Thus they sometimes find out what they do *not* want to do, a revelation just as important as discovering what they do or might want to do someday.

These job-shadow experiences, which happen once a semester, keep kids in conversation with themselves, as do the other opportunities they have. They are in the process of forming themselves, testing out who they are or could be, trying on different selves. All of this is an essential part of the experience of creating and fostering an academic identity, as they hear again and again that to be a firefighter, for instance, they need a degree in fire technology and advanced technological and medical knowledge. School then, for some, becomes a solution to a problem they face and now want to solve: how can I learn what I need to know to be able to live the life I want—as a chef, for example?

## *Reading Buddies*

In addition to the weekly guest speakers, some kids go around the corner to Washington Elementary School to work with kindergartners in Alexia Bogdis' class. Sue Glick, our service learning coordinator, runs this program for us, taking care of the permission slips, arranging with Alexia when to begin, finding out how many kids Alexia needs and what special qualifications (e.g., speaking Spanish) the Reading Buddies should have. As part of the selection process, I have all students, even those who do not want to be eligible, fill out the application in Figure 4.13.

This application process reinforces much of what different speakers have said regarding responsibility, experience, and general qualifications in the workplace. It gives me the chance to talk about handwriting on applications and how to handle applications when you have trouble spelling words (e.g., make a copy of the application and use it as a draft; then complete the original when you have corrected the spelling and mechanical errors).

1. **Name:** Marina

2. **Age:** 14

3. **Previous Experience(s)**

I read to my nephew and I read 2. books in a month, And if i do go to Washington it would help me feel like a stronger reader because one of my fears is reading allowed and i think this will make me feel more confident.

4. **Qualities and Qualifications**

I babysit my best friends little sister who goes to Washington. I'm really helpful and I'm responsible enough and mature enough to walk over and read to the kindergardeners.

5. Write a brief summary outlining why you should be one of the few chosen to work with children at Washington Elementary School on Wednesdays. Be specific and discuss what contribution you would make to the classroom.

I really would love to go to Washington school because i like reading and i also think little kids are so interesting and fun. I think that this will make a huge impact with my reading confidence and i think they will enjoy it just as much. I can be responsible enough to walk there and be on there campus with just as much respect as I have for my school. One of my weaknes -es are reading out lowed because I'm self conslous and I think, or I know this will help me and make a great reading expierence for me and the Washington students.

FIGURE 4.13. Marina's application to work with kids at Washington Elementary School.

The kids who do go to Washington benefit from the program in so many ways it is hard to know where to begin. First, they must be responsible not only in the kindergarten class (as role models, helpers, and mentors) but on the way there. They are, as I emphasize, functioning as adults in this setting, as role models to the kids but also as representatives of our school. Another aspect of responsibility is getting there on time. When they go depends on the period in which they have ACCESS, though it is generally first or second period. They must get themselves to Washington Elementary School on their own (it's three blocks away). So they must learn to manage their time and obligations. They gain confidence in themselves as they handle the different requests from the teacher. Some work with groups of kids; others might help individual kids one-on-one. Sometimes they read, but other times they help with other academic tasks or group activities. (See Figure 4.14.) Given that my students have identified reading difficulties, it is ideal for them to be in a kindergarten class, for while my kids read well above that grade level, they are still uncertain, as one

FIGURE 4.14.   Antonio, one of four kids who goes to Washington each week, discusses a book with Justin and Whitney, two kindergartners in Alexia Bogdis' class.

student said: "I am afraid that I will forget how to read when I am in front of the kids in Ms. Bogdis' class." Instead of avoiding that fear, however, the student confronts it, and overcomes it, gaining crucial faith in her own abilities not just as a reader but also as an emerging adult who can handle difficult situations. Reflecting on her experience at Washington, one student wrote:

> Washington is really fun. At first, I was kind of scared to read out loud. It was easy after the first book. If you have really good social skills it's a lot of fun. You *cannot* be shy or you won't have fun and neither will they. We work with random kids each time, but it's fun. They're so cute!

There are other benefits worth mentioning. Parents dropping kindergartners kids off see these responsible teenagers and, after hearing their children talk about how wonderful the Reading Buddies are, realize that teens are not the monsters the press and some adults make them out to be. The kids go to the school by themselves, meeting first at Burlingame to get their permission slips; thus they have to manage not only the responsibilities of school but the challenges of walking into a strange place (the elementary school) and working with adults (the school secretary, with whom they must check in, the teacher's aid, the teacher, the kids, and any parents who might be volunteering on that day).

We rotate the groups throughout the course of the year, choosing who goes based on their commitment and interest but also on their grades and performance in school. This program, which I began years before ACCESS existed, transforms kids, confirming some girls' identity as loving, helpful people and revealing these and other qualities in some of the boys who go. I express my pride in their work through periodic notes such as this one:

November 17

Dear Danny, Marina, Alice, and Antonio:

The best part of every Wednesday is when I show up and see that none of you are in class. This means that you have once again remembered to go to Washington Elementary School to work with the kindergartners in Ms. Bodgis' class. I'm proud enough that you go over there and help the kids in all the ways that you do. What impresses me even more is that I have never had to remind you, and you have never missed a day (except when Danny broke himself up playing football and had to wear a cast).

Your consistent commitment to those kids and their teacher says so much about your character. Last year I tried to send some kids who were great kids but not entirely responsible. My hope had been that if they got to do something like go to Washington that it would turn them around. While they did some good work over there, they were not consistent and sometimes even asked if someone else could go in their place. This made Ms. Bogdis wonder if the program should continue this year. You four have so completely restored her faith in me, our program, and the kids at Burlingame High School that she can have no doubts about the value of ACCESS and its Washington Reading Buddies program.

I almost came over this morning to see you in action but could not get away in time. I will try to come next week, which will be your last week as Group A before helping Group B take over where you left off. You will see the kids there again; whether you go as a sub for someone in Group B or we all go at the end of the semester and the year, you will maintain your relationship with the kids.

I have wanted to thank you and tell you how proud I am of you for some weeks. Today, however, reminded me all over again how impressive you have been. Since you didn't go last week, I worried that you might forget since the routine had been interrupted. But no, you went, without a reminder. You've set a strong example and high standard for the others in the class and in this way you have all provided leadership not just within our class but in the school and the community, as well. You can be *sure* those kids you work with go home and tell their parents over dinner all about you and how wonderful you are and how the day you come is their favorite day of the week. I know, because this is what my daughter does when she speaks of her reading buddy who comes to her kindergarten class.

The kids there are lucky to have you as their teachers, their mentors, and their buddies.

Sincerely,
Your Proud Teacher
(aka Mr. Burke)

P.S. Next time you see her, thank Mrs. Glick for all she does to make that experience at Washington happen.

Only through constant reflection on what works and what does not am I able to improve the program over time. This means not only writing and thinking myself but having the kids and, in the case of Washington, the kindergarten teacher think about how her kids and my kids benefit from the experience. In the following exchange, we discuss a year from which we learned important lessons:

Hi Alexia,

We'll be there on the 20th. I'll confer with Jim re: numbers. Jim and I just spoke in the hallway and I was just going to e-mail you re: your reflections about this year and then I read your e-mail. I appreciate your comments and I know Jim will value them as well. My main thought is that it is important to hear your comments particularly when there are concerns as soon as possible. I'm forwarding your e-mail to Jim so we can assess for next year. I'm looking forward to hearing from Carol as well.

Thanks again for your cooperation.

Sue

Alexia Bogdis replied:

Hi Sue,

I am fine with the 20$^{th}$ . . . and would like to offer my reflections on this semester of buddies as it compared with the other years I have done this. I'm not sure of what happened with the kids involved, but it was not as reliable as before. Sometimes I would have 2, or 3 never knowing until they came. The tutors came at 9:20 and would confer among themselves, sometimes coming over from Carol's room at 9:50 to go. If they liked the activity they would stay until 10:00, otherwise they'd say they had to go. On Tuesday I heard them saying they didn't have to be back for Brunch. (Don't know the time.) In the past they would always show up at the same time, usually the same number, and leave at the same time every week. It seems that the group as a whole didn't see this as seriously as the kids I've had before. Carol may have some other observations to share . . . I just got the feeling they were cutting out to go somewhere or do something before going back to school, or take a break. When I asked they said they had to leave at that time. Just didn't have the same impact on my class this time and I hope to have buddies again. We were both overwhelmed this year and I apologize for not contacting Jim sooner.

Hope this feedback helps in the future.

Alexia

I then responded with:

Dear Alexia and Carol:

First and foremost: Thank you both for inviting my kids into your classroom this year. Thank you very much. This program has made a big difference in the lives of the kids who have gone in the past. This semester has given me some important insights into the conditions necessary for the program to succeed. I thought I would think about them out loud there and invite you to respond. (Sue shared Alexia's email last week: I appreciated the honesty of it.)

Programs can only be as successful as the people involved. That's why Sue Glick is so important: she adds consistency, integrity, and organizational capacity I could not manage on my own if I were trying to juggle the Washington program and teach the class at the same time. It's also why Alexia (and now Carol) are so important: consistency and commitment ensure the success of the program. Of course the final and all-important participants are the kids (mine) themselves. Without going into the details, I made choices as to who should go this semester based on some different principles than we have followed in the past. Alexis' comments last week say best what I felt: despite some successes, this semester has not been up to the standards of the past. In the past I have specifically chosen kids who were making accelerated progress and who needed (and would feel rewarded by) the additional challenge that going over to Washington offered. I chose some kids this semester whose lives lack the stability and success that makes them see the Washington experience as a reward, a recognition of their increased responsibility. Only lately has it become clear to me that "all the pistons were not firing" as they have in the past. I would ask that you maintain your commitment to the relationship we have established these last few years and trust me to choose the right kids next year who will be there, on time, ready and willing as they have in the past.

As far as bringing this year to a close, I would like to suggest that we call it a wrap and learn from my mistakes this semester. I am very open to your counterarguments: if you feel your kids need closure to the year with my kids and you want to have that final gathering, I'm committed to it. If, however, you feel the connection is lacking and any get-together would not give that sense of conclusion, then it seems best that I just thank the kids and say it's over for the year.

Please let me know what you want and how you think we can improve the program for next year. I will do whatever I must to ensure that the program continues and does so in a way that meets your and your students' needs.

Thank you both for your support of my kids this year. Whatever balls they dropped, whatever glitches have happened, one thing is always clear to me: They love and enjoy your kids and see in them some of the joy they once found in school before it got serious and difficult for them.

Sincerely,
Jim Burke

Finally, Alexia responded:

To: Jim Burke
Subject: Reflections on Reading Buddies—and Gratitude
Date: May 13

Hi Jim,

Carol asked me to reply for both of us . . . it is Open House day and the natives are restless!

First of all, our kids loved having the experience of the older buddies coming in. The first semester definitely was more what we would like again, but the second semester was still a great gift to our kids. Just from our standpoint,

## HOMETOWN

# Teaming up for success

**BHS Reading Buddies
program may soon
face elimination**

BY SABRINA CRAWFORD
*Independent Newspapers*

SUSAN CALDWELL

Burlingame High School teacher Jim Burke and BHS student Luba Kalinina listen to Washington Elementary kindergarten student Caroline Sharpe talk about how her mom had braided her hair, at an end of the year Reading Buddies party in the classroom of Alexia Bogdis.

BURLINGAME — Walking through the hallways of Washington Elementary, you can hear the laughter of children echo.

And once you step inside kindergarten teacher Alexia Bogdis' class, it's easy to see why.

Inside the alphabet-covered walls, children eagerly line up for fruit cups and juice — indicating that today something extra special is happening.

When a group of teens walk in, the kindergarteners wave their arms brightly,

"Hi, Ben. Hi. Monica. Sit next to me, Greg," they call out.

As the teen tutors scoot into kiddie chairs, books in hand, banging their adolescent knees against the too-tiny table tops, the 5-and-6-year-olds squeeze next to them and beam.

For Sue Glick, head of the Reading Buddies program, watching this kind of interaction is what makes her job so worthwhile. For the past seven years, Glick has built this program — which sends Burlingame High School teens to local elementary schools to help the young students learn to read and write. She's lovingly crafted it from the ground up.

But now, as the San Mateo Union High School District scrambles to find extra dollars amid the statewide budget crunch, Reading Buddies — and the entire community service learning program it's a part of — is on the chopping block.

PAWS (People, Action, Work, Service) was started in 1996 with special grant funding to help BHS students learn to serve in the wider community. Since then, Glick, also a BHS parent, has helped students organize food drives, fund-raisers, tutoring sessions and even a senior oral history project. But among the crown jewels has always been Reading Buddies.

"It's an amazing program." Glick said. "It takes a lot of coordination with the teachers to get them over here, but the kids and the teens both get so much out of it," she said.

But the original three-year grant has long since run out. In order to keep the $25,000 program going, the principal and parents agreed to fund it for one year. After that, the district took it over. But with SMUHSD looking to cut $4.5 million from next year's budget, special grant-launched programs like PAWS are facing the axe.

Now Glick fears her job and PAWS will come to an end unless BHS is able to find some alternate source of funding, such as a grant or private donor, to save the day. In the past few months, she's sent out several grant applications, appealed to local clubs and recently also to the BHS parent group who saved the program once before. Now, she's keeping her fingers crossed — that somebody will come through again.

"If we lose this, it's really going to have an impact," Glick said. "Not all kids learn by black-board teaching — some of them really need something else to help them along."

Bogdis, who has been teaching kindergarten for five years and participating in the Reading Buddies exchange for two, agreed. "I would hate to lose it next year," she said. "It really helps the kids. This way they get extra one-on-one attention that

they can't get during regular class time."

On the other end of the spectrum, BHS English teacher Jim Burke said Reading Buddies enriches the lives of his students.

One of the first teachers to sign up for the program, Burke sends a small group of teens who have volunteered their study hall period twice a week to help Washington Elementary children learn to read.

"I've seen students grow so much in this program," Burke said. "Some of them have never been around young children. They may not have siblings and getting to mentor these kids — to have the chance to be tutors and role models — is so good for them."

One year, a junior he taught was so inspired that he and his classmates wrote a grant proposal — and raised $2,500 to buy books for their buddies.

Looking around the room, it's easy to see that this kind of spirit will carry on as long as the program continues.

At one table, kindergartener Brennan Lynch carefully fills in his journal. Wearing a navy 02 jersey, he bites down on his pencil and squints — trying to think of the right phrase.

"How do you spell 'because?'," he asks 15-year-old freshman Ben Pierce.

Pierce looks back at him and smiles, "You know how, Brennan."

The younger boy looks a little uncertain but then sounds it out, "b-e-c."

"Keep going," Pierce encourages him.

"a-ummmm-u."

"That's right."

"s....e!" Brennan clamors triumphantly.

"All right," Pierce claps his hands. "See, you knew it."

Emboldened by his accomplishment, Brennan continues writing, then looks back up for a minute. "I did it, " he says. "I knew it!"

Pierce, who had never worked with children before Reading Buddies, is among those who think they may have found a true calling. "I really love working with little kids," he said. "They learn a lot from me helping them and I learn from them, too. I hope they don't end this. I really hope they don't."

FIGURE 4.15.

it was all that we emailed back and forth . . . So I hope that those kids you selected this semester got out of the experience what you hoped they needed.

So we can end here and tell our kids it is time for the tutors to have exams and say that they loved coming, and you can tell the tutors we loved having them and thank them so much.

I know that I am very looking forward to continuing the partnership in the future and the children of next year will love the experience. Hopefully Sue will still be able to connect us and your time at school will be with a group who can come and help. I'm not sure about Carol's plans for next year . . . will depend on assignment and class, etc. Anyway, thank you and have a great summer.

See you next year.
Alexia

## *Other Opportunities*

Reading Buddies, Toastmasters, guest speakers—these are all scheduled opportunities that take place in the controlled environment of the classroom. Throughout the year, unexpected opportunities arise, opportunities that generally require a level of maturity or abilities that not everyone has yet. As these events come up, I evaluate whether I have any students who would be appropriate for that event or program. Beth Pascal will typically send an email telling me about an upcoming Women in Business conference in San Francisco to which high school girls are encouraged to come. She will take mostly juniors and seniors but will also save a few spaces for current and past ACCESS students who I think will benefit. On other occasions, a program like the NXTAGE Foundation Leadership Skills Workshop Series for High School Students will solicit students. Beth will send me the papers and suggest that I recommend someone for it if I think I have someone who's eligible. In this way, she (like Sue Glick and Lori Friel, the college advisor) consistently advocates for not only the kids but the program, helping me through her nudging and encouragement to challenge the kids. Such programs often provide experiences that help the students develop greater purpose in their lives. Here, for example, is the schedule of events for the NXTAGE Foundation Leadership Skills program, which offers a monthly workshop series for the academic year:

- Leadership Magic: The Magic of Listening, Learning, Leading, Living
- Successful Leadership Styles
- The Magic of Managing Conflict
- Leadership in the Real World
- Understanding Organizational Behavior to Enhance Your Leadership Ability

I choose five students who show promise but also demonstrate the willingness to commit to such a program. I am also guided by the need to balance the opportunities, to find the right ones for the right kids without overwhelming them through such experiences and thereby undermining their efforts to succeed in school. Here is the letter I wrote to the kids in one of the leadership programs, which they enrolled in during their fall freshman semester:

November 17

Dear Danny:

I know you have another leadership meeting today and just wanted to tell you how proud and impressed I am that you have made the commitment to that program and, more importantly, to your own growth as a person. We must challenge ourselves if we are to grow and to improve. Every speaker who has come to our class has said something about this: it was hard for me, but I did it, and having done it gave me confidence that I could do it again, do it better, and do other things. Such experiences teach us to believe in ourselves.

You continue to set an important example for others in the program and the school itself. Look at you: you are freshmen, and yet you commit your time and energy to go to these leadership meetings after school. You're all incredible and I'm grateful for the chance to watch you go through this process.

I can't wait to hear about your next meeting and to see what you will do in the weeks, months, and years ahead. Nothing will surprise me; instead, you will only confirm how successful I already knew you would be if given the chance to show the world who you are and what you can do.

Keep up the fine work.

Sincerely,
Mr. Burke

P.S. You might look for a chance to stop by and thank Mrs. Pascal for all she has done to set up this opportunity for you.

Here is the letter Danny wrote to Mrs. Pascal about the early stages of the leadership program in which he participated:

Dear Mrs. Pascal:

This is a letter to thank you for pushing me to go to the leadership classes at the Recreation Center. I just think it's fantastic how you go the extra mile to help kids be successful in life.

The first class at the Rec Center was based on leadership. It was amazing how many parts of leadership there are. I always thought leadership was getting players fired up on the football field, but that is a different kind of leadership. There is a difference between football leadership and street leadership. I know I have the football leadership, but I need to work on my street leadership.

The first session taught me the different qualities of leadership. It gave me the urge to want to do better and be a better person. Leadership is the best way to help be a better person. And whether you know it or not, you have a lot of leadership. I greatly appreciate your urge to help other kids be successful.

Thank you,
Danny Glover

As I mentioned earlier, ACCESS is a freshman class, but my commitment to the students and their success extends beyond that year. Julia Heredia and Zaniesha Woods, both former ACCESS students, applied to the Youth Leadership Development Program when they were juniors. Julia's application shows the way my relationship with the students—in this and other circumstances, such as applying to college or for scholarships—works in the long term. She came to me with her application, requesting a letter of recommendation but also asking if I would review her application. She had many mistakes, a result of her difficulty with spelling; I suggested she get a clean copy, duplicate it, and use the copy as a draft. We also talked about this as a strategy for the following year when she applied to colleges. Here is the note I wrote her after going over her application:

> Julia,
>
> I am *thrilled* that you are pursuing this leadership program. You can *always* count on me for guidance and recommendations. One thing: take advantage of the fact that your note is in pencil inside your application. Fix *all* spelling and grammar errors (I can help), and write in your *best* handwriting. I'm very proud of you. Go Julia!
>
> Mr. Burke

Her application itself demonstrates the initiative kids begin to take if they develop a passion for something and commit to their own success. Julia wrote:

1. Why are you interested in the Youth Leadership Program?
   *I always wanted to stand up or represent my thoughts and ideas but always felt scared to say them out loud. I believe that I could give out good ideas and become a good leader.*

2. Please explain what you hope to gain from participation in the Youth Leadership Program.
   *I hope to get more confidence on saying out loud my ideas. I want to be a leader and I feel this could be my starting point.*

3. How did you hear about the Youth Leadership Program?
   *I heard about it from my English teacher. She said it would be a great opportunity for us to understand the full process of becoming a leader.*

4. What do you do after school?
   *After school I go to water polo practice and then I go home and do my homework.*

5. In what kinds of community organizations, committees, or groups would you like to become active?
   *I would like to become active in school activities. Helping and running things, or maybe organizing activities.*

6. What school organizations, committees, or groups have you been a member of?
   *I have been in a few clubs but have not really been involved in the real action.*

Finally, she needed someone to write her a recommendation, something I was more than willing to do. Here is what I wrote:

> Julia Heredia embodies all the principles that your program strives to honor. I have known her since she arrived at Burlingame High School. She entered our school (and my ACCESS program) reading at the sixth grade. She worked *so* hard to learn and succeed that she not only raised her scores to grade level by year's end but excelled in all her academic courses. I have followed her progress and success closely. She is ready to extend her efforts to involve leadership. I recommend Julia to your program with *no* reservations.

> Jim Burke
> ACCESS Teacher

## Making the Most of High School

The people who make the most of high school, who leave having learned the most about themselves and the world, are the ones who make use of the school and its resources. Not everyone knows how to do that, though, nor are all inclined to do so. The opportunities I discuss in this chapter force kids to dig down inside themselves and find what they have. Some, of course, find that there is not much there, which begins the conversation within themselves about what they want to do, who they are, what they bring to the table. I end this chapter with two short reflections, one that I wrote and another from Rofida Morsy, who represents everything this program strives to achieve. Because she is Muslim, she could not always take advantage of the opportunities I encouraged her to take. Instead, she made the most of her time in class, going on to win the

Toastmasters best speaker award for that year. But first a short letter I wrote to some colleagues outside of school after bearing witness to my students' work with kids at Washington Elementary School, where we all went to have a cookies-and-punch party at the end of the year.

Friday was an amazing day to me, one of those days when you marvel at kids and what they can do if given the chance. Every Wednesday this semester, four kids from my ACCESS class have walked over to Washington Elementary School to work with and read to a special needs kindergarten class. Most of the kids who go are boys and, for what it's worth, Latino. I've marveled at their commitment to it right up to the end. Friday the kindergarten teacher asked all the kids to come together for a celebration. Her students, some of whom have serious disabilities, sang the rainbow song, they laughed, they sat and had breakfast with my kids while I and their parents looked on. The kids, hers and mine, could not have been more happy. Finally, it was time for what apparently has become a ritual: time to play tag while the playground was all theirs prior to recess. My wonderful big high school kids were as six-year-old as you could ever be, yet at the same time big kids, kids who had grown into newer, older selves willing to take responsibility for others. Paulina and Jorge held little kids aloft and carried them along on the monkey bars, making the little kids feel a strength and ability they did not have. Cristian Tajimaroa was dishing out high fives to any who would take them. When we left, the teacher hugged each of my kids, who had to say good-bye to their kindergartners. A number of kids were dabbing at their eyes, even the toughest of the kids. Only days before, four of my boys had spoken to our entire faculty about what it means to work with these kids and why schools need to provide kids such an opportunity to contribute to their community and, thus, to their own growth. These four boys, standing up in front of 80 adults in a library. Daniel Chu saying he loved working with the kids so much that if he wasn't in class, . . . "Well, you know where you can find me." Big deal, so they read to little kids, some say; it's a reading class, they are supposed to be sitting down reading! Oh, I forgot to mention: all four boys end the year having reached grade level (in reading) and earned at least a 2.5 GPA. But such measures are nothing alongside Jorge's smile, the way Daniel's voice sounded when he talked to the faculty about the work, the pride Tony takes in sitting with AJ, who looks at him as though Tony is the mentor he has, in fact, become and will continue to be.

Also written at the end of the year, this letter from Rofida represents the effect we hope these opportunities will have on kids:

Dear Mr. Burke,

Thank you very much for your help and the time you dedicated to help. I appreciate it. Your class has unexpectedly been a great help to me. I am now very sorry that I ever didn't want to be in this class. With all of the great work and effort you put to give us all opportunities I feel that you have truly personally changed my life.

I just want to let you know that the time you gave made a difference. I look now at myself, a person who has grown smarter, more confident and has definitely built in some self-esteem. All of the things we worked on like the speaking book, Toastmasters, and even the many worksheets taught me a lot about myself and threw in my brain much more knowledge than I thought I might ever receive. This class skilled me in accomplishing more than what I think.

Thank you for giving me the opportunity to tell people who I am and teaching me to allow myself to share my personal opinions without hesitation. I also want to thank you for giving me a time of my own for reading. This was a pleasant chance for me to improve my reading level, my skills, and my vocabulary. Through my years of school I had never opened my mind to my positive side until this year.

Rofida

# FIVE

# *Students*

As I stood before several hundred people at a national convention, speaking about my ACCESS program and the strategies I use in the program, my students were, in the substitute's words, "disappointing . . . abysmal." He went on to describe in greater detail what happened in my classroom while I was away, celebrating the progress they had made that year:

> It took ten minutes to *begin* silent reading. If I put a timeline on the board to show their progress toward fifteen minutes of sustained silent reading, we would be in negative numbers. They lost the privilege to play chess. I sent Sammy to see the Dean for throwing a pencil into the ceiling. I actually only saw him jumping up and pulling it out of the ceiling, but it was positioned directly above his seat (he was in the second row, first seat). Among other out of control behavior, I was struck by a heavy piece of cardboard thrown across the room and a hacky-sack ball I confiscated for the period was removed from your desk. This is pretty typical ninth grade behavior for Fridays, but I am sure this is not what you expect. Probably fifty percent of the class read and worked quietly. The pencil incident was the culmination of a steady series of requests and instances to sit down and get to work on something.

I include this unflattering glimpse into the class in order to emphasize the objective reality of my class at a point in the year when I was not there. They are first and foremost freshmen, and mostly freshmen boys, so they are *works in progress*. (I'm also enough of an optimist to see the "probably fifty percent" as a sign of real progress!) While I would love to return the following Monday and find a sub report filled with wonder at their decorum, I know better than to expect it. Besides, it's not what they *did* that matters as much as what they *do next*. What they do, how well they will do it, *if* they will do it—these ends depend on my understanding of the students in my program, for they will not try to understand me and what I have to offer if I do not quickly understand who they are and what is important to each of them.

Some programs, notably those that recruit specific student populations, create a profile of the type of student they seek. This profile might be based on the purpose of their program (e.g., urban African American boys, kids who come from families in which no one has gone to college). However, ACCESS has no say over who comes into the program. Thus I have had to learn to identify different types of kids in my program by way of understanding their different needs. Far from stereotyping the students, I seek only to identify recognizable patterns of behavior and need so that I can be sure that what we do helps them all move along the performance continuum (Figure 5.1). These profiles also help me streamline my efforts early on when I am trying to decide which students, for example, are ready and appropriate for certain opportunities (e.g., Reading Buddies, leadership programs).

Using the performance continuum to provide a context for each student's progress, I have identified the following four student profiles. These are not so much discrete types of students as patterns of academic performance and a

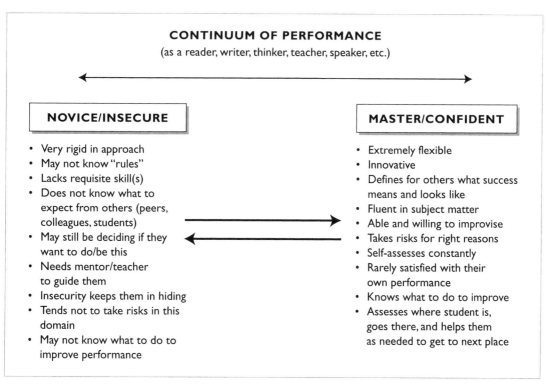

FIGURE 5.1.    Continuum of Performance. From *The English Teacher's Companion*, Second Edition, by Jim Burke, © 2003 (Heinemann: Portsmouth, NH).

measure of their commitment to academic success at a certain point in time. The different profiles focus on students' progression along the continuum, which for some is linear but for others is intermittent or even arrested.

- Accelerated progression
- Steady progression
- Variable progression
- No progression

## *Accelerated Students*

Some kids enter the ACCESS program feeling they have been miscast for a part they don't want to play. Not all, but some, resent being placed in the ACCESS program. Sometimes this attitude stems from class attitudes, kids from success-ful families who feel they do not belong in such a class with "those kids." Other kids come in and accept their placement as a challenge they immediately intend to meet on their way to great success. Early on, I found myself feeling anxious or defensive in response to such kids, some of whom think if only they are surly enough, they will be turned loose to take a different class. Over time, however, I have learned to see their resistance as a great engine that drives them to get the most out of the class and, in the process, creates a great sense of momentum that carries them through the remaining years. Not all of them, of course, dis-play such an attitude, as you can tell from the following letter of recommenda-tion I wrote for Marcy Vega when she was a senior:

> November 24
>
> To Whom It May Concern:
>
> I am writing to recommend Maricela (Marcy) Vega for admission to your program. Marcy did not solicit this letter; thus you should read it as an hon-est expression of my faith in her as both a student and a person. Of the many students I have had the honor of teaching, Marcy Vega deserves spe-cial recognition not just for what she has accomplished and learned but for all that she has taught me and those with whom she has worked over the last four years.
>
> Upon entering Burlingame High School, Marcy was assigned to my ACCESS (Academic Success) program, as her reading ability at that time was not ready for the demands of high school work. Her score on the Gates-MacGinitie placed her just below the sixth grade in September. Her response to this challenge was immediate and impressive: she worked harder than any-one else in my program. By year's end, she improved her reading abilities well beyond all the others; by June she was reading at almost the eleventh grade.

Her remarkable success was further reflected in the impressive grades she consistently earned in her academic classes.

Her commitment to her education has not wavered these four years. Instead, it has only grown deeper and more serious as she prepared for college and explored her interests with children through the school's Service Learning program. What transcripts can't show is the effect a student like Marcy Vega has on others around the school. When my current freshmen see her reading the morning news on the school's televised news program, they see someone who sat where they sit and faced the same challenges they face. I routinely celebrate Marcy's success and use her example to remind the students in my freshman ACCESS classes what hard work and big dreams can help a student achieve. It is not only students who are inspired by Marcy; faculty, too, show an obvious commitment to her. I often see the service learning coordinator, Sue Glick, talking to Marcy about new opportunities; Lori Friel and Beth Pascal, who run the College and Career Center, routinely contact Marcy about colleges and opportunities they think might interest her.

Marcy contributes ideas and energy to any class she has; she contributes to the school and its surrounding community. To know Marcy is to also know how important family is to her. Her parents have supported her, seeing in her success the realization of dreams that brought them to this country in the first place. The values they have instilled in her—respect, discipline, integrity—are the same values that will ensure her success in your school and in life. They are also the same values that will allow her to maintain her commitment to school and to her family. Such support and connection are crucial to a successful transition into college.

Maricela Vega brings to your school not only her intelligence but her generous spirit and leadership. She will contribute to your school in ways that you will immediately appreciate and long remember. I am proud to know her and to have watched her work so hard to make her dreams come true. I recommend her to you without reservation. If you have any questions, please don't hesitate to contact me.

Sincerely,
Jim Burke
English/ACCESS Teacher

Luba Kalinina, another student who realized her potential, wrote the following letter to incoming freshmen:

Dear Freshman,

Welcome to Burlingame High School. I'm sure your first day at school is very different from the middle school that you went to. Don't be nervous or scared because you will meet a lot of new people and will have a lot of fun throughout the year. You will soon have a senior buddy that will show you around and tell you more about this school.

My name is Luba Kalinina. I went to Burlingame Intermediate School for some of my 8th grade. Personally I think it was a lot harder to be a new student at a school after the year has started, rather than going to high school with all your friends. Being a freshman might be kind of frightening because you are the youngest again, but you get used to it and remember everyone had to go through it.

High school is a step in your life that will help you succeed in the future. You have to take it serious as you have fun because if you mess up one year it will be very hard or maybe even impossible to make up the credits. In order to pass you have to do your homework because if you don't you won't learn and will fail the tests. Also, you have finals twice a year that go over everything you learned within the past half a year.

Most important, colleges look at your high school years and if you did bad you won't be able to get into a good college. Make sure that you just don't mess up because you will wish that you didn't later.

By the end of freshman year I learned that you could do anything if you believe in yourself. I found myself as a student who has the ability to do anything only if I try.

When I started the year I had a GPA of 2.5. Then it dropped to a 2.3, that's when I realized why do I go to school if I'm not going to get anything out of it. When I began doing all of my homework I saw my grades go up every grading period. On my last report card I had a 3.333. I believed in myself and followed through with my plan and reached my goal. Also, I was one of the students who went to Washington Elementary every Tuesday to tutor kindergarten students. Seeing the smiles on those kids' faces when they see you makes you happy inside. Even though it wasn't a big deal for me, they couldn't wait until the week passed so we could come again. Seeing them be happy made me happy inside. Not only that I taught little kids how to do things, I learned a lot about myself.

The ACCESS class that Mr. Burke teaches helps you a lot during your freshman year. When I first came into it I thought all we would do is read, but we didn't. You do read for 15 minutes everyday, but also you learn how to study for your tests, how life works, and what high school is all about. Mr. Burke is always there for you in or out of class to help you if you have any questions. He talks to you privately about your progress, he tries to help you anyways possible. Also, you get study hall so you could do your homework from other classes and have help right there if you need it.

Overall, high school is a lot of work, but very fun. It is way different from middle school and in my opinion a lot better. Just make sure that you get good grades and you will be fine. Have fun in Mr. Burke's class, it really helps you find yourself and see what you can do. Try to stay out of trouble because detention is not fun at all. Good luck in high school and I hope you have fun.

Sincerely,
Luba Kalinina

These accelerated kids often move through the four years guided by their desire for a life no one in their family has lived, which makes it one they cannot easily understand. As Marcy approached the end of her senior year, having distinguished herself throughout the four years, she encountered resistance from her parents, which led me to write the following letter:

Dear Marcy:

Mrs. Friel sought me out today to tell me that you were running into some trouble with your college goals. I don't know all the details but got a sense of it from her.

I just wanted to send this one short note in case it helps somehow. Some months ago Judge Marta Diaz, the San Mateo Superior Court judge, spoke at the Latino Community Summit here at BHS. She spoke in my ACCESS class also the last two years. But at the summit she said some things that I had not heard and wanted to briefly share with you.

She came from a family in which no one had ever gone to college. She excelled, much like yourself, in school and her parents supported that but did not understand fully the world for which she was preparing herself. She got into Cal, where she worked hard all week as a student and lived in the dorms. Because money was tight and her parents couldn't cover it all, she drove home every weekend to work at the racetrack down in San Mateo to make money to pay for college, then got back Sunday night and kept right on studying. While some who had money worried about which party to go to, or which weekend trip to take, she kept her focus on education and earning the money needed to help her parents pay for that education.

I did much the same when I went to UCSB. I worked in a knife store. (All right, I admit it: It's the ONLY job I was ever fired from—but that's because I sat at the counter when there were no customers and studied my college textbooks until people came in.) I parked cars, weeded yards, collected tickets at the movie theater, and did time as a playground monitor at an elementary school—whatever it took to make it through. The truth is there are always jobs for wonderful people like yourself near the college campus; some restaurants would pay good money to just have you stand there and smile as people came in, so radiant and friendly is your smile.

What am I saying? Do whatever you must to get to that UCSC campus, take one less class if necessary so you can work three more hours, so you can help to pay for it. Trust me, it will work out and be worth it—because YOU are worth the best education you can get, the one you have worked these years to achieve. A UC degree is all the more valuable now as the standards are raised and it gets more expensive.

You know I'm here to guide and advise as needed. Right now, the only thing I can do is tell you that everything you have done leads up to this moment and the choices you have made—which are the right ones. Your parents, like mine when I entered college, perhaps can't understand the road ahead because they have never traveled this road before. The uncertainty of it perhaps scare them, seems too much of a risk.

A school like BHS has so many rich kids in it that it seems like all college is about is going to some beautiful place with fun people and having a great time. When I got to UCSB, though, I met many (I was one) who worked while others partied, who studied while others surfed, but who also had fun and enjoyed themselves. They got work study jobs that allowed them to work in the university health clinic or, like my wife, work in the cafeteria, to contribute toward the education that is expensive for some and nothing for others.

You know what I'm saying here. I'm proud of you whatever you do, but sometimes you have to be the teacher to your parents and help them realize what is possible and remind them of the depth of your own commitment by showing them what you are willing to do, how serious you are about your dream to graduate from the University of California.

Don't hesitate to let me know how I can help. Can't wait to see you graduate Friday.

Sincerely,
Mr. Burke


Before my first group of kids graduated, I conducted a senior success survey, asking ACCESS (and other) kids to discuss a person, event, or experience that most significantly contributed to their success. Marcy wrote:

When I first read this question, I couldn't really think of anyone off the top of my head because I didn't know how I would know who made an impact on me. Then I started thinking . . . how do/would I know when someone has made a difference on me? Well it's when you start considering someone as more than a teacher or friend; it's the person that you want to make a difference for and do much better. It's that someone that shows they really care, and for me that someone was Mr. Burke. Throughout my four years here at Burlingame, I've never had a staff member take interest in a student as much as my freshman reading teacher. Showing that much enthusiasm in a student can really make an impact on someone, it did for me. It showed me that someone cared about what I did and how I did in school. He made me want to be someone better. He encouraged me to keep fighting and try my hardest. Almost near the end of high school I was willing to give up, I was at the bottom of the pit. But he picked me up and encouraged me to climb up. He made me realize that I did not go through these four years for nothing. He is who helped me get through these four years. I want to say thanks now, but I know that's not enough, so when I'm up there holding my bachelors degree; please realize it will be in your honor. Anything I achieve after high school will be in your recognition. I will never forget you. Thanx.

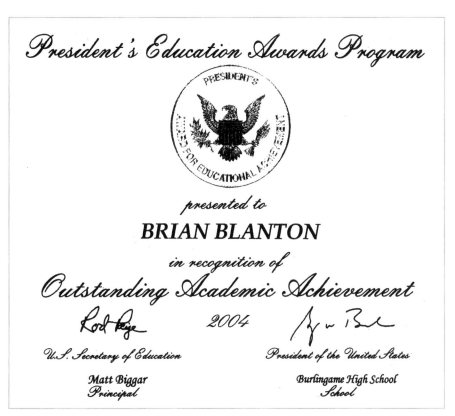

*President's Education Awards Program*

*presented to*

**BRIAN BLANTON**

*in recognition of*

*Outstanding Academic Achievement*

2004

*U.S. Secretary of Education*

*President of the United States*

*Matt Biggar*
*Principal*

*Burlingame High School*
*School*

FIGURE 5.2.  Brian Blanton and Jessica Batchelor, both ACCESS students, received the President's Education Award for Outstanding Academic Achievement their senior year.

These are, of course, rewarding letters to receive; Marcy's and Luba's continued success makes me very proud, but what about the boys? There are boys each year—Rex, Michael, Omar, Matt, among others—who also excel. Brian Blanton, who was in the first group of ACCESS students, received a Outstanding Academic Achievement award from the President's Education Awards Program, a remarkable achievement that testified to Brian's hard work for four years. (See Figure 5.2.)

## Steady Progression

Typically, there are only a few, but usually more than one, accelerated students in the program. I say more than one because they tend to seek out and find others who can reinforce their own ambition, usually in the form of collaboration, but sometimes in the form of rivalry for the top spot, as if there were going to be a chance for only *one* to get out. More common, representing as much as 50 percent of the class, are those students whose progress follows a steady progression along the continuum from the beginning.

Some students may have more to learn than the accelerated students, or may have more to overcome (e.g., emotional obstacles or developmental differences such as actual cognitive disorders). Still, they are a determined lot, a group of students who see the course as the solution to a problem they want to solve but cannot do so by themselves. Dominic Mitchell, reflecting back on his year in ACCESS, wrote the following:

> I think that the ACCESS class helped me grow my academic ability to do better in school. Mr. Burke really influenced me to keep my grades up and to look for college to start my career. We really need to strengthen ACCESS so that more people become involved in the class and hopefully look into their careers and make the right choices. I think that all the guest speakers we had helped me in a way to find out what the outsides are all about and how to manage your way to success. Another person that helped me change my ways around Burlingame is a really good friend of mine named Jessica who is currently a junior at Burlingame. Jessica [another ACCESS student] has really helped me along the way to do better in school and to succeed. Jessica is a type of person that would always be there for me and would always help me on my homework whenever I needed help. So those two people really helped me change who I am today at Burlingame.

Daniel Finnegan describes his progress as a student in another year-end reflection, emphasizing his more global academic progress:

> Some people this year can say that they received a 4.0, some people this year can say that they were athlete of the year, that they were homecoming king or queen. I feel that I did not make these but did have many other accomplishments that don't mean anything to the person sitting next to me in English, but to me, and me alone. I have done things such as participate in a freshman sport, gotten an A on an algebra test that I would have gotten a D or F on in middle school. I have made more friends in one semester than was in my whole class last year. I have tried new things and failed at some, but I feel that the few accomplishments that I have made are worth every single one of the mistakes that I have made and will make. I have seen things that scared me and heard things that shocked me. I felt that even though I was not the best student and got a 2.0 and a 3.1, that does not make me stupid because I have accomplished more in my freshman year than most can. I look back on everything that has happened and I see that I succeeded.

In some respects, this is the most important group in the class, for while the accelerated students set the standard for achievement, the steady kids provide the more reasonable example to the rest of the class. In a program like ACCESS, kids have developed a very clear notion—based on some combination of others' opinions and their own experience—about what they can and cannot do. Many of the kids are quick to say that they just can't take tests, or aren't good students, thereby giving themselves permission not to try to do better. If those who struggle compare themselves only with the accelerated students, they feel defeated, believing they cannot do what those kids do, that those kids are smarter, that they have qualities that the lower-performing kids do not. The steady performers overcome such judgmental voices, learn to hear new voices, and teach those voices to tell them that they *can* do better, even well, if they work smarter, not just harder. I like to tell them that, "Smart is not what you are but what you *do*." Gina San Pietro addresses this steady trend of improvement in her final letter:

This year has been a great time for me in many ways. I feel I've grown so much, not only as a reader but as many things. As a student and a person; before I came to BHS I was really unsure about a lot of things. I think high school is a time in your life where you are just trying to figure yourself out. I feel this year ACCESS has done that.

Before I entered this ACCESS program I was not a reader. I would hate to read and I would never read any assigned books. When I got into Mr. Burke's class I thought it was just a big joke, so I never really took it seriously; until I listened to what he was saying one day then I started to think "Hey this class is probably good for me." I started paying attention, I started reading more and building up my confidence in reading and I started feeling more comfortable with reading books. Shortly after I would just start reading books when I was bored as a past time, which I never did before. If I could do this class again I surely would because it was an awakening, you learn stuff about yourself that you would never learn in a regular class.

I think me, as a student is something I'm working on, now and the years to come. I still get lazy, I still do not do my homework at times, but every student does that. But I still am figuring out what is good for me, and what I can handle, and what I can't handle. But I think I've made a lot of progress learning about myself as a student, I have discovered my weaknesses, and my strong points; now I am just working on putting them all together.

The one thing I am the most proud of is the results in my reading, when I first went to summer school for reading so I wouldn't have to take it freshmen year I got a 4.7 reading average. When I came into freshman year I had received a 7.5. Leaving the freshman year I had achieved a 10, which is at 10th grade level. I was shocked but then looked back on all the effort I had made, over the year and I just thought all the trying had paid off. I was extremely pleased with my progress, and myself. I think ACCESS is the best class for anyone who is really coming into high school very unsure of where they are, or who they are, or how they are as a student. I can honestly say it's built a foundation for me in pretty much everything from: self-esteem, academics, friends, how to deal with situations, how I look at my self and how I want to present myself. It's been a great freshmen year, and when I look back on high school, I think this year would have to be my favorite year, when it comes to growing and learning.

Thank you,
Gina San Pietro

While Gina focuses her observations on the her improvement as a reader, Simone Torres concentrates on the role of more global skills, such as organization and time management:

Dear Mr. Burke,

I have improved on many different qualities. The main thing was my reading capability and to bring up my level of reading. I have read several different books out of my own interest and not because it is a homework assignment. My study habits are much better than before. Before I would just study things I really didn't need to study and I would also study the things I already knew, but now I study in ways that will help me on my tests. When we had a map quiz I figured out what I didn't know already and study those things. While taking my test I look for hints and key words to help me find the answer. I would also eliminate the answers I know were wrong so it would narrow it down. After I started taking my tests smarter some of my scores went from F's to D's or D's to C's and so on. One of the other things that I have improved on was my organization. Organization is not just keep you papers in order it's also preparing writing assignments or projects. Like my speeches for toastmasters, I had to brainstorm and then put it all together to make something that makes sense. Sometimes I might be a little messy and unorganized but I have learned to change and organize myself. And it has helped me a lot. Not only in my school work but at home also.

Simone Torres

## *Variable Progression*

Some kids appear to be steady students, at times even working like accelerated students, and then they stop, taking a few steps back or even falling off the academic wagon. For some, it is a two-steps-forward-three-steps-back progression, one determined by what is going on at home, which home they are living in (e.g., one girl lived one week with her mom, who demanded nothing, and the next with her dad, who made her do her work), or whether they even have a home. Other kids fluctuate depending on the teacher they have, responding to the culture and demands in that class. Still others simply have yet to develop the stamina they need to keep going or the insight into how success actually works (that it is a fire you must keep feeding).

Ben Pierce, a great kid who transferred into ACCESS after the fall semester, and whose performance throughout high school has continued to fluctuate, offers an insightful narrative of his years in school as part of his academic autobiography. (Figure 5.3 shows a graph he drew to illustrate his academic career.)

> I am a freshman in high school and I have had a crazy life. Ever since I was born.
>
> First it was kindergarten and that was an o.k. year, no troubles, no problems. I was just growing up. I remember when kids used to look up to the big kids at school who have gone through what I was going through. I couldn't wait to get into the first grade, but then I did.

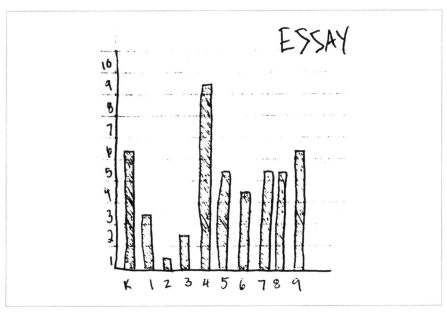

FIGURE 5.3. Here Ben graphs out his years in school (as did everyone else in class), visually telling the story of which years were up years and which were not so great. Giving kids the chance to communicate ideas in other forms or media often allows them to see connections and express themselves in other ways.

I was in the first grade and well that teacher always told me I was fooling around in class. I always got a red card. I didn't even do anything though. I was a quiet kid and kind. I wouldn't have done a bad thing.

Second grade came, ohhh that was a bad year. Nothing wrong with friends. I've never had a real problem with that. "You're stupid, what's wrong with you, kid!?" That's what she told me one day. I didn't know how to read. I also used to bring popcorn at lunch for the other kids. She used to tell me, "Why do you do that for people who don't even care about you? You're a bad kid" she used to tell me. But I don't understand. I just wanted to make people happy.

Then it was the third grade. I didn't know multiplication. Everybody laughed at me. That was not a good day. It was a new school and I was still trying to fit in. The next day was even worse. "Ah, I cut myself. I'm bleeding! I feel a little . . ." I fainted, hit my head on a chair when I fell. I ran out of the room saying that I couldn't see. I couldn't. The next day there were some kids making fun of me. It was a bad year.

When fourth grade came I just pushed the third grade out of my mind, like it didn't even happen. It was the year of Ms. Marshall. She believed in me. She got me into drama, into history, into writing. She said I was smart and funny. But sadly the year after that she died of cancer. Fourth grade was such a good year. My baseball team even won the championship. But then it all went away when fifth grade came.

When I entered the fifth grade, I made my first best friend. We made movies together at home. They were good horror movies, too. I was happy when he moved next door to me. We got into Pokemon. That's when I felt like my childhood really began. But then sixth grade came and my childhood had already ended.

Evan and I weren't hanging out anymore because I was now in middle school and he was still in elementary school. I was sad. We were best friends, went through our troubles together, but never saw each other. And a year after that he moved.

But that's when I met Marcus, my next and most recent best friend. Once he left my grades just lowered each quarter. Lower and lower. All the way to eighth grade. Now it's ninth grade and I am still struggling with grades. And that's life and there's nothing like it.

Sergio Torres entered ACCESS as a quiet boy who loved cars and wanted to be left alone to drift in the margins. His performance rarely varied: he produced little writing, seeming to struggle from what Mel Levine (2003) has termed "output failure." Looking back on his first semester in high school and my class, Sergio wrote:

I'm having a hard time starting to write because I have no idea about how I have changed because it is practically the same thing that happened last year. I hadn't done any serious reading. Every time I try, it's the same thing over again. I get lazy and go to sleep or watch TV. It wasn't always like this. I used to get A's and B's on every report card and I used to do everything with maximum efficiency and never get lazy. I used to finish my homework in less than an hour. Now I take about two hours with sloppy work that my teachers don't accept or that is all wrong. I know how to do all the things I'm supposed to do but when I finally get to it I get lazy and put it away, not even doing 50% of it. I really want to do all my work but I just can't. . . . I just really can't do it anymore. I just need another chance to improve. I'm trying to do better in some of my classes but I can't improve anymore and I am now getting warnings that I might go to summer school and at home my parents don't believe me anymore and think I am useless and I can't do anything right. Mentally I can do everything but physically I can't because I have this laziness I can't get rid of.

I came to know Sergio's mother through the Latino Parents Group meetings I attend each month. There, over food and in between presentations, we talked as Sergio stood by, hearing how much his mother cared, remembering that they came to the United States specifically for him to get a good education. So I worked that angle, not shaming him, but reminding him that his mother would be proud. In May, he represented his progress that year as a continuum, using adjectives to describe how he felt at different stages of the year (see Figure 5.4).

A month later, in a final reflection on the year, Sergio wrote the following for his graduation speech for ACCESS:

> My name is Sergio Torres and when I first came to this school I felt nervous. I was scared that I would fail and not make any friends. When I arrived, I was reading at the sixth grade reading level. But ACCESS really helped me learn new strategies and gave me a new sense of hope. The teacher told me that smart is not what you are but what you do that really helped me because all my life my family had lost faith in me. They would tell me that I was a lost cause and that my life would never amount to anything and that I should quit while I was ahead. In the first semester, I got a 1.3 GPA, but now I have a 2.7 GPA. I know this is nothing compared to others but to me it feels great because now I know that if I put my heart and mind into it I can accomplish anything.

While Sergio eventually evened out that second semester, some students are much more volatile in their progress, resembling the stock market's daily rise and fall as they struggle to understand their own value and whether or not they are worthy of investment. No one better represents this variable progress than Michael Calkins, a kid with all the makings of a great success who comes from a family so dysfunctional that I spent the year trying to figure out (and never succeeding) whom he lived with and why. At one point he mentioned that he

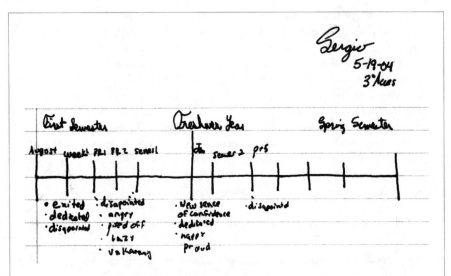

- The first week of school I felt both excited and disappointed because all my friends were going to Capuchino and my parents made me come here. I also came very dedicated because I really wanted to change academically. I wanted to show my parents that I could do my work and that my brother wasn't better than me.

- At the end of the first semester I felt angry and disappointed because I knew that I had failed in my goal and from there I became lazy and uncaring. I stopped doing my homework and stopped studying. I didn't care anymore because I felt like nothing I did made a difference.

- At the beginning of the second semester I felt proud of myself for achieving a 2.6 GPA even though it was puny compared to others but knowing that achieving my goals is possible and I got a new surge of confidence and started working harder and doing better in school.

FIGURE 5.4.   Sergio uses a time line to chart his freshman year.

had lived in thirty-two different foster homes; yet this didn't always add up, for it was typically his grandmother who came to school when Michael got in trouble. Figure 5.5 shows Michael's academic time line for the year, followed by his final reflection on the year before he headed off to summer school to make up the classes he had failed.

Some kids struggle with school all four years, in large part because they struggle with themselves. Some of these problems are institutional, having to do with the culture of the school or the class and that student's inability to ever find a comfortable place there. Other problems stem from cognitive disorders that follow them wherever they go. And some troubles are more psychological. These different problems can make the time in high school a trial for some kids

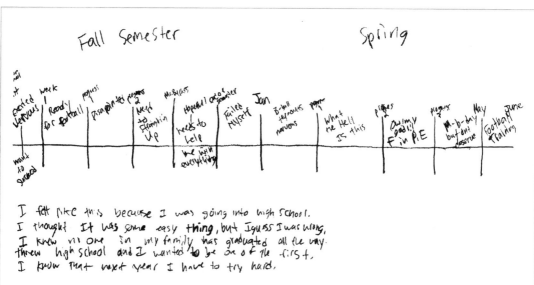

I felt like this because I was going into high school.
I thought it was some easy thing, but I guess I was wrong.
I know no one in my family has graduated all the way
threw high school and I wanted to be one of the first.
I know that next year I have to try hard.

## ALL ON ME

I've completed outrageous goals this year but they were all the kind that I couldn't succeed in life with. I have been going the opposite direction for the past 3 years, and next year I don't want to make it a 4th. I'm going with a whole different strategy. When I first came here to Burlingame I was excited, thinking that high school was all about party's, and girls, but I can tell you one thing when you have a .6 on your first report card you are not doing any partying.

My whole family went to Burlingame High School and it was even better that I got to go. I feel like that since I'm going here I need to keep the family tradition going on. When I came into Mr. Burke's class I didn't know what to think, but to be a class clown. Now I still haven't stopped that, because that's who Michael Calkins is, but he is also a person who can stay on track when he needs to. When I found out I had a .6 I felt like I wanted to cry, but I didn't. I went home and did make up work and studied, and my grade went all the way up to a 2.1. From a .6 to a 2.1 a big jump if you ask me.

I never had to prove anything to myself. This next year coming I'm going to have to. I need to take my head and put it in the game. Instead of staying on the side line watching.

Mr. Burke you have taught me a lot of things in my life and I won't forget it, or you.

FIGURE 5.5.   Michael reflects on a difficult year by using a timeline to get some perspective.

who show promise, who even achieve success over the four years, but lack the capacity to sustain it at that point. Daniel Chu, writing as a senior, represents this type of variable student:

> I don't know what to say, what I want to say has already been said. This is a remake of my first survey. Throughout my four years of high school I've lied to myself and others. I've lied about my homework to myself to a situation with a sub in my physics class. Someone once told me that you lie consistently to cover your first lie, well here I am today still telling everyone I'm going to graduate,

but right now I don't <u>THINK</u> it'll happen. I don't want to do this project, I don't think anyone does but if I want to BARELY pass with a 59%. One of the few things I've done in high school was earn a "B" on a midterm but my pride was soon ruined by my teachers judgment. My teacher thought that a student who was failing the class could not in any possible way, score a "B" on a midterm "He must have cheated." I only have three words for that: THAT'S BULL SHIT! . . . It's little things like this that make a student want to do better, it was something for me to build on. I said to myself, "Hey, if I can get a B on my midterm, maybe I can get an A on my senior project and pass the class."

I was then embarrassed in front of my peers when my teacher abruptly stated out loud. "Daniel, I reviewed your mid-term, and I want you to retake it. I want you to hand-write it." Later, in person, they told me "the vocabulary used didn't seem to match my character." Not only was I embarrassed but I was being judged. Judged by an elder. All of these things can lower a kid's self esteem. I have no point to this story. But it is all perfectly true!

Just before getting this survey and his comments, I wrote Daniel a letter that provides additional context to his story:

Dear Daniel:

Several people came to me on Friday to express their concern about you. I hope you can take time to listen to what I'm going to make time to write today. There is nothing more important for me than to write this letter to you. This is my first point, one you need to accept: Daniel Chu matters, is worth investing in, is worth all the time it takes for you to help him (that is, you) graduate from high school.

Sound familiar, Daniel!? You are surrounded by people who care about you and think you are a very fine young man. I suspect you are partly worried that what you are doing (or not doing) will disappoint them, make them think less of you, so you are trying to avoid them, trying to hide from the consequences of your actions.

I don't have time to be too gentle here: the stakes are too high and time is running out. You must find within yourself the courage to be honest with yourself and those around you. This is something that has been difficult for you at times. As a freshman you told me you weren't supposed to be in ACCESS, that you had no reading difficulties. "Someone made a mistake," you said. And I almost believed you. Then you settled down and began to do the hard work of improving yourself, and you made great progress. You said to me, right outside my room in May, "What about next year, Mr. Burke? Just when I've made all this progress and I sign up for more difficult classes, you cut the program off. I need this next year." So with your words in my head, I went home and created (that weekend) the sophomore ACCESS program—not for you but because of you. Then you had that situation with Mr. Sullivan and the lying (to me and others) about what you did and did not do in the math class.

I don't bring these things up to make you feel bad, but rather to place what is going on right now in some kind of context. You appear to be lying to yourself and, perhaps, some of your teachers and your mom about what you have (or, rather, have not) turned in.

You need to think of yourself as a player who got caught stealing second. Stand up, dust yourself off, and admit your mistakes—not just to those who care about you but to yourself. Then be the responsible, good young man you are and work your butt off to graduate from high school and walk across that stage with a feeling of pride instead of staying at home, hiding in shame from the truth of your mistakes.

This is the most important month of your life so far. This month, beginning today, you will decide to stand up for yourself and to yourself, demanding more from yourself. You know what leads to success in baseball; you also know that the same rules apply to school success, as well as life in general. When I nearly failed out of high school, I was left with the realization that it was no one's fault but my own. Sometimes kids want to blame others—the teacher, the assignments, the school, their family—but that's just hiding from the truth that we are all responsible for our own actions.

I don't mean to sound like a preacher here. That's not my intention. I see a kid I care about very much making bad decisions that will hurt himself and his relationship with others. When Mrs. Friel and Mrs. Pascal express concern and encourage you to use your time in there to study and pass English, they are saying they care. But when you avoid the Career Center and them after they say those things, it makes them worry and wonder if you respect them. Starting today, I'd get in there, apologize, thank them for their concern, sit yourself down, and work hard hard hard on that English and Economics. No one wants to see you fail, but no one will pass you just because they think you're a nice guy.

As for me? Well, you know me, Daniel: I'll help you however I can. I'll help you do assignments you don't understand and give you a place to work to keep you focused. Why do I do these things? Because you are the student I was, and it is my good fortune to be able to help people like you find their way in this world so they can have the life they want, the one they deserve if they are willing to work hard for it.

I hope this letter helps. Don't give up on yourself.

Mr. Burke

## *No Progression*

Some people believe in the eighty-twenty rule: the idea that you will always have 20 percent (of your students, employees, teammates, community) who will fail and 80 percent who will pass. While I don't argue with this notion, my experience is that you can never tell who will be in the 20 percent, so you should treat them all as if they are in the 80 percent group. I have had macho, silent Latino boys who made no progress sit next to other, similar Latino boys who took off and achieved great success. I have seen rich white girls have academic meltdowns, doing no work, often not coming to class at all just as often as I have seen other kids whom teachers had dismissed wake up and do great work. My point is that while I have kids who make no progress, it happens for different reasons, and they still benefit from the ACCESS program, as Rami shows in his letter:

Dear Mr. Burke,

When I first came to this school I was a struggling failure coming out of middle school. I feel that my overall progress has been given to me, my work ethics are pathetic and I struggle to break bad habits. But I have slowly gained confidence as a person not a student. But I have gained knowledge on how to be a better reader without a doubt.

I have read eleven books through out the year and I feel my skill as a reader has greatly increased and I find it easier to read for longer amounts of time than I have ever been able to. All year I have been saying to myself I will do better next semester, those words might as well have been shadows in the dark because those goals were never seen.

Now I find myself in the home stretch with a .833 grade point average and nothing but my bass to accompany me. I plan to turn my life around sophomore year because if not I will just go further down the gutter than I already have. I just need to find a way to succeed and do something with my life.

Rami Khoury

Other students come but never seem to be present mentally, for they have problems that keep them so preoccupied that school seems absurd. Guiselle, for example, cared about school but had such serious problems in her life that she could not concentrate on school even though she was usually there.

Dear Mr. Burke,

It's not like I don't care, is just that right now I have a big problems of my own and I can't concentrate with all of what I have in my mind. I try to think about what I'm reading, but I just can't and the problem that I have, not the family one, but mine, is going to ruined my life, and I don't know what to do, I don't know if I should keep studying in school or drop out and find a job. My best friend Joanna, she tries to keep me in school and tells me to get my education, to not drop out, but it's hard for me. I don't know what to do, I don't want to make the wrong choice. People think that I don't care about my education, but I do, I just don't show it, and right now I'm like if it's going to ruined my life, then why be in school if it's not going to help me with my problem. What I want to do is to graduate, but I don't think I'm going to be able to. Just don't know what to do. I'm very confuse. I want to get help from my teachers, especially you, Mr. Burke, because I trust you more and I think you might be able to help me, and my counselor, Ms. L—.

I don't know what to do with my life.

Guiselle Hernandez

Still others come and seem not to be mentally present, but are; they just have yet to find in themselves the courage to commit. Carlos, for example, was a nice boy who came, smiled, often shook my hand, responded to my words— and did no work, a philosophy that got him in such deep trouble that he was transferred by the end of his freshman year to the district's alternative school since it was mathematically impossible for him to graduate if he stayed. Looking back on his year, Carlos wrote:

In January I didn't like to come to that class. I thought this class was pointless. After a week or so I really liked the class. You do your job very well. I think all the students like you. You really talk to kids well. I think a lot about what you tell me I think my reading has improved. I used to think reading was really boring but now I think its alright. I liked that you supported me when everyone else didn't.

These are the kids who come but do no work. More confusing to me are the kids who, at fourteen, never come. Crystal missed about one hundred days of school her freshman year. This attendance pattern created a cycle of diminished expectations that eventually made success impossible. For some reason, no matter what grade they have, kids always come to class on the day of the final exam. On that day, Crystal reflected on her freshman year:

My first year as a freshman wasn't as good as most freshmen. A lot of people said there freshman year was pretty fun, I wouldn't know though. Most of my freshman year I wasn't even here so I wouldn't know. Most of the time I wasn't here just sitting at home or with a friend. I didn't really get to go through my first year. Now that it is coming to an end, I really miss being a freshman, [I'll] never be able to be a freshman again. I might have to take the courses over as a freshman but never as a "REAL" freshman. I had a lot of trouble during this year. Not that that's an excuse or anything but I have. As you can tell my mom obviously doesn't care if I attend school or not. Which most parents do care about. The only time she cared is when the school tried to tell her that it was child abuse and she could be sentenced to jail. That was the only time she tried to make an effort to get me in a school. We tried going to a school in San

Carlos called West Bay High School. It's a private school but it was too much money for my mom and dad to handle. Even though that school would have been the best thing I could have done. But now theirs three more days of school left and I've been back for about 3 weeks now. Now that I've been here for a while I know I will miss all my friends that I've made and people I've met, and all the times I've spent here even though its not that much time, but to me its a lot.

It is easy, when thinking about the kids in this no-progress category, to dismiss them as lost, or even as losers, kids who don't care (so why should we?). But kids always care, even (or especially) when they appear not to; after all, it's their life, and everyone wants happiness. What we must realize is that the moment hope for success expires, so will all effort. No one, ourselves included, will work for success that cannot possibly be achieved. Jeremy Sandoval wanted to do well, cared about school, but never seemed to get his foot in the door:

> At the beginning of the year I was doing better than I am now, but I feel I've learned more than I knew before. I say this because when we did finals the first semester I felt like I didn't know most of the things I was doing. Then when STAR testing came I felt like I knew a lot more of the things I was doing. Now that I'm toward the end of the year I feel like I know what I need to know as a freshmen even though it doesn't show in my grades. I still want to learn how to read faster and be more organized but I still have time to work on that so I'm not to worry.
>
> I feel I am now capable of being a better test taker because I am confident when I take tests. I also feel like I can get into a book I like now and before I would just read and be lost and not understand it. Now while I take test I know how to maintain my pace so I don't have to worry about keeping up with the rest of the class. I don't feel I've committed myself to my classes as well as I should because I didn't do a lot of my homework and I just blew it of knowing I shouldn't have.
>
> When I first started high school I was confident and didn't want people to get the wrong impression of me. Then a little while later I gave up and began to blow off my work. Now toward the end of the year I want to turn my grades around and do better but there's not that much time to do it. Next year I'm going to come in with a different attitude and do better.
>
> Sincerely,
> Jeremy Sandoval

In the end, failure is inevitable, but we don't know who will experience it, so we must come and be the best teacher we can for all our students. In ACCESS, my relationship with the kids extends far beyond that freshman year, which is important to the kids and to me, for some kids wake up later, after they leave the program. The reasons for their failure are as different as the reasons for their subsequent success. Still, it is essential that we realize and remember that kids don't all progress at the same rate and that they are works in progress. Jenny Jones, for example, failed all her classes freshman year, missing more than one hundred days of school. When she came, I saw the potential, but she kept asking to be put in special education classes, something I saw no reason for, given what I saw she could do on her best days. The following year, going over the second set of progress reports for all students who were and had once been in ACCESS (I had not been able to obtain copies of the first-semester progress report data), I saw her name listed, which surprised me because I had assumed she would have been long gone, reassigned to the continuation school, if nothing else. Then I looked at her grades: nearly a 3.0, and in all college-prep classes. My amazement was matched only by my faith that this was entirely possible. What impressed me all the more was that it was two-thirds of the way into the semester; so this was not a moment's change but a new way of working. The girl who, when she came, asked some of the best questions but read at a sixth-grade level found herself on the other side of a line she didn't mean to cross. Realizing what she did *not* want to be led her to realize what she did want to be: successful, respected, proud. Returning in the fall of her sophomore year, she made the necessary commitment, developed the requisite knowledge and abilities, and worked hard to improve those capacities such as speed, stamina, and confidence that allowed her to achieve the success I knew could be hers all along if she embraced the Four Cs.

# SIX
# *Teachers*

It is summertime in San Francisco, a beautiful day, and I am sitting in Mission Cliffs, an indoor rock climbing school where my twelve-year-old son, Evan, is enrolled in a summer climbing camp. School has been out for a few weeks and I am settling into the routine of the summer months, which means more time with my family, the chance to read more books for my own pleasure, and the opportunity to think about something other than school. And it's working: I'm at my ease, enjoying a novel, looking up periodically to watch Evan, when I suddenly realize that this rock climbing school is a perfect analogy for my role as an ACCESS teacher, or for any teacher in an academic success program.

The facility is filled with walls, each with a range of paths of varying difficulty, which Evan must learn to climb on his own. Instructors begin by teaching the kids a range of strategies to solve different problems they will encounter during their ascents. Thus the teacher serves as an experienced guide, showing them (by modeling) how to do everything; he knows what will give them difficulty because he has surveyed the wall, evaluated which aspects of it will make success elusive, and then figured out which techniques he can give them to help them quickly experience success. Then each student must suit up with the harness, which they then hook to a rope that connects to the teacher. For the rest of the lesson, the teacher ensures that the student will not fall, even as he teaches them (in context) how to climb that wall, reminding the student at every turn that he or she can do it, explaining how, and telling the student *why* that technique is the right thing to do.

School *is* a series of walls for the kids who come in; some of the walls are mental, others have more to do with a lack of knowledge or necessary skills, and some relate more to (real or perceived) limitations (e.g., stamina, speed, strength). Running through it all is the question of commitment: How badly does that kid want to scale that wall, which is to say, what is on the other side that is worth all the trouble and potential risk? Moreover, does that teacher genuinely *believe* that each kid can find his or her way over that wall?

When you teach a class like ACCESS (or any other AS program), you are never "just" a teacher. A short job description might say that an AS teacher will:

- *Assess* students before, throughout, and at the end of the year to identify their strengths and needs as well as their progress toward improving in those areas.
- *Reach out* to all invested parties—teachers, parents, counselors, support staff, administrators, and, of course, students—to help that individual student succeed in class and at school.
- *Be a mentor* to kids in the program all four years during which they are in the school (e.g., via notes, conversations, greetings, meetings).
- *Communicate* with teachers, administrators, and parents about what students need, what you are doing, and how your AS class can help students succeed in other teachers' classes.
- *Advocate* for your students and program to ensure the conditions necessary for both to succeed are met.
- *Instruct* your students in the use of all appropriate strategies that will lead to personal and academic success in and outside the classroom.
- *Manage* program data and resources for consistency and continuous improvement as well as to ensure that you have the evidence needed to defend the existence of or argue for additional support for your program.
- *Coordinate* people and programs to ensure consistent and effective implementation of program elements (e.g., opportunities).
- *Believe* that each student can succeed and that your efforts can and will contribute to the student's academic and personal success.

I end with this last requirement because without that faith—in the student as well as yourself—nothing can happen. Lisa Delpit wrote, "Perhaps more significant than what [our teachers] taught is what they believed . . . They held visions of us that we could imagine for ourselves. . . . They were determined, despite all odds, that we would achieve" (1996, 196). Such teachers are what Benard and her colleagues (2000) call "turn around teachers"; they emphasize that such teachers:

- *Provide connection* between kids, to the world, as well as to the students' own interests, thus making the classroom one where kids feel safe to take the risks they must if they are to improve and develop a sense of pride in their accomplishments.

- *Build competence* in the kids, giving them the skills and knowledge they need to meet the academic and social demands of school.
- *Provide opportunities for students to contribute* to not only the classroom (by asking questions, participating in discussions, making decisions about what they read and learn) but the community (through community service). Such opportunities give students a sense that they *do* have ideas worth sharing, that they *do* know things, that they *can* do what teachers asked, and that they *do* matter; they have value both as students and as *people.*

While these guiding principles are useful, teachers of AS programs find themselves working in increasingly hostile, results-oriented environments where the only connection that seems important is the one to the school's test scores, where the only contribution anyone seems to care about is measured by points, not pride. Being an AS teacher can be a lonely position, one that leaves you feeling unwelcome at meetings where people are talking about how "*those* kids" are lowering the scores, causing trouble—in short, making the school and some teachers feel unsuccessful. The AS teacher often feels connected to all academic departments but belongs to none, sometimes functioning as a sort of conscience for the school, reminding teachers that *all* students deserve the education the school—and the society—can provide them. Theresa Perry (2003) argues that "the task of [academic] achievement . . . is distinctive for African Americans because doing school requires that you use your mind, and the ideology of the larger society has always been about questioning the mental capacity of African Americans, about questioning black intellectual competence" (5). These same doubts stand like walls before the ACCESS kids who enter the school, except for those few accelerated and steady performers I discussed in the previous chapter. Perry poses the following questions from the perspective of the students entering school:

> How do I commit myself to achieve, to work hard over time in school, if I cannot predict (in school or out of school) when or under what circumstances this hard work will be acknowledged and recognized?
>
> How do I commit myself to do work that is predicated on a belief in the power of the mind, when African-American intellectual inferiority is so much a part of the taken-for-granted notions of the larger society that individuals in and out of school, even good and well-intentioned people, individuals who purport to be acting on my behalf, routinely register doubts about my intellectual competence?
>
> How can I aspire to and work toward excellence when it is unclear whether or when evaluations of my work can or should be taken seriously?
>
> Can I invest in and engage my full personhood, with all of my cultural formations, in my class, my work, my school if my teachers and the adults in the

building are both attracted to and repulsed by these cultural formations—the way I walk, the way I use language, my relationships to my body, my physicality, and so on?

Will I be willing to work hard over time, given the unpredictability of my teachers' responses to my work?

Can I commit myself to work hard over time if I know that, no matter what I or other members of my reference group accomplish, these accomplishments are not likely to change how I and other members of my group are viewed by the larger society, or to alter our castelike position in the society? I still will not be able to get a cab. I still will be followed in department stores. I still will be stopped when driving through certain neighborhoods. I still will be viewed as a criminal, a deviant, and an illiterate.

Can I commit myself to work hard, to achieve in school, if cultural adaptation effectively functions as a prerequisite for skill acquisition, where "the price of the ticket" is separation from the culture of my reference group? (5)

The AS teacher, in other words, must see students not only for who they are but who they could be; they must believe in these students when others do not, coaching them up the wall by those paths appropriate to that kid, but holding the rope all the while so the students will not fall, even as they learn to do the climbing themselves. The teacher must also think through and define their principles so that they can, in the face of resistance (or worse), stand strong and know where they are going, why they are going there, and that they will get there if they stay the course. Some will want to define the course, as in my case, as a mere reading course, seeking to reduce it to skills; some will seek to make it a remedial English course or a study skills class. Underneath these terms, however, lie the assumptions about the kids and what they can do, what they are worth. In *Lifers: Learning from At-Risk Adolescent Readers*, Pamela Mueller (2001) reflects on what she has learned after years of teaching "lifers," kids who got trapped in remedial classes and never seemed to find their way out. Mueller writes:

As a secondary school reading educator I have always seen my role as one of empowerment, supporting all students in their quest to become independent learners capable of succeeding when they leave high school. With each group of lifers that arrives at Daniel Webster [Regional High School], my challenge has been to do what I can to help these at-risk readers escape the label. Where in the past many educators have stressed keeping up as they interact with this group of adolescents, I prefer to emphasize catching up. My reasoning is simple: if Alexis, Kayla, and Mick manage to keep up with *Of Mice and Men* but fail to catch up on their ability to read novels independently, what will the future bring for them except more of the same? Once a lifer always a lifer.

Therefore, over the past six years I have sought to change the way we teach these students, creating a corrective reading curriculum that helps them improve their abilities to decode and make sense of text while transforming the way they look at themselves. As lifers change their view of themselves, it often happens that teachers who work with them do the same, eradicating once and for all this insidious label and all the baggage that comes with it. (135)

Focusing on the "roles of the reading specialist," the International Reading Association (2004) stresses three roles that apply just as well to the AS teacher:

**Instruction** The reading specialist supports classroom teaching, and works collaboratively to implement a quality reading program.

**Assessment** The reading specialist evaluates the literacy program in general, and can assess the reading strengths and needs of students and communicate these to classroom teachers, parents, and specialized personnel such as psychologists, special educators, or speech teachers.

**Leadership** The reading specialist is a resource to other educators, parents, and the community.

## Roles and Responsibilities

As I discussed the first two roles (as defined by the IRA) in other sections of the book, here I will focus more on the leadership the AS teacher must provide within the class and the school. Many of my ideas in this area stem from *Lincoln on Leadership* (Phillips 1992), a small but insightful book that examines the traits that made President Lincoln so successful. Of the fifteen qualities, the ones most important to me in my role as an AS teacher are:

PEOPLE
- Get out of the office and circulate among the troops
- Build strong alliances
- Persuade rather than coerce

CHARACTER
- Honesty and integrity are the best policies
- Never act out of vengeance or spite
- Have the courage to handle unjust criticism
- Be a master of paradox

## ENDEAVOR
- Exercise a strong hand—be decisive
- Set goals and be results-oriented

## COMMUNICATION
- Master the art of public speaking
- Influence people through conversation and storytelling
- Preach a vision and continually reaffirm it (1)

All of these traits serve one penultimate goal: to create a sustainable program that results in academic and personal success in the short and long terms. Such a program begins by defining what it *is*. To this end, I had to communicate effectively to a range of people (teachers, counselors, administrators) who should *not* be in the program. In the first year of the reading program (i.e., before it became the ACCESS program), the counselors put kids from all different grade levels in there. Such a mix made success impossible because the students' needs were too disparate. So I wrote the following letter toward the end of the first semester to start defining the program:

TO: English Department Chair, Head of Counseling, Principal
FROM: Jim Burke
RE: Developmental Reading classes

As the semester works its way toward its conclusion, several questions arise:

- What are the criteria for exiting this class?
- How should we identify freshmen for the class next semester—and based on what criteria (e.g., a failing grade is not appropriate as the primary criteria since kids can be geniuses and fail)?
- What is/should be the time line on that process?
- What role can/should I play in that process (i.e., how can I help?)?
- What should we do with the 10–11 grade class?
- If it is to continue to exist, how can we identify 12–14 more 10–12 graders to be in the class next semester?
- Note: I suggest only 12th graders who have yet to pass the reading competency test be considered eligible for the class.

What I know at this point:

- Academically dysfunctional (but not intellectually challenged) students like Daniel O are entirely inappropriate for such a class. He came to the school with a history of failing classes but reads at approximately the 12th-grade reading level.

- These students' reading difficulties almost invariably belong to a larger set of problems I would call academic illiteracy. Thus an essential part of the course curriculum is and will remain academic literacy skills.
- Kids are benefiting from the program.

I don't know what to suggest in terms of follow-up, but I keep having these quick little conversations with each of you about one aspect of this course or another. My objective here was to put the issues on one page and bring it to those I depend on for guidance and support.

I would welcome the chance to meet with anyone sooner rather than later so we can begin planning the next semester's roster (i.e., recruiting kids). I would be happy to meet with any kids who have doubts about taking such a class.

Thanks for your continued support and your attention to this note.

Jim Burke

As the years have passed, it has become clearer which kids should be in the class; still, I monitor closely who is placed in there so that those who should be are included. For example, our school has made a commitment to help our Latino students succeed in and feel more a part of the school. While my ACCESS class is not predominantly Latino, I usually have more than a few. One year, going over the entrance information in August, I noticed the number of Latino students was unusually low. My role as the ACCESS teacher demands that I reach out to all who should be in the program; thus I contacted the assistant principal to make sure we were not missing anyone. She replied:

Hi Jim:

The placement for ACCESS students comes from the test scores and/or teacher recommendations from the students' middle schools. When we are scheduling, we follow those recommendations. I went over all of the recommendations this past summer and made sure we had everyone appropriately placed or had the Waiver forms. Many of the students who needed support were either Special Education students or ELD students. I hope the low number means that our students are reading better. Let's continue the conversation.

Jackie

In addition to defining the program for counselors and administrators, however, I must make it especially clear to teachers what the class is and how it can help them. In the following letter to a freshman teacher, I addressed his concerns about students missing class to have the final celebration for Toastmasters:

Dear Steve:

Thanks for approaching me today to ask about the event on Friday. As I said, I am very sympathetic to your concerns—even frustrations—about the kids missing class for the Toastmasters ceremony. I thought I would sit down and use the occasion to think it through so that I can better understand what I am trying to accomplish and clarify my support for whatever decision you make.

Toastmasters and other such experiences in my program fall under what I call "opportunities." In many ways, they are inspired by experiences like the one you have provided kids through Sojourn to the Past (i.e., occasions to which they must rise, during which they must find inside themselves what they have, what they are here to do). Of course, going to Washington Elementary School to mentor kindergartners is not the equivalent of traveling to Washington, D.C.; nor is going to Berkeley for a day the same as hearing Senator John Lewis. Both experiences, however, demand that the kids dig down deep and act their best, take themselves seriously.

ACCESS students' success will be determined, in large part, by the extent to which they can commit to their own future, to their potential to do and be something more than they are. So I try any way I can to foster a sense of commitment—to themselves, their classes, the school, their parents, whatever works—that will lead to success in key academic classes like English, math, and, of course, Modern World History. Thus when I run into a situation like this Friday—the kids having an exam in your class on a day they are asking to be excused—I'm not at all happy about it. (Nor do I intend this letter in any way as an argument for their release, as I will explain further on.) I see Friday as something like a bug in the program, a flaw in a design, in other words, an unacceptable problem I must find a way to solve if this program is to evolve and improve. My goal is to offer solutions, not create problems.

There is no question that this program remains a work in progress. My commitment to these kids and this program is as deep as it is to teachers like yourself; I want nothing but success on both fronts: theirs and yours. These couple years working with you have given me much to think about and suggested important paths I need to explore so that I can better help the kids succeed in their academic classes, something that will become all the more pressing (and pressuring) if the school board passes its Academic Core proposal that would make the UC entrance requirements our *graduation* requirements.

I shouldn't use this letter to think through my own plans, but it helps to speak about them with a demanding audience like yourself in mind. As for Friday, I would say this: I'm committed to providing challenging opportunities that will build them up to meet the demands of great teachers like yourself or Diane McClain. I expect you to be as committed to your own class and its importance, and to stand your ground and say, "This test is what matters most now, today." I don't create opportunities like this to inspire conflict between us or obstacles to the kids' success; rather, I do so for those who can and will come. It's a testimony to you and Michelle and the regard the kids have for you both that when either of you has withheld permission, the kids not only accept it but see in it your commitment to them and the importance of doing well in your class. As Stephen Covey wrote, "Saying *No* to one thing means saying *Yes* to another." So please know that I completely support your right (even obligation) to say *No* to missing the period by way of saying *Yes* to their success on the test and in your class.

I wrote you a letter once, some years ago, celebrating the difference you make in kids' lives, the way you inspire them. You were considering leaving the classroom to work with Sojourn to the Past. I said, "Stay. Make a difference here." You have, and you do. It's what I try to do, too.

Thanks for listening.

Jim

This teacher responded with the following note, which helped me clarify for myself the boundaries of the program. In the letter, he expresses his concern about the kids missing class on occasion for outside opportunities. In his Modern World History class, kids had a quiz every day and worked a demanding pace; missing class was not a good idea and I knew it. Through our ongoing conversation, and his letter, I changed our policies about missing class, saving such days only for the trips to college campuses, which happen once in the fall and once again in the spring. Here is Steve's letter:

> Thanks for your thoughtful note, Jim. I understand and appreciate what you are trying to do for these ACCESS students. I believe that these students, more than others, need to be challenged in different ways in order to connect with school. My main concern is that the classroom connection has become secondary. Field trips and guest speakers [that require kids to get out of class] give students great opportunities, but instilling in students a strong work ethic and the importance of a basic education seem to get overlooked. I will let each student decide for themselves whether they would like to attend the upcoming event. It then becomes their responsibility to make up the test they are missing.
>
> Steve

Such conversations—whether they take place at the photocopy machine, in the mail room, via email, over lunch in the faculty lounge (which my school does not have, thus making a centralized professional community that much more elusive), or during department meetings—have the potential to form alliances between you and academic teachers who can, if you create such a relationship, see you and your program as a solution to one of their most pressing problems: how to help their struggling (D/F) students succeed. A similar discussion, via email and in the halls, with the social studies teachers one year brought these helpful ideas for how we could support their work:

## SPECIAL EDUCATION/READING DEVELOPMENT SUPPORT
## FOR SOCIAL SCIENCE CLASSES

1. Check planners daily (review assignments, homework, get students organized).
2. Special focus on essay answer writing instruction—i.e., how to take the question and incorporate it into the answer as a topic sentence. Use sample questions to practice with students.
3. Developing cohesive and factually supported sentences and paragraphs for essays and writing assignments. This would strengthen student writing skills across all curriculums.
4. How to read and interpret questions and reading assignments (analytical skills).
5. Test-taking strategies for multiple choice questions, fill-in-the-blanks, matching, chronology, map and chart reading. Use sample tests to accomplish this.
6. Read and interpret supplemental readings to coincide with social science units (historical novels, short stories, primary and secondary source documents).
7. Vocabulary and spelling support for unit content.
8. Mapping and clustering of content standards to help students see themes and the "big picture."
9. Showcase content-related videos, plays, and other media to enhance the historical content of the unit.
10. Encourage and support peer-tutoring, senior buddies, and the homework center as alternatives for students who need extra help and support.

The AS teacher, however, must be careful about letting their class become a mere support class that exists only to tutor the kids and give them time to work on assignments for, in this case, Modern World History.

On other occasions I try, not always successfully, to communicate to teachers what we are doing and why. Again, I have no extra periods, as one might if they were a literacy coach. So I have no dedicated time to meet with or support teachers outside my own class. Thus I must resort to more informal support by giving teachers:

- Handouts (e.g., with graphic organizers and other instructional support techniques)
- Articles
- Books
- Assignments
- Letters

Here is one such letter, which I sent out to those who had ACCESS kids in their classes. I sent it out about a month into the semester.

TO: Teachers of Students in the ACCESS Program
FROM: Jim Burke
RE: ACCESS Program

I do apologize for taking so long to get this out, but I wanted to wait until enrollment stabilized in the ACCESS classes. I wanted to take a moment to tell you what the program is, who is in it, and what we are doing.

Let me begin by asking you a favor: Please do not refer to the class as "the reading class." Refer to it instead as "ACCESS," which stands for **Ac**ademic Suc**cess**. It is about much more than reading; to be specific, we focus on what people are beginning to call "academic literacy." While I cannot guarantee that our work will translate into immediate and stellar success for all students in all their academic classes, I am confident that the program will develop the skills and confidence they need as the year rolls along.

Here is a brief description of the program and its goals:

ACCESS is for those students who want to do well in academic classes but lack the confidence or skills. ACCESS students develop habits and strategies that will ensure success in school and the world of work. ACCESS offers a network of tutors, resources, mentors, and opportunities that will prepare and inspire students for life after high school. It's a program for those who are willing to work hard today to gain access to their dreams tomorrow.

ACCESS is for those students who:

- Want to succeed in school and after graduation
- Lack the academic skills and knowledge they need to succeed in academic classes

- Need support and tutoring they are not getting through other programs
- Are willing to work hard to succeed
- Want to explore careers, gain access, and contribute to their community
- Want to be prepared to begin work or go to college when they graduate
- Want to learn and work within a small, supportive community of students

Here are a few things we are doing to improve their academic skills and personal confidence:

- Keeping a Weekly Record organizer to teach them to prioritize, organize, and monitor their work in all their classes
- Participating in the Toastmasters International Youth Leadership Program every other Friday
- Hosting motivational guest speakers every other week (including people like the mayor of Burlingame, Sen. Jackie Speier, and Lisa Rosenthal, founder of *San Francisco Peninsula Parent Magazine*)
- Teaching them note-taking methods (Q Notes and Cornell Notes) and test-taking strategies
- Teaching them how to read and write about a variety of texts, especially textbooks at this point
- Talking about how they can be more successful students and people

The students have identified certain techniques that help them do better in classes:

- When giving directions, try to set it up so they can read as well as hear the directions. Most students, but especially those in the ACCESS program, have difficulty processing information if they only hear it. They say it is ideal if the teacher writes the directions on the board, then previews the homework/reading with them or models how to do the assignment before sending them home for independent work.
- Try to provide examples of what successful work looks like so they know what they are supposed to try to accomplish.
- Write down homework assignments on the board so they can be sure to write this information down correctly.
- Help them understand what, out of all the information they encounter in your class, is important (e.g., when taking notes, when studying for a test, when reading).
- Use techniques that can help them see what they are learning: graphic organizers or other such tools to help them organize information as they read or prepare to write about it.
- Teach them how to read the different types of texts they read in your class.

My prep is third period, but please let me know anytime (by email, a note, a quick chat in the hall) if I can help you. Here are some examples of ways I have helped others so far:

- Worked with the freshman history teachers on how to take notes and prepare for tests
- Met with Matt Vaughn to help him prepare to teach the kids how the science textbook works and how to read it
- Provided a range of graphic organizers to different teachers when they asked.

I would be happy to meet with you to discuss some of these tools and techniques. You can download all the different graphic organizers. Thank you for all you do to help your kids, especially those we have in common.

Sincerely,
Jim Burke

A program like ACCESS, as I have discussed throughout the book, involves so many people, all of whom play crucial roles; these, too, must be coordinated to meet the evolving needs of both the students and the program. So while focusing on getting the class off to a sound academic start through the curriculum, I must communicate with other key players like the service learning coordinator, the school-to-career coordinator, and the college advisor through such memos as this:

Dear Sue, Beth, and Lori:

I know you are busy settling into your new digs. I wondered if the following were possible this Friday:

You would all come in and introduce yourselves, explain what you do for the school and for the ACCESS program, and then you could have them list out some interests on 3 × 5 cards that solicit their interests for job shadows, schools, and service learning ideas. It would wrap up the week by giving them a sense of what the program is, what is possible, and things to look forward to, all of which will further increase their commitment to school and the program. If not Friday, I'm open to other days. And if you can't all come in together, I understand, but I think it would be ideal if we could do that so as to present ourselves as more of a program and team to the kids.

Let me know your thoughts. If you have other ideas as to how to adjust what I outlined here, please send them along. More minds equal better ideas than mine alone can dredge up.

Thanks!
Jim

On other occasions the AS teacher, in a way core academic teachers do not, might need to seek out or advocate for program resources they need to do their work or accomplish their program's goals. While not all schools have parent groups to which teachers can apply for money, teachers can write grants to local, state, and national organizations for resources (see Burke and Prater 2000). Here is a sample minigrant to the parents group at my high school:

TO: BHS Parents Group
FROM: Jim Burke
RE: Funding Request
March 12

Dear Parents Group:

I begin with continued thanks for your past support of my ACCESS program and the kids in it. Your efforts and, more specifically, your contributions, make a daily difference in my classroom and the lives of my students. The requests below will benefit approximately 40 students, all of whom are in my ACCESS program (Academic Success, aka Developmental Reading).

I am requesting funding for several projects, each of which I will describe below.

1. *Info-kids* books. A recent book called *Info-kids* (Stenhouse 2002) talks about kids who are passionate about information and facts. These students often find themselves in reading classes, as their intellectual attention and motivation undermine their success in other, more academic classes. As part of my commitment to improve students' ability to read, I look for books that will engage them. Books like *The Guinness Book of World Records* and *Encyclopedia of American Cars* offer strong support for the early phases of students' reading development, especially for boys. Short but well-written texts about subjects that really interest them improve their speed and stamina, not to mention their commitment as readers.

   **Request: $300.00 to purchase nonfiction, information-oriented books at Borders for my classroom library.**

2. *Reader's Handbook.* Students must learn to read a variety of types of texts in their academic classes if they are to succeed. This book, designed specifically to teach students "to read a variety of types of texts," has several unique features that will help me get kids off to a quick start in the fall and thereby help them succeed in English, science, and social studies. Specifically, the book:

   - Teaches students the elements of and how to use a reading process for all classes and texts
   - Focuses on effective reading and writing strategies that help each student think strategically

- Uses examples from many of the texts they read in their primary academic classes; for example, the chapter on reading history textbooks uses the same textbook our kids use to demonstrate the techniques. This is especially helpful given the difficulty of the Modern World History course they must all pass this year
- Offers structured but *short* sections that are ideal for in-class use, something that allows me to provide focused instruction around "mini-lessons" about those issues most important to the kids in ACCESS

One last item deserves special mention as it may raise some questions. I intend to give the books to the kids to use and keep as their own. This serves an important instructional purpose: by annotating the text they will be working as much more active readers, doing what the president of the International Reading Association said in a recent article is the single most useful reading strategy: reading with a pencil in their hand. This gives them purpose and permission to engage and interact with the text. I hope the book will also become, as a dictionary often is for our ESL students, a trusted guide through the remaining four years at our school.

**Request: $800.000 (40 books @ $18.95 + taxes and handling)**

**Total Request: $1100.00**

Thank you again for your continued commitment to my students and the ACCESS program. I'm grateful for all the work you do and the difference it allows me to make through my teaching. If you have any questions, please contact me.

Sincerely,
Jim Burke
ACCESS Teacher

Mentoring and advocacy come in many forms, sometimes direct, other times behind the scenes. The indirect form means tracking the performance of any current and former ACCESS students every progress report period. It means comparing the latest data with the long-term pattern of their academic performance and judging what might help. In some cases, I might go around to their class and speak to them; it might also mean writing them a note telling them how impressed I am with their latest performance or reminding them that they have done well in that class in the past and should be able to do better than they are doing now. It might also mean keeping my eyes open for them as I move around the school. I know, for example, that I can count on seeing Danny Martin outside my classroom door every day, even though he is a senior, because his locker is right there. So when the progress reports come out, I check in with him. These conversations and notes inevitably include reminders that they can always come by for help or a chat if they need to. And this open-door policy pays off: Omar sends his college application essays for feedback; Julia stops by for help on her *Scarlet Letter* essay; Michael visits to just check in, let himself get a bit of a pep talk he knows will come if he plugs me in and tells me he is getting lazy. They know they are always welcome because I tell them but also because I never forget them. I try to always get out into the halls, walking around when I can; when I see an ACESS student I *always* say, "Hi, Danny!" "Hey, Brad, how's baseball going?" "Sutton, how's that English class going?" and so on. Another inevitable part of these mentoring efforts is maintaining the high expectations I tried to establish while they were in the class. So when I'm not checking on their standing or encouraging their general efforts in classes, I am talking up college, asking them if they have thought about it, been to see Mrs. Friel about college, the PSAT, the SAT.

This focus on college, and particularly on Lori Friel, the college advisor, grew out of a conversation with her about the PSATs. She mentioned in passing that many kids had been coming in to sign up for the PSATs, saying that I told them they should think about it. Whereas the kids in my AP English class had mostly signed up for the SAT and the ACT before they were out of diapers, AS kids don't know how this process works, don't know whom to see, where to go, when to do it. Now I send Lori a list of all the former ACCESS kids when they are juniors and encourage her to summon them in to sign up. A list of thirty kids might net as many as fifteen kids who never thought about signing up and weren't ready to start considering college. This PSAT rouse also has an added benefit: the kids are in her lair, surrounded by college posters, applications, visiting speakers from those schools, all of which lead to opportunities. This is the kind of note I try to send to Lori, which is easy to remember to do when she tells me what kind of difference it makes:

> Lori:
>
> Here is the list of ACCESS kids broken down by graduation year. If you talk to any kid who wants to take the SAT test but says they cannot do so because of money, let me know. We could try to approach the administration or the Parents Group. Also, did the SAT prep class scholarships get awarded last year? I was under the impression that kids could apply for those as a condition for making the prep program/class available on our campus. Also, thanks for hooking up Tyler [a former ACCESS student] with that University of Oregon rep; Tyler came by afterward to tell me about it and seems genuinely motivated to make that happen. Thanks for all your help.
>
> Jim

## The Home Connection: Parents

Sometimes there are things you can't accomplish through teachers or administrators because they are bigger, deeper issues. For these, you must go to the parents, to the home. This has become somewhat easier with *some* parents as email has become more common. Our school's website, as with most, features my name and a link to my email address, so parents will write me, as Russell's parents did about a month into school:

Mr. Burke:

We enjoyed meeting with you before school started. Your course looks great and we are hoping that Russell [will] benefit from it. Can you please send us a message to let us know how he is doing so far? Does he seem to be applying himself and absorbing the material? Any info you can give us would be greatly appreciated.

Thanks and regards,
Tim and Maria B—

Here is my response:

Hello Mr. and Mrs. B—:

Nice to hear from you and thanks for taking time to write. First, before I forget: Russell has not gotten the CSM permission slip signed so if you could help with that, I'd be grateful. We are going to CSM (no other program in the district gets to take freshmen) for a College Day on 10/28. It's a good day and they get to see interesting things and get hooked into the idea of college, something you have no doubt established as a value in your home for Russell.

I am working hard to get to know the kids, what they need and who they are. I think he is settling into high school and seems comfortable socially with kids in the class. He talks to me, seems comfortable in the class. I don't mean to imply that being "comfortable" is the big goal of school or my program, it's just an important litmus test for me in terms of a student's initial response to the climate of high school. He works better some days than others. Today was interesting: I had all the kids fill out applications (that I created) for going to Washington Elementary Wednesday mornings to mentor kindergarten students for the period. (We have always done this, and they never miss class.) Only about 5 kids can go, so I make them argue their case, outline their qualifications and so on. I'm pretty sure you know what Russell's handwriting looks like on most days. I told the kids about the importance of handwriting and how it reflects on them when applying for a job. Russell's handwriting on his application was entirely improved, which says that he took it very seriously. I don't know if it will work out for him to be one of the kids who gets to go, but it suggested to me that he wanted to and took it seriously. We are working closely every day on a set of mental habits and skills that I think lead to success in other academic classes. Progress reports go in on Tuesday of next week. You should get them Saturday (next), but the important point about that is that by the time they arrive at your house, it's already the end of the seventh week. I look very closely at these first progress reports as a global indicator of their performance in other areas and then after that make adjustments in the ACCESS program that I hope will help.

If I didn't answer your question well enough, please write back with other questions. Thanks and don't hesitate to write in the future. We're in this together.

Jim Burke

Of course, not all parents are allies; some, in fact, are the source of their child's troubles. I have had ACCESS kids who attended school 10 percent of the time and whose parents never responded, not even when threatened by the school with criminal charges for neglect. I have had classes where several kids lived in foster homes after years of abuse at the hands of their biological parents. Most of the kids come from supportive families and their parents, if absent, are simply working extra jobs to help the family get by. Still, I often find myself feeling like a parent for the kids at times, giving Lidia a dollar for food when she admits that she doesn't feel well because she didn't eat that morning or reminding others to make sure they get to some meeting or talk to their counselor. Kids need adult guidance, even when their behavior and attitude imply otherwise. The AS teacher must provide an environment that maintains high academic expectations while meeting their sometimes high personal expectations for help when there is no one else to turn to as this student's note shows:

Hey Mr. Burke,

I'm better at writing things down than actually telling people. I'm trying hard in school but my home life isn't that good and if I told you my cousin past away last week and I don't really have too many good friends. And a lot of stuff in school requires a computer which I have but no internet, no library card because I owe money, and our phone just got turned off. So there's *so* much stuff going on in my life, and I've been kind of depressed and I cannot fail and I don't want to, because I didn't graduate eighth grade well at least not on stage, so I know what it's like to fail. It was hard to give this to you but I wanted to let you know what's going on and if you could talk to some of my teachers that would be great or I could but it's hard for me to actually just go up to them. But yea, thanks!

From: Maria

Such a letter demands a serious, sincere response; this student risked so much. After talking to a couple of her teachers, both of whom changed Maria's seat assignment to help her get away from kids who distracted her, I wrote:

November 10

Dear Maria:

Thank you for trusting me enough to write that letter yesterday. I know how hard it is to do that, especially when you feel the way you do now. I'd rather talk to you in person, but wanted to say a few things and share the poem below with you. First, I talked with Ms. C a bit to let her know what's going on, and met with Mrs. B—, your counselor, who I think is a gifted counselor. She has helped many girls just like yourself through important decisions and hard times; you're lucky to have her as your counselor (though Mr. S— and Mrs. L— are also great!). I want you to let her coach you through things; trust her as you would me. She knows what she is talking about.

A few other questions:

- How much do you owe the library? The BHS library? Or the city library?
- Do you know you can use my computer before school and during lunch?
- Do you know you can go to the library after school every day and use their computers and have a place to study?

What successful people do, Maria, is what you are doing: they find people who can help them, admit they need help, tell those people how they can help, then accept the help, and, years later, help others who, like themselves when they were young, want to succeed but do not know how to accomplish it. Mrs. P will help you in many ways if you go in and ask. She's a wonderful person and has helped many kids in my program. You can use their computers in there for some things; so next time you have time, go in and visit Mrs. P and let her know what you need and find out what she has to offer.

There was a girl very much like you five years ago who arrived at BHS and found herself in my ACCESS program. She had to learn to trust her own mind, to have faith in her own intelligence, and to learn new habits that would help her find the success she wanted so badly. She had to learn that she was, in fact, very intelligent, generous, and, ultimately, a role model to others. She went to Washington as you do. She got involved in community service as you are doing. She was selected for a leadership academy, as you have been. And she worked hard for four years, improved, and arrived at her senior year with a very high GPA and the realization that she did not have the money to go to college, which is what had motivated her for four years. Her name was Marcy, and when I learned that she did not have the money to even apply to college, I created the ACCESS college scholarship (a $1000.00 scholarship) for such an ACCESS student. Why do I tell you this? Because I see in you not just who you are but who and what you could be and am willing to do what I can to help you make that story come true. When you arrive at the end of your four years, you will find people like me and Mrs. F who will move heaven and earth to arrange the money you need to attend the college you want. Here is one more detail: Marcy is in college this year, a freshman—at *UC Santa Cruz* [a school Maria often spoke of wanting to attend].

Some people have to walk a longer road, even a harder road than others, but it teaches them things, shapes them into who they are, Maria. What you do not have will teach you to provide for yourself, to seek out what those around you cannot provide; you will learn that you must—and *can*—provide for yourself. To the extent that people see your story as a happy one, a winning one, they will want to contribute to your success however they can. You are at a school with many people who will do for you what others may not: care about you, support and encourage you, guide you, and, when you graduate, celebrate you and send you on your way, proud of all that you have done to make yourself the success I know you will be.

All I ever think when I see you is how great you are and what incredible things you will go on to do while here at this school. The school is full of people who can't wait to know you, to be your friend, to help you succeed.

Here, in the meantime, is a poem that relates to much of what I am talking about ["Autobiography in Five Chapters," by Portia Nelson]. Enjoy it. Live it.

Faithfully,
Mr. Burke

## Conclusion

I became, as most do, an AS teacher to help, to transform the kids only to find that the work transformed me. To paraphrase Steven Covey's eighth habit, I have found my own voice (as a teacher, a person) by helping others find theirs. Mina Shaughnessy captures this evolution best in her metaphor of "diving in," in which she divides the "Basic Writing" teacher's developmental progression into four stages:

1. *Guarding the Tower*: During this stage the teacher is in one way or another concentrating on protecting the academy (including himself) from outsiders, those who do not seem to belong to the community of learners . . . The teacher assumes that he must not only hold out for the same product he held out for in the past but teach unflinchingly in the same way as before, as if any pedagogical adjustment to the needs of the students were a kind of cheating.

2. *Converting the Natives*: The teacher has now admitted at least some to the community of the educable. These learners are perceived, however, as empty vessels, ready to be filled with new knowledge. . . . The teacher's purpose is

the same: to carry the technology of advanced literacy to the inhabitants of an underdeveloped country. . . . [Eventually] it occurs to [the teacher] that perhaps these simple things—so transparent and compelling to him—are not in fact simple at all, that they only appear simple to those who already know them. . . .

3. *Sounding the Depths*: [The teacher] turns now to the careful observation not only of his students and their writing but of himself as a writer and teacher, seeking deeper understanding of the behavior called writing and the special difficulties his students have in mastering this skill.

4. *Diving In*: [The teacher] who has come this far must now make a decision that demands professional courage—the decision to remediate himself, to become a student of new disciplines and of his students themselves in order to perceive both their difficulties and their incipient excellence. . . . Diving in is simply deciding that teaching them to write well is not only suitable but challenging work for those who would be teachers and scholars in a democracy. (Corbett, Myer, and Tate 2000, 99)

By such criteria I should perhaps call this book *Diving In*, for this last stage describes best my feelings about my work with these students. It *is* difficult work, but it is also *important* work, work that gives me the chance to contribute not only to an individual's improvement but the community and even our country. I come to school each day to teach both advanced classes and ACCESS classes, arriving equally prepared to be the best teacher I can be for all my students. Both classes, and all students, challenge me, reward me, and frustrate me in their own ways, but it is the small victory in the ACCESS class that I think about when driving home, wondering how I can nurture it into some larger gain the next day for that kid or the class, so that my ACCESS kids can, themselves, dive in to the wider waters of the world for which school seeks to prepare them.

# *Epilogue*

It is the last day of the school year, the period during which we are supposed to have a final exam. Instead of another big, long test like the ones they have taken all week, we have a graduation ceremony. Kids who entered nine months before feeling unsure and indifferent, lacking a direction, now stand before us delivering speeches as they learned to do in Toastmasters. Sitting in class with us are Beth Pascal, Sue Glick, and Lori Friel as well as Matt Biggar, the principal and a big supporter of the ACCESS program. At the back of the room, the kids have spread food out on the table; for once it is OK to have a big bag of Cheetos in the room.

Before the kids begin to give their graduation speeches, which they worked on the previous week, I give a commencement address, bringing to it the full measure of my voice, for I want them to feel like this is truly a meaningful ceremony. Here is what I say:

**GRADUATION**
1a. Conferral or receipt of an academic degree or diploma marking completion of studies. b. A ceremony at which degrees or diplomas are conferred; a commencement.
2a. A division or interval on a graduated scale. b. A mark indicating the boundary of such an interval.
3. An arrangement in or a division into stages or degrees.

Life is a series of graduations. We graduate from crawling to walking; from training wheels to the skinned knees of independent riding; from elementary school to middle school; and so on. This week my daughter graduates from preschool to enter kindergarten in the fall. My son graduates from elementary school so he can begin to swim in the wider waters of middle school. And you graduate from freshman year, from this class, from one identity to another.

The word *graduation* relates to words like *gradation*, and *gradient*, even *grade*, all of which suggest that we move from one point to another, sometimes quickly, sometimes slowly. It also suggests that you cannot graduate if you are not moving forward, reaching, trying to accomplish some next step, for to get from one stage to the next, one must move.

It is only when we move past these divisions, when we graduate from one phase to the next, that we feel some sense of achievement. The depth of our pride and satisfaction is a measure of the effort we invested in achieving that goal. We feel no accomplishment when we wake up in the morning; it was going to happen. We didn't have to work at it.

Becoming something we were not, but wanted to be; learning something that was not easy for us, but we know we need to succeed—these are accomplishments we should celebrate. And so we do today. We celebrate not only the readers and students you've become but the lives you will enjoy due to your investment in yourself and the society. For to improve yourself in any way is to improve the society in which you live.

Thus to speak of graduation is to speak of what you not only have done but will do. Your work this year has purchased you greater chances for success in the years ahead. But this year's gains are only a down payment on all you will need to know and be able to do in the years to come.

Graduations are only beginnings; they are never endings. You worked all year to get to this moment only to graduate to the next phase of your education. You will work these four years to graduate from high school only to enter another school, which might be on a college campus or at a company.

So as I stand here today to celebrate you and all you've accomplished, all you've learned, I wish you a hunger you can never satisfy, a hunger that leads you always toward—what is next, what is better—for you and those around you. This hunger will make your life a long series of graduations that lead to a point, years from now, when you can look back, just before that final graduation from this life to the next, and see with pride all that you learned . . . all that you lived, all that you loved along the way.

When the period is over, the year is over. But the story is not, nor is my relationship with these kids. After a nice lunch and a change of clothes, I head over to the performing arts center to watch the seniors graduate, kids who only four years earlier stood before my class telling us all they intended to do. And now that time has come for them to take over, to become their own teachers, to teach themselves how to live, to make their life a story worth telling.

# Works Cited

Benard, Bonnie, Nan Henderson, Nancy Sharp-Light, and Emmy E. Werner. 2000. *Mentoring for Resiliency: Setting Up Programs for Moving Youth from "Stressed to Success."* San Diego: Resiliency in Action.

Block, Cathy Collins, Linda B. Gambrell, and Michael Pressley. 2002. *Improving Comprehension Instruction: Rethinking Research, Theory, and Classroom Practice.* San Francisco: Jossey-Bass.

Burke, Jim. 2002. *Reading Handbook: A Student Guide for Reading and Learning.* Wilmington, DE: Great Source.

———. 2004. *School Smarts: The Four Cs of Academic Success.* Portsmouth: Heinemann, 2004.

Burke, Jim, and Carol Prater. 2000. *I'll Grant You That: A Step-by-Step Guide to Finding Funds, Designing Winning Projects, Writing Powerful Grant Proposals.* Portsmouth, NH: Heinemann.

Coogin, Michael D., ed. 2001. *The New Oxford Annotated Bible.* 3rd ed. New York: Oxford University Press.

Corbett, Edward P. J., Nancy Myer, and Gary Tate. 2000. *The Writing Teacher's Source Book.* New York: Oxford University Press.

Covey, Stephen R. 1990. *The Seven Habits of Highly Effective People.* New York: Free Press.

Delpit, Lisa. 1996. "The Politics of Teaching Literate Discourse." In *City Kids, City Teachers,* edited by William Ayers and Patricia Ford. New York: New.

Dorsey, David. 2000. "Positive Deviant." *Fast Company* (December): 284–86.

Druian, Greg, and Jocelyn A. Butler. 1987. "Effective Schooling Practices and At-Risk Youth: What the Research Shows." Northwest Regional Educational Laboratory. www.nwrel.org/scpd/sirs/1/topsyn1.html (accessed September, 17, 2004).

Freedman, Jonathan. 2000. *Wall of Fame: One Teacher, One Class, and the Power to Save Schools and Transform Lives.* San Diego: AVID Academic.

International Reading Association. 2004. "Teaching All Children to Read: The Roles of the Reading Specialist." International Reading Association. www.reading.org/resources /issues/positions_specialist.html (accessed December 5, 2004).

Lampert, Magdalene. 2001. *Teaching Problems and the Problems of Teaching*. New Haven, CT): Yale University Press.

Langer, Judith A. 2002. *Effective Literacy Instruction: Building Successful Reading and Writing Programs*. Urbana, IL: National Council of Teachers of English.

Levine, Mel. 2003. *The Myth of Laziness: America's Top Learning Expert Shows How Kids—and Parents—Can Become More Productive*. New York: Simon and Schuster.

Marzano, Robert, Debra J. Pickering, and Jane E. Pollock. 2001. *Classroom Instruction That Works: Research-Based Strategies for Increasing Student Achievement*. Alexandria, VA: Association for Supervision and Curriculum Development.

Morris, Tom. 1995. *True Success: A New Philosophy of Excellence*. New York: Berkely.

Moses, Robert P. 2001. *Radical Equations: Math Literacy and Civil Rights*. Boston: Beacon.

Mueller, Pamela. 2001. *Lifers: Learning from At-Risk Adolescent Readers*. Portsmouth, NH: Heinemann.

National Council of Teachers of English Commission on Reading. 2004. "A Call to Action: What We Know About Adolescent Literacy and Ways to Support Teachers in Meeting Students' Needs". National Council of Teachers of English. www.ncte.org /about/over/positions/category/literacy/118622.htm (accessed November 11, 2004).

O'Connell, Jack. 2004. "High Performance High School Initiative: Improving High Schools from the Inside Out." *High School! A Newsletter for California Educational Leaders* 3, no. 2.

Perry, Theresa. 2003. "Up from the Parched Earth: Toward a Theory of African-American Achievement." In *Young, Gifted, and Black: Promoting High Achievement Among African-American Students*, edited by Theresa Perry, Claude Steele, and Asa Hillard III. Boston: Beacon.

Phillips, Donald T. 1992. *Lincoln on Leadership: Executive Strategies for Tough Times*. New York: Warner.

Positive Deviance Initiative. "Positive Deviance Initiative." www.positivedeviance.org (accessed September 23, 2004).

Rose, Mike. 1989. *Lives on the Boundary: A Moving Account of the Struggles and Achievements of America's Educational Underclass*. New York: Penguin.

Rymes, Betsy. 2001. *Conversational Borderlands: Language and Identity in an Alternative Urban High School. Language and Literacy*, edited by Dorothy S. Strickland and Celia Genishi. New York: Teachers College Press.

Schmoker, Mike. 1999. *Results: The Key to Continuous School Improvement*. Alexandria, VA: Association for Supervision and Curriculum Development.

Schoenbach, Ruth, Cynthia Greenleaf, Christine Cziko, and Lori Hurwitz. 1999. *Reading for Understanding: A Guide to Improving Middle and High School Classrooms.* San Francisco: Jossey-Bass.

Sparks, Dennis. 2002. "Amplifying Positive Deviance in Schoool." National Staff Development Council. http://www.ndsc.org/library/publications/results/res 4-02spar.clm.

———. 2004. "From Hunger Aid to School Reform." *National Staff Development Council* 1, (Winter): 46–51.

# *Index*

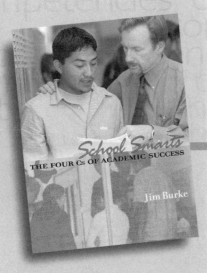